HOCKEY GODS

HOCKEY GODS

THE INSIDE STORY OF THE RED WINGS' HALL OF FAME TEAM

Nicholas J. Cotsonika

TRIUMPH
B O O K S
CHICAGO

Editors: Alison Boyce Cotsonika, Gene Myers

Designer: Bob Ellis

Copy editor: Brad Betker

Cover designer: Christoph Fuhrmans

Photo editor: Diane Weiss

Project coordinator: Dave Robinson

Special thanks: Mitch Albom, Laurie Delves, Carole Leigh Hutton, Heath J Meriwether, Mitch Rogatz, Helene St. James.

Library of Congress Control Number: 2002107273

This book is available in quantity at special discounts for your group or organization. For further information, contact:

Triumph Books
601 South LaSalle Street
Suite 500
Chicago, Illinois 60605
(312) 939-3330
Fax: (312) 663-3557

Published in cooperation with the Detroit Free Press

Printed in the United States of America
ISBN 1-57243-481-3

To Alison

Contents

Prologue
The Hockeytown Pantheon

The entrance to the Hockey Hall of Fame isn't impressive. You walk into a Toronto office/retail complex, go down an escalator, make a U-turn, pass a couple of food-court-type restaurants and arrive at what looks like a glorified gift shop/arcade. You buy a ticket, mush through a turnstile, see more minor league and strange international sweaters than anything else on exhibit and end up watching kids shoot plastic pucks on a pretend ice rink in the interactive area.

But then, you find a set of stairs off to the side, and you climb up and into another world—wood-paneled walls, a stained-glass ceiling and a faint sound above the whispers of visitors: a scratchy recording of an old radio broadcast piped in from the past, Foster Hewitt, the man who made a certain phrase famous. *He shoots! He scores!* Straight ahead, past the Conn Smythe Trophy and the Hart Trophy and the Prince of Wales Trophy and the Clarence Campbell Bowl, surrounded by glass plaques of the inductees, the Stanley Cup sits upon a pedestal, like a silver chalice upon an altar. It's called the Great Hall. It's a converted bank, but . . .

"It's like you're in a church," said Leslie Meader, a fan from Orange County, Calif., there for the first time in the summer of 1999. "It's awesome."

When the 2001-02 Detroit Red Wings won the Stanley Cup, no fewer than nine of the players seemed destined to have their names on glass in the Great Hall. Chris Chelios. Sergei Fedorov. Dominik Hasek. Brett Hull. Igor Larionov. Nicklas Lidstrom. Luc Robitaille. Brendan Shanahan. Steve Yzerman. And their coach, Scotty Bowman, had been in the Hall of Fame for more than a decade. They were all quite human, with flaws and quirks, as you will see. But in the context of their sport, they were immortals, or soon to be, and at first blush, the title of this book is used in that spirit.

The Hockeytown Pantheon

The title also reflects the Wings' stature in the city of Detroit—and by the Wings' stature, I mean *all* the Wings: from their nine potential Hall of Famers to their Grind Line guys, Kris Draper, Kirk Maltby and Darren McCarty, who must have a larger, more loyal following than any other checkers in the history of the National Hockey League. People worship winners, and in Detroit, a place with a depressed self-image, people worshiped the Wings. They were icons in a community that adopted a marketing concept, Hockeytown, as an alternate identity. Fans named their newborn children after them: During the playoffs, one family named a son Yzer. The Arena family named a son Joe Louis.

Finally, the title gives a nod to the hockey gods, the unearthly forces you curse when you hit the post and thank when the other team does. In many ways, the season these Wings had was a miracle. Not because they won the Cup. Somebody wins the Cup every year. But because of *how* they won the Cup. How they were assembled. How they came together. Who they were. What they had done. The little dramas. The milestones along the way. As you will see, for these stars to align the way they did, the stars had to align.

—*Detroit, July 2002*

Chapter 1
Mr. Holland's Opus

I t said IMPORTANT MESSAGE across the top. Still, Ken Holland thought nothing of it. As general manager of the Detroit Red Wings, he made his living on the phone. He saw so many little, purple IMPORTANT MESSAGE slips every day that he knew how few of them were ever really IMPORTANT.

Darcy Regier had called. Holland had known him for years. They had played against each other in juniors, they had played with each other in the minors and now Regier was general manager of the Buffalo Sabres. He could have wanted to talk about anything—or maybe nothing much, just the latest goings-on around the National Hockey League.

Sitting at his desk in his office at Joe Louis Arena, Holland called back. He and Regier gabbed a little while. The conversation was casual.

Then Regier got to the point.

"We're going to move Dominik Hasek," he said. "Are you interested?"

Dominik Hasek? Was he kidding?

"Absolutely we're interested," Holland told him.

Wasn't much more to say. Soon they hung up.

Holland was dubious at first.

"I've been on many, many phone conversations with other general managers and a name has come up," Holland said. "That might be the last you ever hear of it, because maybe they change their mind for any number of reasons. 'Are you interested?' And you hang up. And that's it."

And this was Dominik Hasek they were talking about. He was a future Hall of Famer, one of the game's greatest players—the "Dominator." To keep him another season, the cash-strapped Sabres had to exercise an option in his contract, costing them $9 million plus bonuses. Even so, how could they let him go?

"You don't think it's going to happen," Holland said.

Mr. Holland's Opus

But a day or two later, in the late afternoon of Wednesday, June 13, 2001, Regier sent Holland a fax. It gave him until the 23rd to talk to Hasek's agent, Rich Winter, about a new contract.

"At that stage of the game," Holland said, "I now in my own mind am saying, 'It's gonna happen.' "

The Sabres were serious: Hasek was going to be traded. The only question was: To whom? To the Wings? To the Wings' Central Division rivals, the St. Louis Blues? To someone else?

The next night, Holland attended the NHL Awards at Toronto's Air Canada Centre. As Hasek stood on the stage, receiving his sixth Vezina Trophy as the league's best goaltender, Holland sat in his seat, daydreaming, fantasizing. Hasek was wearing a tuxedo; Holland was imagining him in a Wings sweater.

"That's how it starts," Holland said.

The 2000-01 season ended in a nightmare.

The Wings never lost more than two straight games. They lost four total after Jan. 30. They finished with 111 points, second-most in the league, second-most in franchise history. They won their first two playoff games against the Los Angeles Kings, dominating the second, 4-0.

"We looked like world-beaters," forward Darren McCarty said, "and then it all fell apart."

The Wings lost four straight one-goal games. Twice, they took a lead into the third period, blew it and lost in overtime. They fell in the first round for the first time since 1994, when the San Jose Sharks upset them in seven games. They lost to a seventh seed that had to fight to the finish just to make the playoffs, to a team that hadn't won a playoff series since '93.

Every elimination is disappointing.

But this one . . .

It wasn't even May yet, let alone June. The season ended April 23. The Wings hadn't been done so soon since 1991, when they lost Game 7 of a first-round series with the Blues on April 16.

"It really stinks," forward Pat Verbeek said. "Looking back on the season, I think we felt we had a real shot at winning the whole thing. . . . It was out there on the line, and we didn't take it."

Injuries were a significant factor. Captain Steve Yzerman missed all but one period with a fractured left fibula. Forward Brendan Shanahan broke his left foot blocking a shot in Game 1 and returned in Game 5, as best he could. Defenseman Chris Chelios played with a broken left thumb, defenseman Todd Gill with a broken foot, McCarty with a sore right ankle.

The Kings improved as the series progressed, too.

But that shouldn't have mattered. The Wings prided themselves on their depth, and they should have won, anyway.

"We're not going to make excuses," center Kris Draper said. "Come on. Look at what we did in the first two games. We beat them, 4-0, without (Yzerman and Shanahan). We can't make excuses. It's not because Stevie didn't play or Shanny didn't play. It's how the guys that played played. That's what the problem was."

The turning point was Game 4.

A victory would have given the Wings a 3-1 series lead, all but sending them to the second round. Entering the playoffs, 181 teams had taken a 3-1 lead in a best-of-seven series, and only 16 had lost the series.

The Wings had a 3-0 lead with less than 6½ minutes left in the third period. Then it was 3-1. And 3-2. Then it was gone. The Kings scored three goals in 5:14, the last two with their goaltender pulled, the last with 53 seconds left.

Then, 2:36 into overtime, the Kings scored again.

The Wings lost, 4-3.

How could this happen?

"There's no easy explanation," forward Kirk Maltby said.

Let's start with Scott Thomas. Unlikely comeback, unlikely hero. He played only because fellow forward Steve Kelly had the flu, and he played only 54 seconds the first two periods. But he scored the Kings' first playoff power-play goal against the Wings in 40 tries over two years.

The Wings were humming along, then forward Martin Lapointe went off for slashing center Jozef Stumpel. Moments later, defenseman Mathieu Schneider fired the puck from the point, and Thomas tapped it in.

Let's continue with the second goal. Unlikely collapse, unlucky breaks. Lapointe battled along the boards with Schneider and ended up off for interference. While conceding he deserved the first penalty, Lapointe fumed about this one.

"If the score's 3-2, I don't think the referee calls that," Lapointe said. "It's refereeing the score, you know? It's 3-1, and it's an easy call to make, and he calls it. That's not the way it should be."

Moments later, from the corner to goaltender Chris Osgood's right, Stumpel sent the puck toward the slot. It went off one of Chelios' skates and squeaked between Osgood's right pad and the left post. Whether it crossed the goal line was questionable. Video replay officials allowed the goal, and Osgood fumed.

"The fans started cheering as if it had gone in, and their goal judge flicked the red light on," Osgood said. "I think there's absolutely no way it was in."

Let's finish with the finish. Perhaps stunned by their bad luck, the Wings panicked. They failed to clear their zone. Coach Scotty Bowman never called a time-out. After a scramble, forward Bryan Smolinski tied the game.

In overtime, forward Adam Deadmarsh, a notorious Wings-killer who used to play for the archrival Colorado Avalanche, threw the puck out of the corner to Osgood's left. Forward Ian Laperriere tipped it. Streaking in off a line change, center Eric Belanger put it high into the net.

The Wings went off looking dazed.

Before the third period, Los Angeles coach Andy Murray motivated his players by reminding them of the "Miracle on Manchester," the greatest comeback in NHL playoff history. On April 10, 1982, the Kings rallied from a 5-0 deficit and beat the Edmonton Oilers, 6-5, at the Forum, on Manchester.

"Let's make one of our own," Murray told them.

After the players obliged, the L.A. scribes tried to, too. Because the Staples Center was located at Figueroa and 11th, at different points the Los Angeles Times called the thriller the "Frenzy on Figueroa," the "Fantastic Finish on Figueroa" and "Eleventh (Ave.) Heaven."

The Wings called it embarrassing.

"We just did some stupid things," Draper said. "Just played stupid hockey."

"What happened," defenseman Nicklas Lidstrom said, "shouldn't really happen."

But it did.

"We didn't recover from that point," defenseman Larry Murphy said. "It took the wind out of our sails. We just never got that type of game that we needed to take the series back. It had an effect on us."

"It's funny that you evaluate a whole season on six minutes," associate coach Dave Lewis said. "That's a hard thing to swallow."

The Wings played with little passion in Game 5, a 3-2 loss, deflated further when the Kings scored just 1:15 into the first period. Osgood said some of his teammates didn't even show up.

Bowman literally didn't show up for practice the next day. The Wings played hard and got some breaks in Game 6, scoring their first goal when a puck went in off two Kings, after a controversial L.A. penalty. But the Wings blew a 2-1 lead when Deadmarsh scored in the third and lost when Deadmarsh scored again in overtime.

"We're here just shaking our heads, sick to our stomachs," Draper said. "We have no one to blame but ourselves. We're going to be shaking our heads here for the next couple of weeks, just wondering, 'What if?' "

Everyone else was wondering, "What's next?"

The Wings won back-to-back Stanley Cups in 1997 and '98. But they followed them with back-to-back second-round playoff losses to the Avs. Now this. The trend was decidedly downward. The Wings had the league's second-highest payroll, at about $55 million, but they were its oldest team, with an average age of about 31. The Detroit Free Press ran a large photo on the front of the sports section, showing the players consoling each other. The headline: "PAST THEIR PRIME?" The Wings looked like a classic car, proud but sad at the same time, a glorious Motor City machine that couldn't keep up anymore.

The day the Wings cleaned out their lockers, a local dealer received a shipment for Shanahan: the 1949 Cadillac convertible he had ordered.

"I need to fix a couple of things," the dealer told him. "It's not ready to run."

"Aw, well," Shanahan said, "I'll chance it, because, you know, the guys want to see it. Today's the last day."

Shanahan made it to the rink all right. But on his way home, top down, crutches in the back seat, the car sputtered to a stop on the Lodge Freeway.

Yzerman drove past Shanahan—and kept going. He was doing a radio interview on his cell phone, and he told his listeners about his teammate's trouble.

"He bought a new car, a new old car that he was really proud of, and he's broken down on the side of the road," Yzerman said. "So if anyone can help him, please do."

About five minutes later, the TV trucks started showing up. Chelios, another classic car buff, came to Shanahan's rescue, whisking him away.

"Needed a five-dollar part," Shanahan said.

Holland didn't look at a newspaper for days after the L.A. debacle. He flipped on sports talk radio for a minute one morning, but the venom was too much to bear, so he quickly flipped it off. He didn't need to read. He didn't need to listen. He knew.

"We have a lot of disappointed fans in Detroit and all of North America," he said. "But I think everybody in our organization is just as disappointed with what transpired in the past two weeks. I'm terribly disappointed. It was a devastating loss. We had great hopes, and all of a sudden . . ."

His voiced trailed off. He sighed.

"It's going to take some time," he continued. "It's going to take a lot of thought and planning. We need to do some things. I don't know exactly what. You really have to take the emotion out of it. I'm really emotional right now."

Over the next month, Holland began reshaping his roster. He decided not to re-sign Gill, Murphy and forward Doug Brown; while Gill eventually signed with Colorado, Brown and Murphy retired. He told Verbeek he would wait and see with him; he ended up not needing him, and Verbeek signed with the Dallas Stars. Holland re-signed center Igor Larionov, and he signed free-agent defenseman Fredrik Olausson, a 14-year NHL veteran who had spent the season in Switzerland.

The big question was whether Bowman would be back. Owner Mike Ilitch had said Bowman could coach as long as he wanted.

But Bowman was 67, he had been year-to-year for years and, while the Wings were underachieving in December, he said he might not return if the Wings failed to improve their playoff performance.

"Let's face it: A coach, if he doesn't do well, isn't going to be back, doesn't matter who it is," Bowman said. "That's the nature of the game, and it's the way it should be. . . . We're a pretty high-profile team, we've got a high payroll and the expectations are high to do well in the playoffs."

Bowman always took his time deciding. In mid-May, he was announced as a finalist for the Jack Adams Award as coach of the year, based on regular-season performance. Associate coach Barry Smith said that encouraged Bowman. On vacation in Florida, Bowman said he would return to Detroit soon to discuss his future and thought he would have his mind made up by the end of the month. By May 22, Bowman still hadn't talked to anyone yet, and Ilitch showed his displeasure in a TV interview.

"If I don't hear from him within a short period of time, I will pick up the phone," Ilitch told Fox Sports Net. "I told Kenny that he's got to put pressure on Scotty and (Scotty) had to give us an answer right away, because we don't want to be looking around for a coach at the last minute. It wouldn't be fair to us or the fans. I think we're going to get a quick response out of him now."

Asked whether he had a gut feeling, Ilitch smiled.

"He's so unpredictable, I don't want to say it," Ilitch said. "But, yeah, I think he'll come back."

Bowman did come back. But he didn't announce it until June 7, after passing his annual physical—and trying unsuccessfully to get Holland to fire Lewis and goaltending consultant Jim Bedard. Bowman was notorious for blaming others when things went wrong. He always looked after Smith, who had been his assistant with the Pittsburgh Penguins in the early 1990s and with the Sabres in the late '80s. But Bowman sometimes was hard on Lewis, who had been with the Wings before he arrived. He thought Bedard was too friendly with the players.

Holland met with Ilitch in late May. Ilitch knew his classic car needed much more than a five-dollar part, but he had no desire to break up the team, to ditch all the old guys and plug in young pups, as some were suggesting he should. The Wings had kept

7

their core largely intact for years, and they still believed it was one of the best. They had Yzerman. Ilitch bought the team in 1982 and hired Jimmy Devellano as general manager a month later, and Yzerman was the first player Devellano drafted, in '83. At 21, Yzerman became the youngest captain in franchise history. Now, at 36, he was the longest-serving captain in league history—one of its most accomplished players and most respected leaders. The Wings had five other potential Hall of Famers: Chelios, the veteran warrior; Larionov, the wise Russian; Lidstrom, the master of the subtle arts; Shanahan, the charismatic sniper; and center Sergei Fedorov, the enigmatic talent. They had valuable role players. Forward Tomas Holmstrom took beatings in front of the net. Draper, Maltby and McCarty made up the ever-popular Grind Line. Ilitch hoped to re-sign Lapointe, whose scoring touch had blossomed, and then add, not subtract.

"We wanted to try to do something with a real impact to our hockey club," Holland said. "We had to do something."

Ilitch, an entrepreneur who made a fortune in the pizza business, had taken his hometown team from awful to awesome by taking risks and going after big names. Risks? Devellano gave the go-ahead to his scouts to select Soviet players at the 1989 draft. The Wings picked Fedorov and defenseman Vladimir Konstantinov—then helped them escape from behind the Iron Curtain. In the summer of '90, they sneaked Fedorov out a side hotel door after an exhibition in Portland, Ore., and flew him to Detroit in Ilitch's private jet. In the spring of '91, they gave cash to an intermediary, who bribed Soviet doctors to fake a cancer diagnosis so that Konstantinov could go abroad, ostensibly for treatment. Names? While the Wings worked on building a foundation through the draft, they worked on rebuilding their relationship with the fans by acquiring players like Brad Park, Darryl Sittler, Borje Salming, Bernie Federko, Dino Ciccarelli, Mark Howe, Paul Coffey, Mike Vernon and more. They brought in coaches like Jacques Demers and Bryan Murray and finally, in '93, Bowman.

"I'm big on names," said Devellano, now senior vice president. "I'm big on personalities. I'm big on the show-business aspect of sports. I believe it's entertainment. I've always felt that way. I don't like dull. I don't like drab. I like pizzazz. . . . In many cases, we got players really on the downside of their careers, but we tried. . . . In a lot of towns, people accuse the owners and management of not trying to win. That's the one thing no one's been able to accuse us of. That's the one thing we've constantly tried to do."

Why stop now? The Wings had to fight the natural inertia of professional sports. Championship teams are supposed to decline, because that's the way leagues are structured. The bad teams draft first, the good teams last. The bad teams are supposed to get better, the good teams worse. The standings are due to flip. The Wings had won more games in the regular season (363) and playoffs (70) than any other team since Bowman arrived. No team had won more Cups. The standings were overdue to flip on them, but Ilitch had money and momentum on his side.

In March, Ilitch said he would do "whatever's necessary" to keep the Wings in Cup contention. Some were skeptical. In the spring of 2000, Ilitch had told his Detroit Tigers he would do "anything to win," and he had ended up cutting costs and declining to bid on free agents. Ilitch was burned by the heat he took from the fans and media. But this was different. Baseball was a more expensive game, the Tigers were terrible and the Wings were something special.

As Devellano said, the franchise was "in the Detroit River" when Ilitch bought it—for only $8 million. The average crowd was maybe 7,000 fans. There were 2,100 season-ticket holders. There was no waiting for anything. Concessions? Bathrooms? Step right up. The Wings were giving a car away every game. Now Joe Louis Arena had been sold out for about 15 years. There were 17,000 season-ticket holders. There was a waiting list. The Wings didn't have to give anything away. Everyone in the city seemed to have a Wings sweater, and countless cars had Wings flags flapping from their windows.

In the mid-1990s, a suburban Detroit marketing firm, Bozell Worldwide of Southfield, had about two weeks to come up with an ad campaign for the Wings. As the staff brainstormed, someone wrote "Hockeytown" on the board.

"I just pointed to the wall and said, 'That's it right there,'" project leader Gary Topolewski said. "We just kind of knew. . . . It was very true."

The ad campaign became a long-term brand, and the long-term brand became one of the city's alternate identities, like Motown. The word was plastered everywhere in big, black arrogant letters, from signposts on Jefferson in the heart of downtown to the middle of the circle at center ice. Detroit was Hockeytown.

Ilitch remembered when the Red Wings were better known as the "Dead Things." He didn't want them to slip back toward that, especially with the way the Tigers were playing.

"The Red Wings are so much a part of the city now, you just want to keep it that way," Ilitch said. "Once the city gets used to it, you get used to it. . . . We're going to fight like the dickens. . . . We've got to do anything we can."

Around the time Regier called Holland about Hasek, agent Carl Lindros called Holland about his top client, his son.

Eric Lindros was a winner of the Hart Trophy as the league's most valuable player. He was big enough to bruise at 6-feet-4, 235 pounds, and he was a skilled enough center to have scored a whopping 659 points in 486 regular-season games. But he hadn't played in 13 months. In the 2000 playoffs, New Jersey Devils defenseman Scott Stevens gave him his sixth concussion, and now, as a restricted free agent, he was in a bitter battle with Philadelphia Flyers general manager Bobby Clarke.

At first, Lindros demanded a trade to the Toronto Maple Leafs. Then, three days before the March 13 trade deadline, he added three teams to his list: the Wings, Blues and Washington Capitals. The Lindroses had approached Holland several times, and Holland never had been interested. He had been turned off by Eric's concussions, his high salary hopes, the way the family had held out and demanded trades to get what it wanted since Eric's junior days.

But Holland had to show some interest this time. When you're a GM, you have to investigate all your options, especially with a player of Lindros' caliber, even if just to make sure the deal doesn't work for you. That's especially true when the player in question is a buddy of some of your prominent players, including your captain. Lindros knew Chelios and Shanahan. He had a cabin on the same Ontario lake as Yzerman. In public, Yzerman said he would like the Wings to acquire Lindros. In private, Yzerman lobbied the Wings hard—even suggesting they trade Fedorov for him.

The Lindroses lived in Toronto, and with the NHL Awards there, Holland scheduled a meeting for that Thursday. He was supposed to arrive at about noon, but his flight was delayed. He wasn't going to get in until about 3:00, so he called Carl.

"Can we postpone this thing till next week?" he asked.

Carl said sure. They set up another meeting for Monday. So after watching Hasek win that Vezina, and Lidstrom win his first Norris Trophy as the league's best defenseman, Holland flew back to Detroit. And after having numerous conversations over the weekend with Winter, Hasek's agent, Holland flew back to Toronto. He met with the Lindroses for a couple of hours or so.

"It was a good meeting," Carl said. "Eric and Ken did most of the talking."

"Nothing really happened," Holland said. "He just wanted to meet, express his interest in coming to Detroit, talk about his health and the medical reports and where he was at."

Holland flew home feeling no urgency about Lindros. The next day, he flew to Ft. Lauderdale, Fla., for the general managers' meetings and the draft in suburban Sunrise. He had until Saturday—only five more days—to talk to Winter, so they talked often. A potential contract was just one subject.

Winter told Holland that Hasek had asked for a trade. The Sabres were willing to exercise their option to keep Hasek another season, even if it would cost them $9 million-plus. But between the trade deadline and the playoffs, Hasek told Regier he wouldn't be back. He wanted a fresh start. After the playoffs, Hasek submitted a short list of teams to which he was willing to be traded. The Wings were on it. Hasek had a good relationship with owner John Rigas, and because of all Hasek had done for the Sabres, taking them to the 1999 finals, winning two Harts along with those Vezinas, Rigas agreed to send Hasek to whichever

Western Conference contender Hasek felt would give him the best chance to win his first Stanley Cup.

Winter told Holland that Hasek had doubts about Detroit. Because he played in the Eastern Conference, Hasek saw the Wings twice a season, tops. He didn't know much about them firsthand, and all he had been hearing and reading was how they were still a good team but, because of their age, in decline. He thought some of the teams on his list were better. Holland spent countless hours trying to convince Winter to convince Hasek the Wings were his best option. So did assistant general manager Jim Nill, who grew up with Winter in Alberta. *We're going to make some changes. We have some great players: Chelios, Fedorov, Larionov, Lidstrom, Shanahan, Yzerman . . . tell him to think of what he could do with them.* Nill had joked with Winter about Hasek's coming to Detroit long before Hasek was available. Winter would call him about his clients in the upcoming draft, and he would ask about the Wings' needs.

"Goalie," Nill would say.

"I don't have any goalies," Winter would say.

"Are you sure?"

Winter told Holland one more thing: Hasek was promising one season of service, no more. Hasek, 36, had been talking for years about retiring and taking his family back to his native Czech Republic. Holland was confident that if he could acquire Hasek, he could convince him to stay longer by selling the Hockeytown program—from the youth hockey opportunities for his 11-year-old son, Michael, to the fans' passion. When the Wings won the Cup in 1997 and '98, police estimated a million fans flooded the normally desolate downtown for the parade. If Hasek came and the Wings won their third Cup in six seasons, how could Hasek look into such a crowd and not say he was coming back?

Time ran out on the Wings and Winter the first day of the draft, but Holland and Nill had made progress. Hasek seemed excited about the Wings. If he went to Detroit, he would accept $8 million—$1 million less than he would have made in Buffalo but the same as the Wings' highest-paid players, Lidstrom and Yzerman—unless the Wings won the Cup. Then he would make $9 million. The deal would be for one year, with club options for two more. Holland spoke to Regier, but Regier was so busy trading holdout captain Michael Peca—to the New York Islanders, in the end—that he had to put Hasek on the back burner.

"I'm still figuring it's a summer project," Holland said. "Sometimes you really work at things, and then they kind of die, and then they pick up sometime down the road and you finish it off—or else they die and you never hear about it again. I'm thinking, at the very worst, Buffalo will pick up the club option and retain rights. Then they can do something at some point during the summer."

All wasn't quiet, however. During the general managers' meetings, word had gotten around that Holland had met with the Lindroses. Rumors are rampant in the hockey world. They spread into the media quickly, and this one was big news. A Detroit sports talk radio station reported a Lindros-to-the-Wings deal was done, and that sent the fans into a frenzy.

"It was chaos," Holland said. "The city was nuts. They figured people were at the airport waiting for Eric to be flying in."

Holland set things straight. He said there was "no truth to all the rumors." He acknowledged he had met with the Lindroses, and he even said he had had "exploratory discussions" about a trade with Clarke. But he added he hadn't spoken with the Lindroses since the meeting and hadn't spoken with Clarke that day, and "that should tell you where we're at."

But Holland also dropped a little hint.

"Given the way we lost in the first round this year, we're exploring everything: We want to make our hockey club better," he said. "Stay tuned."

At the draft, Holland had heard some teams had asked the Phoenix Coyotes for permission to speak with superstar center Jeremy Roenick before July 1, when Roenick was scheduled to become an unrestricted free agent. Back in Detroit that Monday, Holland called Phoenix general manager Cliff Fletcher.

"I was wondering if it was true," Holland said.

It was. Fletcher told Holland he had spoken to one team about Roenick. The Coyotes were not going to re-sign him, so as far as he was concerned, anyone who called and asked for permission could have permission. Holland thanked Fletcher and right away called Roenick's agent, Neil Abbott. Holland and Abbott talked again Tuesday. Abbott asked for a contract proposal Wednesday.

"We made a proposal—a very good proposal," Holland said. "I know we were in the mix."

The Wings offered Roenick about $37.5 million over five years. Abbott called Holland that night and told him Roenick wanted to have a look around the Detroit area. They booked flights. Roenick and his wife, Tracy, landed about 4:00 P.M. the next day, and Holland picked them up at the airport. Holland wined and dined them at Forte, a swanky restaurant in the upscale suburb of Birmingham. He left them at their hotel, the Townsend, about 8:30 or 9:00.

"Thought we were in the mix," Holland said.

About 10:00 the next morning, the phone rang. The person on the other end told Holland that someone in the Wings organization had heard Roenick had signed with Philadelphia. Holland immediately called Abbott. Yes, Roenick was a Flyer. Abbott had called Holland, but Holland had turned off his cell phone, so Abbott had left a voice-mail message.

"I felt bad," Roenick said. "Ken Holland was more than gracious with me. But sometimes decisions have to be made—and made quickly."

Roenick was close to coming to Detroit.

"Very, very close," he said.

But after Holland dropped off Roenick, Roenick's cell phone rang. The Flyers. An offer. Five years, $37.5 million. Take it or leave it. Within a half-hour. Roenick said the Flyers told him they had other options but would drop them if he signed. Now.

"That all could have been a ploy on their part," Roenick said. "But it kind of put me in a position where I had to decide."

Roenick called a friend, the Flyers' Rick Tocchet, and told him he had 10 minutes. Philly or Detroit? Not surprisingly, Tocchet told Roenick to pick Philly.

In the end, money wasn't the issue, of course. The deals were almost identical. Roenick's wife was accomplished in equestrian, and she felt Philadelphia's suburbs were better for horses than

Detroit's suburbs. Roenick said he worried about the Wings' age and was "a little wary of the goaltending situation."

Statistically, Osgood ranked second only to legend Terry Sawchuk among Detroit goaltenders, second in games (389), second in wins (221), second in shutouts (30). He was 28. At 28, Patrick Roy, the league's all-time wins leader, had 225 wins in 418 games and 20 shutouts.

But for all his big saves, Osgood made some big mistakes. With only 41 regular-season games of NHL experience, he found himself in the net in the first round of the 1994 playoffs, after starter Bob Essensa lost twice to the Sharks. In Game 7, Osgood strayed from the net, played the puck—and sent it straight to forward Jamie Baker, who scored the winner with 6:35 left. In the dressing room afterward, Osgood sobbed and kept repeating, "I'm so sorry," and some people never got over that. Osgood played most of the '96-97 season, but Bowman went with Mike Vernon in the playoffs, and Vernon won the Conn Smythe Trophy as the playoffs' most valuable player as the Wings won the Cup. The Wings won the '98 Cup with Osgood in goal, but many remembered only the 90-footers he allowed to the Blues in the second round and to the Stars in the third.

"Because of that," said Draper, one of Osgood's best friends, "I don't think he's gotten the credit he deserves."

"There has been the perception out there that when the Red Wings win, we win because of our skaters," Holland said, "and when we lose, we lose because of our goaltending."

After Holland heard the bad news about Roenick, he worked on Hasek that Friday afternoon. Over the phone, Regier wondered how they would put together a deal that made sense for both sides—this was a strange situation, but Hasek still was a franchise player—and they started talking about packages of a player and draft picks.

"We tossed some ideas around, and at the same time, I know there's another team involved—at least one other team," Holland said. "I can't say things were heating up on June the 29th, but we were talking a fair amount."

At about 5:00, Regier called Holland. He told him he wanted to trade Hasek before July 1, when he would have to pick up his option. That meant the deal would be done tomorrow. By midnight.

"You now want to make it happen," Holland recalled.

Holland spent Saturday evening at home in his den with Nill. They didn't have anything to eat; they didn't have anything to drink.

"You're not in the eating mood; you're not in the drinking mood," Holland said. "You're anxious."

Starting at about 6:00, Holland began going back and forth with Regier. They would talk, trade ideas, take a 5- or 10-minute break. They would talk, trade ideas, take a 5- or 10-minute break. This went on for about three hours. Sometime between 9:00 and 9:15, Holland spoke to Regier.

And then the phone went silent.

Nill used his cell phone to keep in touch with Winter. But otherwise, he and Holland made small talk. They imagined what it would be like to acquire Hasek, but they talked about the two goaltenders they already had, too. Holland believed Osgood was a very good goaltender, and although Osgood slumped miserably in the regular season, he wasn't the reason the Wings lost to Los Angeles. Backup Manny Legace was 28, too, and he had finished the season 24-5-5. *You know, we're pretty well set up here for six or seven years with these two guys. You might not have Dominik Hasek, but you've got a great 1-2 punch that should only get better. You hope they push one another, and they've got a great rapport. . . .* As the clock kept ticking, Holland and Nill knew midnight meant July 1. There were a lot of unrestricted free agents out there. They even wondered if Roy would be willing to leave Colorado, not knowing he was about to re-sign.

"So we're talking about Plan B," Holland said. "You're saying, 'OK, when we hit 12:05, if things don't happen, what do we do? We've got to make some calls and make sure we've got our ducks in order, make sure they know tonight we're ready to go tomorrow morning.'"

At 11:00 o'clock, the phone was still silent.

Holland turned to Nill.

"We're out," he told him. "The deal's being finalized somewhere else."

Holland and Nill figured Hasek was going to St. Louis. Nill decided to make a last-ditch effort with Winter.

"Hang in there," Winter said. "You're still in it."

Winter told Nill not to give up too much for Hasek.

Wait. Had Hasek picked Detroit?

The phone rang at 11:10.

It was Regier. He told Holland he was very close to a deal with another general manager, but he didn't know if the other GM was in or if he was out. He said the other GM was taking some time to think, but he had 50 minutes and didn't have time to think.

"He wasn't going back," Holland said. "If he could do a deal with me on this phone call, it was done. Like sudden-death overtime."

Yes, Hasek had picked Detroit. The Wings were in the driver's seat; Regier's hands were tied. Regier rattled off a few things. Holland rattled off a few things. They talked a little bit about the draft pick, and in a matter of minutes, they agreed: The Wings would get Hasek. The Sabres would get forward Slava Kozlov, a first-round pick in the 2002 draft and future considerations. If Hasek played in '02-03, the Sabres would get a second-round pick in the '03 draft. If Hasek played in '02-03 and the Wings won the Cup, the pick would be a first-rounder.

"I'm done, Darcy," Holland told Regier. "But give me 10 quick minutes here to get Rich Winter on the phone. I just want to double-check to make sure what I talked to Rich Winter about a week ago is still done. I don't want him changing his mind."

Holland called Winter.

"Rich, I've got a deal done with Buffalo to acquire Dominik Hasek," Holland told Winter.

Holland reiterated the contract terms.

"Is this acceptable to you?" he asked.

Winter said it was.

"Let me call Dominik," Winter said. "I'll call you right back."

Winter hung up and called Hasek. About five minutes later, he called Holland back.

"I talked to Dominik," he said. "We've got ourselves a deal."

Winter gave Holland Hasek's cell phone number, and Holland quickly called Hasek. He welcomed him aboard, gave him the glad-to-have-you, told him they would talk soon about bringing him to Detroit, this and that.

Holland called Regier back.

"I'm all done with Rich Winter and Dom," he said. "We've got ourselves a deal. We're done."

"How are we going to go about releasing this now?" Regier asked.

It was about 11:30. Regier quickly set up a conference call, and he and Holland walked through the deal with league officials from about midnight to 12:30. Afterward, Regier and Holland agreed to release the news first thing in the morning, at 9:00 Eastern. But as they were talking, Regier's cell phone rang. It was his public relations director. He had been inundated with phone calls.

"People have somehow heard," Holland said. "So now we said, 'Holy cripes. It's a quarter to 1:00 in the morning.' Now we said, 'You know what? We'd better release it.'"

Holland told Regier to have his PR guy release it at 1:00.

"Give me 15 minutes," Holland said.

Holland called Kozlov's agent, Scott Lites. He knew he wasn't in his office, but he wanted to leave a voice-mail message.

"Scott, it's Ken Holland," he said. "We made a deal. Slava Kozlov's been traded to the Buffalo Sabres."

Holland called Osgood.

"Chris, Ken Holland," he said. "Got some bad news. We've acquired Dominik Hasek. Give me a call as soon as you can."

When Holland finally finished, he and Nill sat for 15 minutes and had a beer. They were obviously ecstatic, but they couldn't celebrate too much. It was July 1, and they had to be up and available at 7:30 or 8:00, so they could work the phones again.

"You've got to get some sleep," Holland said.

Chapter 2
Wings

Dominik Hasek became a Red Wing so late that Saturday night—or early that Sunday morning, rather—the news didn't make the Sunday papers. A lot of fans found out by watching television, listening to the radio or logging onto the Internet. But more than a few found out by word of mouth, hearing from some excited friend who couldn't wait to tell them. The city was abuzz.

If traffic was ever low at the Wings' Hockeytown Authentics store in suburban Troy, it was in July. But not this July.

"It was like flipping a switch when we got Hasek," said Jim Urban, the Wings' senior director of merchandise. "There were phone calls right away. 'Do you have Hasek jerseys? When are you going to get them in?' "

Hasek jerseys went on sale immediately.

As Jim Nill drove back to Ken Holland's house to get back to work, he heard the radio reports about Hasek—and Doug Weight. The St. Louis Blues had acquired Weight in a five-player deal with the Edmonton Oilers and signed him to a fat, five-year contract. Nill was surprised. The Wings had approached Edmonton general manager Kevin Lowe at the draft, told him they were interested in Weight and asked him to call them if something was going to happen. Lowe never called.

As it turned out, Lowe had discussed a possible deal with St. Louis general manager Larry Pleau at the draft. Pleau made a strong pitch for Hasek. Some said he offered him $1 million or more than the Wings had; he said he offered the same amount or maybe $500,000 more. He thought for a while he was going to get Hasek, but when Hasek went to Detroit, he called Lowe and nabbed Weight.

Oh, well. Weight would have been wonderful. He was from the Detroit suburb of Warren, and he was a top playmaker. Too bad he went to the Blues. But this was July 1, the start of the

19

free-agent feeding frenzy, and the Wings had to move on. They dabbled in a lot of things that day. At one point, a representative for Los Angeles Kings left wing Luc Robitaille called Holland and asked whether he was interested.

"We have interest," Holland told him. "Right now, we're talking to some people. We're not sure what direction we're going to go in."

Holland told the representative to stay in touch, to call if Robitaille was close to signing somewhere.

"I don't want to be left out of the loop," Holland said.

Holland and Nill spent most of their time, from about 11:00 A.M. to 7:00 P.M., trying to re-sign Martin Lapointe. The Wings drafted him in 1991, and he spent 10 seasons with them developing leadership, physical presence and scoring touch. Scotty Bowman spoke strongly of how badly he wanted him back. But Lapointe had unusual leverage. He was unrestricted at 27—instead of 31 or older, as usual—because he had made less than the league's average salary for 10 seasons. Plus, skating on scoring lines instead of checking lines, he broke out that season with 27 goals, 11 more than his previous career high. Although some NHL scouts thought Lapointe might never score so much again, several teams pursued him, driving up the price further.

At the end of the day, Lapointe was going to the Boston Bruins.

"It wasn't out yet," Holland said, "but I knew it."

The Wings' final offer was four years, $16 million. Lapointe got four years and more than $20 million. His salary was more than four times the $1.25 million he had been making. One Wings executive said Lapointe "won the lottery."

"I love Marty," Holland said, "but we weren't prepared to pay that kind of money for Marty."

Holland assessed the situation, and his conclusion was simple: Now he needed someone who could score some goals. Lapointe and Slava Kozlov combined for 47 goals that season, more than 18 percent of the Wings' offense. Holland had spoken some with Mike Barnett, the agent for Alexander Mogilny, the New Jersey Devils right wing who scored 43 goals.

"I knew the next morning was crunch time," Holland said. "Either you were in and made a deal or you were out."

The next morning, the Wings introduced Hasek at a news conference at Joe Louis Arena. Hasek, a quirky fellow, came in a cardigan sweater. But a little after 10:00, he pulled on a Wings sweater—No. 39.

"Looks good," Holland said, beaming.

Hasek spoke for about a half-hour in his heavy Czech accent, mixing up the words a bit. He talked about how excited he was "to go to this hockey city, Hockeytown, to just be here and win." He said at first he had given Darcy Regier a list of three teams to which he would be traded, then he picked the Wings, although another team had offered more money. He revealed he had called Regier about 10:30 the night of the deal—and helped Holland get it done.

"I told him, 'No, no, no,' " Hasek said. "He was asking for too much, and I said, 'I won't go to Detroit if you ask for too many players.' I told him, 'I need every good player on this team.' "

Someone asked Hasek about the possibility of playing against his contemporary Patrick Roy in the playoffs. Hasek had won two Harts and six Vezinas; Roy had won no Harts and three Vezinas. But Roy had won four Stanley Cups, including the last one, and three Conn Smythes, including the last one; Hasek had won none of each. Hasek, of course, said it "would be great."

"To win the Cup, that's my goal," he said, "nothing else, nothing less."

The dream, he said, "is what keeps me playing hockey."

Standing behind the reporters, Steve Yzerman smiled.

"My initial reaction is that, come next March, when everybody is jockeying for position, everybody is going to be looking at it and saying, 'I don't want to play Hasek in the first round,' " Yzerman said.

"Having him just makes it that much more uncomfortable for our opposition. You just don't get the opportunity to acquire a player of that magnitude who can have such an impact on your team right away, so it's almost like, if you can get a guy like that, you get him. It's a real coup."

After the news conference, Holland went down the hall to his office and hopped back on the phone. He and Nill worked on Mogilny. For a while, they thought they were going to get him. But then, early in the afternoon, the Toronto Maple Leafs came along with a better offer, and the Wings were out.

Holland and Nill took another look at the marketplace. There was St. Louis' Pierre Turgeon, but he was a center, and they wanted a wing. There was Robitaille and Dallas Stars right wing Brett Hull. Robitaille, 35, had scored 37 goals that season—five more than any Wing had—and 590 in his career. Hull, 36, had scored 39 that season and 649 in his career. Robitaille had made $3.5 million that season, Hull $7 million. Robitaille seemed much more likely to fit into the Wings' budget.

"We made a decision to talk to Luc Robitaille," Holland said.

Holland called one of Robitaille's agents, Tom Reich.

"What's it going to take to sign Luc Robitaille?" he asked.

Reich gave him a number. It was too high.

"We're out," Holland said.

"Whoa! Whoa!" Reich said. "Where are you at?"

Holland, Nill, Reich and Robitaille's other agent, Pat Brisson, talked for two or three hours, Holland staying in touch with Mike Ilitch all the while. About 7:00, the deal was done: two years, $8 million, plus a club/player option for a third year. The Wings had the option to bring Robitaille back at the same salary or cut him loose for $1 million; Robitaille had the option to come back at the same salary if he reached certain statistical marks.

Robitaille had wanted to retire as a King. He had spent 12 of his 15 seasons in Los Angeles, and his family loved it there. But he never was a good skater—he was drafted in the ninth round, 171st overall, in 1984—and the Kings felt he was slowing down. They offered only a one-year, $2.5-million contract—a $1-million pay cut. Robitaille felt they weren't making a commitment to win: They had traded franchise defenseman Rob Blake for financial reasons that season. What's more, like Hasek, he never had won a Cup.

So Robitaille sat down and had a long talk with his wife, Stacia. She told him the time had come for him to go—and go to a winner. "I agreed with her," Robitaille said.

They talked about what that would mean for them and their sons, Steven, 13, and Jesse, 6. Three times in his career, Robitaille had been traded—Los Angeles to the Pittsburgh Penguins, Pittsburgh to the New York Rangers, New York back to Los Angeles. Each time, the family moved as a unit. But this time, it wouldn't. Stacia had a career, too. She was a recording artist with an album, "Hush," coming out in a month. She was president of her own label, Raystone Records. And Steven's school was a big factor. And . . . well, they had to do what they had to do: Robitaille would get an apartment; Stacia and the boys would stay in the L.A. area for a year at least.

"We made the decision together, my wife and I," Luc said. "We talked about it, how we had to communicate, how we would take trips to see each other, how we had to stick together the whole year. We knew it would be hard."

Robitaille's nickname was "Lucky Luc." But it might as well have been "Happy-go-lucky Luc." One of the nicest guys in sports, Robitaille always had a smile on his face, and his smile was huge after he signed. Asked why he would join the Wings, when the Kings had beaten them in the playoffs, he laughed and reminded a reporter the Wings had swept the Kings in the first round the year before.

"Trust me," he said. "They're the better team."

Asked whether Hasek had anything to do with his interest in Detroit, he laughed again.

"Hasek?" he said. "Hasek, Yzerman, Shanahan, Chelios, Lidstrom—there are a lot of great players there."

Told Hasek's goal was to win the Cup, nothing else, nothing less, he laughed once more.

"Well, that's cool," he said. "I think we will do it."

Robitaille said he had "one thing missing" in his career.

"That's to hold the Cup," he said. "It's the best situation for me. I'm so happy to come to Detroit. This is going to be great."

The Detroit Free Press, the paper that had wondered whether the Wings were past their prime, put this headline on the front page: "Detroit dreams anew of Stanley."

The Wings introduced Robitaille at a news conference that Thursday. Afterward, wearing his new No. 20 sweater, he threw out the first pitch at a Tigers game. Holland thought he was done adding to his roster. The Wings had wanted to make an impact, and they felt they had done that with Hasek and Robitaille. Their payroll at about $60 million, they thought they had reached the limit of their budget.

"This is it for high-profile guys," Holland said.

Holland was happy, but not completely. He still had to move defenseman Aaron Ward, who never got along with Bowman and had asked for a trade once again; Ward went to the Carolina Hurricanes on July 9 for what became a second-round pick in the 2003 draft. Worse, Holland had to try to trade Chris Osgood, who had two years and $7.75 million left on his contract—too much for a backup. Few knew how hard that was on him: He had a special relationship with Osgood.

Once upon a time, Holland was a goaltender. He played four NHL games, one with the Hartford Whalers in 1980-81, three with the Wings in '83-84. But he went 0-2-1 with a 4.95 goals-against average, and he spent most of his nine-year professional career in the minor leagues. After Holland finished up in '84-85 with the Wings' American Hockey League affiliate in Glens Falls, N.Y., the Adirondack Red Wings, Jimmy Devellano offered him a job as western Canada scout. Holland was from Vernon, British Columbia.

"The opportunity to remain in the game and have a job in the game after my playing days were over was something I never thought about," Holland said. "But when the opportunity presented itself, I jumped."

Holland set up shop in Medicine Hat, Alberta. He became chief amateur scout four years later, but the general manager in him was starting to come out already. Ball hockey. He had loved it as a kid, running in shoes, wearing shin pads, using a hockey stick to bat around a bounceless orange ball on a rink without ice. He started a summer rec league. It ran from the beginning of May to the middle of July. Games were an hour and a half, from 7:30 to 9:00, from 8:00 to 9:30. Of course, Holland ran a team—and called it the Red Wings.

Hockey Gods

In mid-May 1991, the "Wings" were looking for a couple of players to upgrade the team. Somebody mentioned Osgood, who played for the Medicine Hat Tigers, the same junior hockey team for which Holland played in '74-76. Holland had a couple of Osgood's teammates on the roster, and he convinced them to convince Osgood to come out. He liked Osgood as a prospect, and he wanted to get to know him before the June draft. Osgood was 18, Holland 35. Osgood played forward, Holland defense. After three or four weeks of ball hockey, Holland pulled Osgood aside to talk real hockey.

"We want to draft you," Holland told him. "You've got my word we're going to draft you. Has anybody else expressed interest?"

"Yeah," Osgood said. "I've talked to a few teams."

The Wings took Osgood in the third round, 54th overall. Holland watched Osgood play another season in the Western Hockey League, some with Medicine Hat, some with Brandon, Manitoba, and some with Seattle.

"We developed a big brother-younger brother relationship," Holland said. "I've got four kids. He was like my fifth kid."

Osgood went to Adirondack, went to Detroit as a backup, then became the Wings' on-again, off-again starter. Holland went to Detroit as assistant general manager, then became the GM. Holland lived on a lake in Vernon in the summer, and soon Osgood bought a place down the shoreline.

"He ended up coming out there partly because I was there, partly because he loved the area," Holland said.

In Vernon, they were friends. They golfed—Holland loved golf—but they never talked hockey. In Detroit, Holland was the boss and Osgood was the player. Period.

"It was never something that we discussed," Holland said. "He understood it, and I understood it, and it's business. We had joked on occasion throughout the years that at some point in time I might have to trade him. I didn't think it would be when he was 28, but. . . ."

Osgood didn't return Holland's phone call after the Hasek deal that Sunday. Holland had to leave a voice-mail message on Osgood's cell phone Monday, but he reached Osgood's mother, Joy, whom he had known for 10 years.

"That was a tough call," Holland said. "She was very, very upset. She didn't really understand what was going on. I tried to explain it to her. . . . The hockey players understand. Everybody else doesn't really understand. . . . I ended up telling her to tell Chris to give me a call."

Holland spoke to Osgood the next day. Osgood was upset. There wasn't much to say.

"It was a tough decision," Holland told him. "Chris, it's Dominik Hasek. It's a guy who's won six Vezina trophies. You know, Chris, I'm going to be out in Vernon in a few days. We'll talk then. You're still a member of the Detroit Red Wings."

Basically, all Osgood told Holland was that he wanted to be traded as soon as possible.

"Chris, I've got to take care of the Detroit Red Wings," Holland told him. "I understand where you're coming from. I will try to do that if I can. But at the same time, if I can't, I can't. I'll see you in a few days."

The day after Robitaille's news conference, Holland flew to Vernon. Osgood came over to Holland's cabin one night, and they sat out on his back deck fairly late, until 1:00 or 1:30 in the morning, talking it all out.

Osgood's wishes had to wait. Hasek was hospitalized with a mystery virus.

A couple of days after his introductory news conference, Hasek flew home to Pardubice, Czech Republic. He didn't feel good.

"In order to rule out any complications and to make a thorough checkup, he was taken into a hospital," Jiri Voprsal, Hasek's business partner, told a Czech news agency.

Hasek was supposed to play in a tennis tournament of hockey stars that weekend. Having led the Czechs to the gold medal at the 1998 Nagano Olympics, he was a transcendent athletic idol in his country, as Michael Jordan was in the United States. But to the fans' disappointment, new Wings teammate Jiri Fischer replaced him. He stayed in the hospital. And stayed.

The news broke almost a week later, July 11.

"He came down with a bug, and they couldn't identify it," Rich Winter told the Canadian Press. "They've done all the necessary tests. . . . They're being very careful with it."

Winter said nothing appeared "seriously wrong" with Hasek, they didn't expect "any ongoing problem" and Hasek was in "good spirits." But Mike Ilitch wanted to be sure about his new multimillion-dollar investment. The weekend of July 14-15, he flew his family physician, Donald Weaver, to Pardubice. Weaver found swelling in Hasek's right ankle, tenderness in his left ankle and wrists, and a fever. But the cause, he said, did not have a "definitive diagnosis." Hasek didn't know Wings trainer John Wharton before, but he talked to him on the phone every day.

Hasek was released from the hospital July 19—two weeks after he was admitted—and told to take antibiotics and be back for outpatient treatment. "I'm glad I can go home from the hospital at last," Hasek said in a statement. "Everything will be a bit late, but I believe I will be in shape by the beginning of September. I believe this year will now be as I had imagined it would be."

Hasek said he felt "excellent."

The Wings wished they could say the same.

While Holland was in Vernon, he had two or three conversations with Barnett. They had talked about Mogilny earlier in the month. Now they were talking about Hull, who had taken a look at the Wings' new-and-improved roster, called Barnett and said, "Get me to Detroit."

"Are you interested?" Barnett asked.

"Yeah, we're interested," Holland told him. "But we've got money issues here."

Holland came back to Detroit, and he had about five more conversations with Barnett in early August. Before leaving on a personal trip to Europe on Aug. 8, Holland called Barnett and left a voice-mail message on his cell phone.

"I'm letting you know that I just don't know how we're going to make this thing happen," Holland said. "I think we're out of the mix here with Brett. If you've got something going, make it happen. I'm going to be out of touch for eight days. If you leave messages, I certainly will return my calls."

Barnett kept in touch with Nill, and Nill kept in touch with Holland. When Holland returned, Hull still hadn't signed. Holland had a couple of more conversations with Barnett.

"You know, Brett really wants to come to Detroit," Barnett told him. "He hasn't given up hope."

Holland was in New York on business Monday, Aug. 20. He called Barnett around suppertime, and Barnett said he was flying somewhere the next morning to meet with another team—he was going to Colorado to meet the owner of the Montreal Canadiens—and probably would get a contract done.

"Is there any way we can make this thing happen?" Barnett asked. "Detroit is still Brett's first choice."

Holland spoke with Ilitch, who had a soft spot for Hull. Ilitch had loved watching Hull's Hall of Fame father, Bobby, and when Bobby had represented Brett years before, he had talked to him in an attempt to sign Brett.

"Let's get it done," Ilitch told Holland. "I want to get this guy. Bring him in."

But, Ilitch asked, "Is there any way we can get some financial relief, keeping the team together?"

Holland went back and forth with Barnett, coming up with the basic parameters of a deal, until 11:00 or 11:30.

"Cancel your trip," Holland said.

Barnett canceled.

Holland contacted some of his players the next day.

Earlier, he had checked Hull's character with them. As Sports Illustrated put it, "Holland wanted a cannon from the slot, not a loose cannon." Hull was famous—or infamous, depending on your perspective—for readily sharing his opinions in his raspy voice, sometimes adding his devil-may-care grin. A sniper with a scary shot who scored 86 goals and won the Hart in 1991, he had been forced to complete his game the past three seasons in Dallas, and he didn't always like it. One day at practice, according to the Dallas Morning News, coach Ken Hitchcock preached about positioning and defenses and said goals didn't matter. During the ensuing drill, Hull dumped the puck in a corner on a couple of 2-on-1s. Asked why, he said, "Goals don't matter." Hitchcock threw him out of practice. Hull and Hitchcock got along well away from hockey, gabbing often about music and golf. But Hull hated Hitchcock's defensive philosophy, even though it won the 1999 Cup and got the Stars to the 2000 finals, and the had often had vigorous disagreements about the game. After the Stars lost to the Blues in the second round of the '01 playoffs, they decided to offer Hull only a one-year deal. Hull wanted two years. They never really negotiated.

Brendan Shanahan had played 3½ seasons with Hull in St. Louis. Chris Chelios had played with Hull on the U.S. national team and was one of his best friends. They had been lobbying for Hull, and they gave Holland enthusiastic endorsements. Shanahan said that before Holland could get the name "Brett Hull" out of his mouth, he said, "Sign him."

Now Holland wanted to see about that financial relief. To the best of his knowledge, no hockey player ever had deferred salary so that his team could sign another player. It had happened in the National Basketball Association, but the NBA had a salary cap. The NHL didn't. Shanahan joked that when Holland brought up the idea of deferring money, he told him, "Kenny, Brett's no spring chicken." But Shanahan agreed to defer some salary, as did Chelios and Yzerman—"just enough to make it happen," Yzerman said. Later, Nicklas Lidstrom agreed to do the same.

The deal was done late that night. Two years, $9 million. Hull agreed to take $3.5 million the first year, $4.5 million the next and the last million at the end of the contract, and the Wings agreed to give him $75,000 if he led the playoffs in scoring and $75,000 if they won the Cup.

"Pro sports is a business," Holland said. "It took some people to work with us to make it all happen. I think it's extraordinary. I think it says a lot about Brett Hull and a lot about the people on our hockey club."

"There are a lot of owners and organizations that would take money and profit and put it right in their pocket," Shanahan said. "Here, it seems to always be reinvested, put toward continuing the love affair between the team and the city. Part of playing for a team like this is fitting into a budget."

Even with the players' help, Ilitch was taking a big gamble on a long, lucrative playoffs. The Wings' payroll would bulge well over budget at about $65 million, highest in the league.

"We need a heck of a run," Devellano said. "It can't be a first-round ouster, that's for sure, or we struck out, and it's going to be quite a hit. We're taking a risk most people couldn't or wouldn't do."

Hull? The Wings had Brett Hull now, too? Hockeytown was giddy when the news broke. This time the Detroit Free Press headlines were "Oldies but goodies? Hull, yes!" and "A Hull of a deal." But people also wondered if all this was too good to be true. They knew Hull's personality and reputation. How were all these guys going to play with one puck?

The Wings held their third introductory news conference of the summer the next day. Hull smiled and told the media, "Yeah, you'll hear a lot from me." But otherwise, he calmed fears of an ego overload. He had worn No. 16 much of his career, but he took No. 17, because the Wings were holding No. 16 out of circulation for Vladimir Konstantinov, severely injured in a limousine accident six days after they won the 1997 Cup.

"Numbers aren't important to me," Hull said. "I don't want to make waves."

After he pulled his new sweater over his head, Hull asked, "How's it look?"

It looked pretty good, judging by the jostling photographers in front and their flashing bulbs. But there was a problem for one TV reporter: His camera was blocked. So he yelled, "Down in front!"

Hull just laughed.

"Let's get along now," he said.

How would Hull get along with the coach this time? Well, he sat right next to him and said, "The theory that I have on the game doesn't matter one bit. You do what's best for the group. I don't think that you can look at Coach Bowman and think that he could do much wrong, with the record and resume he has."

How would Hull get along with his teammates? Well, didn't he defer money to be with these guys? And didn't some of them defer money to be with him? They weren't going to be repelled by each other, because they were *drawn* to each other. There wasn't going to be bickering about ice time, worrying about whose spotlight shone brightest.

Hockey Gods

"Hockey players don't act like that," Hull said. "When you've got people like Chelios and Yzerman and guys like Darren McCarty and people like that in the room, those things . . . they don't happen. And if by chance something does happen like that, it certainly isn't going to last long. . . .

"There were some other teams involved, and they made great offers as well. But I couldn't help leaning toward Yzerman and Chelios and Shanahan and Lidstrom and Larionov and Hasek and Scotty Bowman. I'm looking at a team with people I know and admire, with a chance to win the Stanley Cup. To be able to play with those guys is a treat. I couldn't think of anything negative about it. . . .

"It was a no-brainer for me. Putting on this jersey, it is a thrill. Not a lot of people get an opportunity to play on a good team, let alone a team with the quality of people that this organization has, in a city where hockey is such a vibrant part of it. I am looking forward to it."

Chapter 3
Coming Together

On a sunny September morning, a sleek, silver SUV pulled up to Joe Louis Arena. Chris Chelios was driving. Brendan Shanahan was riding shotgun. Brett Hull was in the backseat. They helped each other unload their bags and golf clubs, then stuffed them into one of the Red Wings' two team buses. They were headed to the northern Michigan town of Traverse City for training camp with Sergei Fedorov and Dominik Hasek and Igor Larionov and Nicklas Lidstrom and Luc Robitaille and Steve Yzerman and . . .

"We're talking household names," Ken Holland said, "and a number of them."

Nine.

Nine potential Hall of Famers. And their boss was Scotty Bowman, the greatest coach in hockey history.

"These," Darren McCarty said, "are icons of the sport."

The NHL never had seen a team like this one.

The 1972-73 Montreal Canadiens had 11 eventual Hall of Famers, and Bowman was their coach. The '56-60 Canadiens had 10 eventual Hall of Famers, and Toe Blake was their coach.

But the 1972-73 Canadiens played in a 16-team league, and the '56-60 Canadiens played in a six-team league. The 2001-02 Wings were in a league that had been enriched by the arrival of Europeans, but diluted by the expansion to 30 cities.

And because many of these Wings were in the winters of their careers, many of them already had Hall of Fame credentials. They had made 32 first or second postseason All-Star teams, won 27 major individual awards, made 56 All-Star Game appearances and scored 90 hat tricks. They had four of the top 10 active goal-scorers, and their top five scorers had a staggering 2,683 goals.

Consider the coaches: At the start of the 1959-60 season, the last of that great Montreal run, Blake had won only four of his record eight Cups and still was six years from the Hall of Fame. At the start of the '72-73 season, Bowman had yet to win a Cup. Now Bowman already had tied the record with eight Cups as a coach and had been in the Hall of Fame for a decade.

The Wings looked like world-beaters again. Larionov said he hadn't seen a team so rich in reputations since the Soviet Union's Central Red Army, which had all of Russia's top talent before the Iron Curtain came down. Standing back from the buses in a group of wide-eyed rookies, some of whom ended up asking for autographs up north, coolheaded center Jason Williams cracked, "You could probably take Detroit over to the Olympics and . . . do pretty well."

"We're pleased with our collection of talent; now it has to become a team," Holland said. "It's an important training camp in that we have to build chemistry. The onus is on the players. We have a lot of reason for optimism, but like other teams, we need a lot of positive things to happen for us to have that success."

Before boarding his bus, Hull insisted players weren't kidding when they said they hated training camp.

"The first week is always the worst, but it's kind of a necessary evil," he said. "I haven't been excited to go to training camp in a long time. I'm a very bad training-camp player."

But asked whether he was excited this year, Hull added, "Very . . . very excited."

Hasek was excited, but he was something else, too.

"To be honest," he said, "I'm a bit nervous."

Nervous? The Dominator?

"Just because I'm in a new place, and I know there are big expectations from people and my teammates," he said, surrounded by reporters there just to watch him load his luggage. "I want to prove I can do my job."

Chelios smirked. He always smirked.

"On paper, we look great," he said. "I can't wait to see the product on the ice."

Along with the excitement that morning, there was awkwardness.

Hockey Gods

There was Chris Osgood. As the reporters hounded Hasek, Osgood walked behind them and dragged his bags to a bus. When the reporters spotted him, they left Hasek and hurried over. Osgood boarded without a word, flashes going off in his face.

Holland had been unable to trade Osgood. First, Holland had to hold off because of Hasek's illness. Second, Osgood's high salary was putting off suitors. Teams were asking the Wings to assume some of it, but because of their financial situation, the Wings weren't willing. Third, it was a buyer's market. The Atlanta Thrashers, New York Islanders, New York Rangers and Vancouver Canucks were said to need goaltenders, but the Canadiens, Wings, Los Angeles Kings and Minnesota Wild were said to be offering goaltenders. Buyers could wait, see what they had, let sellers drop their prices and, maybe, pick up someone for free in the Sept. 28 waiver draft.

"There isn't a deal out there for me to pursue," Holland said. "I'm not worried. A lot can happen. . . . It's probably going to be hard on Chris. . . . Unfortunately, (this kind of situation is) part of the profession we all chose."

Then there was Uwe Krupp. He hadn't played in 2½ years, and he was making a comeback—while embroiled in a bizarre, bitter, $8.2-million arbitration battle with the Wings. Just 11 days before, he had gone public with his side of the story in an exhaustive piece by Detroit Free Press columnist Mitch Albom.

When Krupp, a defenseman who played with Colorado, signed a four-year, $16.4-million contract in the summer of 1998, the Wings were thrilled, and Holland said, "We've dramatically improved our hockey club. We like the way he plays—his size, his range. The guy was No. 1 on our list, and he's no-maintenance. He's safe."

Soon the Wings changed their tune. Krupp suffered a knee injury. Then a hamstring injury. Then, after having played only 22 games, he pulled out of warm-ups before a game against the Phoenix Coyotes because of back trouble, and two doctors told him to retire. Hockey is a modern-day gladiators' sport. Men sometimes compete through incredible pain, and the Wings didn't think Krupp was living up to the code.

Holland, Krupp, John Wharton and agent Roland Thompson met in June 1999.

Coming Together

"Here's what happened," Krupp told Albom. "We're in the office, and Kenny's got the letter from (a doctor) saying I need to retire, and Kenny starts yelling, 'What is this shit? What is this shit? You think on the basis of a two-sentence letter you're gonna get out of here? You think we're gonna pay you your contract?'

"My agent says, 'Kenny, what do you mean? His contract is guaranteed. You have to pay it.'

"Kenny says, 'We'll send you to one doctor after another until we find someone who'll operate.' He is really upset.

"My agent goes, 'Kenny, what's the big deal? It's a disability thing. It's insured.'

"And Kenny goes, 'There's no insurance.'

"And my agent goes, 'WHAT?' "

Krupp said a white Ford Taurus pulled up to his remote Montana home the next month. A man who identified himself as Turtle Johnson got out, said he was representing the Wings and asked him to sign a strange letter authorizing a lawyer to examine his medical records, his driving records, any sheriff's reports, any insurance claims, etc. When he refused, the Wings suspended him for failing to turn over medical records.

Then the Wings found out Krupp had been dogsledding—and doing it less than two weeks after his last game. Krupp admitted it was probably a bad idea but said it had no effect on his back. The Wings claimed he had compromised his recovery and breached his contract. They lifted the suspension and gave him a new one.

It was a mess, and it got messier. Krupp said the Wings had hired private investigators, and those investigators had contacted friends, fellow dogsledders and even his ex-wife in Germany. The Wings didn't deny it.

Krupp said he had made progress after months of rehab and was coming back to earn his money and restore his reputation.

"I've had a pretty good career," Krupp told Albom. "I won a Stanley Cup, played in an All-Star Game. But when people hear my name now, they say, 'Isn't he the dumb ass who ruined himself dogsledding?' "

The Wings believed he was coming back just to force them to lift the suspension and to make sure he grabbed that last $4.1 million, and they tried to diminish the distraction.

"We're in the business of trying to win games," Holland said. "The most important thing is chemistry between him and the players. As for any animosity between him and the front office . . . well, let's just say that wouldn't be the first time that's happened in the NHL."

Asked that morning whether he was comfortable joining the team again, Krupp said, "Very. It's a non-issue."

It was Tuesday morning in Traverse City, and the Wings had physicals. Jim Nill stood near one of the arena's two rinks, talking to a reporter about a prospect, when he stopped in mid-sentence.

"What's everybody looking at?" he said.

A bunch of people—players, trainers, reporters, others—were craning their necks to see through a window to the floor above. Nill went over and craned his neck, too. Through the window was a television. And on the television was a plane. And the plane was flying into a building.

Someone said terrorists had hijacked two commercial airliners and flown them into the World Trade Center towers.

It was Sept. 11.

It was surreal. On the television, there was chaos and fire and smoke and death. On the ice, there were Chelios and Yzerman, skating, shooting pucks. On one side of the room upstairs, Wings were grunting on stationary bikes, completing one of their tests. On the other side, people were sitting in front of the television, contemplating the terrible pictures.

Shanahan sat on a plastic chair. Robitaille sat on a table. Behind them, another bunch of people—players, trainers, reporters, others—stood. They were American, Canadian, Russian, Czech, German. By then, the Pentagon was in flames, too.

No one spoke. But there was sound: hurried voice of TV anchor, grunts from Wings on bikes, hurried voice of TV anchor, grunts from Wings on bikes.

The first Trade Center tower collapsed, live, right there, on the screen. A little later, the second collapsed.

One by one, the Wings left. They had a team meeting at their hotel.

Coming Together

When the meeting was over, the players trickled into the lobby. Another surreal scene: televisions carted out and tuned to the news, volume way up; fans asking players for autographs; people on cell phones; people eating lunch; a long line of people—including several New Yorkers—from flights diverted to Traverse City, waiting to check in; golfers carrying clubs, laughing and joking.

"I've got some news," Fedorov said, holding up his cell phone.

"A plane crashed near Pittsburgh, too?" Chelios asked, shaking his head.

"Wow," forward Brent Gilchrist whispered.

"Crazy," Nill said.

In the afternoon, the Wings went ahead with their annual golf outing. It raised money for Vladimir Konstantinov and masseur Sergei Mnatsakanov, also severely injured in that 1997 limousine accident. Fans had paid hundreds, thousands of dollars and traveled to Traverse City to play.

Outside, six or seven people were on a driving range, hitting little white balls onto great green grass. To the left of them, a woman was sitting still in her car. Her radio was on. The news. She was weeping.

At 8:46 A.M. the next day, 24 hours after the first hijacked airliner flew into the World Trade Center, the little arena was full of fans, waiting for the Wings' first practice to begin.

At 9:02 A.M., 24 hours after the second hijacked airliner flew into the World Trade Center, Hasek appeared on the ice for the first time as a Wing, and the fans cheered.

About 40 minutes later, 24 hours after the third hijacked airliner flew into the Pentagon, Mike Krzeminski of Traverse City stood in a corner of the arena. He was wearing a No. 19 Yzerman sweater, trying to explain why he was there.

"It's escapism, definitely," said Krzeminski, 39. "You can only watch the footage so much."

While much of the sports world went silent, the Wings decided not to cancel their workouts.

"It's a delicate issue," Holland said. "Where's the line? How long do you grieve? I don't know what's right. . . . We're here, but

38

I don't know how much everybody's into what we're doing right now. Our hearts and minds are elsewhere."

The Wings were touched by the tragedy, in little ways, in large ways. Chelios' son was on a school trip to Arizona and couldn't get home. Several members of the organization knew Garnet (Ace) Bailey, the former Wing, the Kings' director of amateur scouting, among the passengers on the second plane. Bailey was on his way from Boston to Los Angeles for Kings training camp.

The Wings talked about what had happened. On the bus. In the dressing room. On the bench. Everywhere. Newspapers with screaming headlines littered the arena. As he sharpened skates, equipment manager Paul Boyer looked down at a copy of the Traverse City Record-Eagle sitting on the table. The headline: "TERROR HITS HOME."

"How crazy is that?" Boyer said.

Was it crazy to play hockey? Maybe. Maybe not.

"You know, I think everybody wanted to skate, to try to forget a little about it," defenseman Steve Duchesne said. "I don't know what to say, if we should have, if we shouldn't have."

Was it crazy for hundreds of fans to show up? Maybe. Maybe not.

Jill and Fred Banister, both 58, of Traverse City stood behind one of the goals.

"Just last week," Fred said, "we were on top of the World Trade Center."

Pause.

"It was such a magnificent sight."

Pause.

"I just can't imagine the horror those people must have felt."

The Banisters had felt enough horror of their own. Their daughter and her fiance lived in New York. Their son and daughter-in-law lived in Washington. They had spent hour after hour after hour Sept. 11 just trying to get through to their loved ones, just trying to see if they were alive. Their daughter's fiance worked near the World Trade Center. An eternity. That's what it took for them to find out everyone was all right.

Fred shook his head.

"We saw so much tragedy yesterday. . . ."

Hockey was all they wanted to see today.

They had promised their son long ago they would take an Yzerman poster to training camp and get it autographed. Hundreds of miles away from the rubble, helpless but to hope and pray and maybe give a little blood, they weren't going to break their promise. An autograph is a meaningless thing. Or is it?

"I can't do anything (to help), but this is something I can do," Jill said. "That might sound silly, but. . . ."

She held her head in her hands.

If the Wings didn't know their role in society—as entertainers, as examples—they knew it now. They approached the team's public relations staff and suggested they give blood.

"It just sounded like a good idea," Yzerman said. "We said, 'We should probably do that.' "

The Northwest Michigan Blood Program sent a mobile blood bank to the arena, and about 20 members of the organization gave. Sharon Childs, the program's director of donor services, limited the Wings to 20 pints. The blood itself wasn't as important as what it meant.

"You know," Childs said, "we need national symbols to say, 'Come on, America, stand up and do what you can.' "

Some Wings officials wore pins or stickers of an American flag, even though they weren't U.S. citizens. One fan wore a Wings sweater that had an American flag pinned over the Winged Wheel logo, and he had two American flags sticking out of the top of his hat. The Wings held a moment of silence before each of their scrimmages that week. One night, they listened to a prayer.

Against this backdrop, the Wings started to bond, practicing, scrimmaging, golfing, going to dinner, going to the bar.

Hasek roomed with Hull, which was funny: Hull had dealt him the deepest disappointment of his career. In Game 6 of the 1999 finals, Hull won the Cup for the Dallas Stars by beating Hasek 14:51 into the third overtime. Hull had a skate in the crease, which was forbidden then, but the officials allowed the goal because they ruled Hull had followed the puck there. The Sabres and their fans were furious. "No Goal" bumper stickers became popular in Buffalo.

But as much as the media asked them about the goal—or no goal—Hasek and Hull insisted they hadn't talked about it.

"I'll never mention it, because I don't see any reason," Hasek told the Hockey News. "We are teammates, and whatever happened two years ago, it doesn't matter. I always look ahead."

"I didn't bring up the goal once," Hull told Sports Illustrated. "No way! Why would I do that? I want Dom concentrating about this season and nothing else. Also, I wanted us to get along."

One morning, from behind a window where no one could see him, Chelios quietly watched Hasek practice. Hasek was as known for his work ethic as his unorthodox style. Sometimes, he would ask teammates to shoot at his head. Sometimes, when he had nothing else to do, he would flop on the ice and send his pads skyward—to thwart an imaginary opponent. Every time, he tried his best to stop the puck. "Hockey Night in Canada" once counted how many pucks went past him during a pregame warm-up. Three. Three out of 160. As Hasek explained, hockey was supposed to be fun, and for him, fun was stopping every shot.

"Hey, look in the net," Chelios said to a bystander. "See anything?"

"No."

"No pucks," Chelios said. "Not one." Chelios always smirked. This time, he smiled like a little boy who had gotten a new toy.

One afternoon, Hull walked back to the dressing room and found Larionov, the cerebral center nicknamed "The Professor," playing chess with a team official at a table a few feet from the ice. Shanahan was hunched over, watching intently.

"Oh, boy," Hull said. "Now I've seen everything."

When camp concluded and the boys bused back down to Detroit, they were on their way.

"It's going to take sacrifice from everyone," Hull said. "There are people that will be on the bench in situations where they're used to being out there. For the good of the whole, you have to realize that next time, you'll be out there. Our whole goal is to win 16 games in the playoffs. The sacrifices we make now are what will win for us then."

A big part of the Wings' appeal was their tradition. They were an Original Six franchise, and around Joe Louis Arena were black-and-white photographs of players past: Marty Barry, Ebbie Goodfellow, Syd Howe, Red Kelly, Herbie Lewis, Harry Lumley, Marcel Pronovost, (Black) Jack Stewart and so many others. In the rafters were five retired numbers: 1, for Terry Sawchuk; 7, for Ted Lindsay; 9, for Gordie Howe; 10, for Alex Delvecchio; and 12, for Sid Abel. The Wings had nine Cup banners. Only the Canadiens and Toronto Maple Leafs had more.

When the Wings skated at the Joe that Sunday for the first time, the new players met the man they called "The Link."

Wally Crossman moved from Ontario to Michigan with his family in 1926, the year Detroit entered the NHL. He lived near old Olympia Stadium—*new* Olympia Stadium, that is. When Crossman arrived, there was just a hole in the ground at Grand River and McGraw. He watched workers build the basement, install the brine pipes and lay red brick after red brick. After the Olympia opened in '27, Crossman was a fixture. He worked as a soda jerk at a neighborhood drugstore, so he was never far away. He sat in the balcony for 25 cents. He went to practice for free. After stints as the Cougars and Falcons, after surviving hard financial times during the Depression, the team became the Red Wings when James Norris bought it in '32. The Wings won the Cup in '36 and '37.

"I just hung around and hung around," Crossman said. "I'd go into the building and get acquainted with all the players and the coaches."

In 1940, war duty called the Wings' dressing room assistant, and coach/general manager Jack Adams asked Crossman if he would carry on for him. Crossman jumped at the chance, and so he was there when the Wings won Cups in '43, '50, '52, '54 and '55, when Adams broke up the team afterward, when the Wings went into a nosedive, when they moved into the Joe on Jefferson in '79, when Ilitch bought them, when they became good again. He also married in 1940. So perhaps it's poetic that the only jewelry he wore was a Wings championship ring from the '50s on his left ring finger. The ring had a slender gold band, with a red stone and a Winged Wheel, decorated by a single small diamond.

Crossman had come to the Joe that day to say good-bye. After 61 seasons, less than two months from his 91st birthday, he was quitting to spend more time with his wife, Peg, who was 80 and needed constant care in an assisted-living facility.

"I've had a good life with it," Crossman said. "I've enjoyed it all. Hate to give it up, but there comes a time when you have to do something else. . . . I've smelled enough sweat."

He smiled. "I don't want to stay here till I'm 100," he said, laughing. "That's too long."

As Crossman turned left out of the dressing room and headed under the stands toward the exit, a reporter stopped him. Crossman had seen it all, so what did he think of this Detroit team? How would it stack up?

"Lot of great players," he said. "Just hope they aren't too old."

The Wings opened the exhibition season at the Joe that Monday night, a day late because of the terrorist attacks. They played the Rangers.

"Think of how much we've all been distracted by this," Yzerman said. "Now think about someone right in New York. You can't really compare it."

"They're right in the thick of things," Chelios said. "They saw it. They actually saw debris, everything flying, the smoke."

"It's a bad time for the whole world," Hasek said. "You cannot completely get your mind off what happened last week."

But, Hasek continued, "You have to think about tomorrow. For me, it was a good week of hockey, and now I'm glad the exhibitions are starting. I am telling you: I am nervous, being in a new city."

Hull and Robitaille didn't play. Neither did Eric Lindros, whom the Rangers had acquired Aug. 20: He had a sore knee. But Hasek played, and he received a warm welcome from the fans as soon as he hit the ice.

Security was tighter. The coaches wore red-white-and-blue ribbons on their lapels. During the anthem, the fans cheered when Karen Newman sang "that our flag was still there," and the players stood shoulder-to-shoulder on the red line, American next to Canadian next to Czech next to Swede and so on, Rangers and Wings interspersed, in a show of solidarity.

But as hockey games go, life appeared largely back to normal. Players fought. Fans booed. The Wings lost, 3-2, but they

43

dominated the first 40 minutes. Hasek was long gone by the time the Rangers scored two late power-play goals. He left after 29:09. He had faced only 10 shots, and he had stopped them all so easily that he felt as if he hadn't faced any.

"Barry," he said to Barry Smith, "no shots."

"Well," Smith said, "that happens here sometimes."

After the Wings played their fourth exhibition that Saturday night, Fedorov swerved his black 2001 BMW around a car stopped for a red light at West Fourth and Lafayette in the suburb of Royal Oak, then ran the light at high speed. It was about 3:00 A.M.

Fedorov was born in Pskov, outside Leningrad; grew up in Apatiti, above the Arctic Circle; and went to a special sports school in Minsk. After he left the Soviet hockey team, he found himself at a Detroit-area Corvette dealership. He was told to "pick one," so he picked a burgundy one. In 1994, at 24, he recalled his first speeding ticket with fondness.

"I didn't know this would be bad for my license," he said. "It was dark, the flashing lights. It was like, 'Wow! A detective thing! Like in the movies!' I was excited."

When the lights flashed this time, it wasn't so exciting. Fedorov was 32, and he knew much more than he did then. Police said his blood-alcohol level was .09 percent, below the .10 threshold for drunken driving, but over the .08 for impaired driving. He was arrested. He was in custody for two hours.

And he was in the news again.

Fedorov was the Wings' resident rock star. Of course, he had the money: millions upon millions. But he also had the look: high cheekbones, flowing blond hair, flashy clothes. He had the charm: big smile, teenager's playfulness, trouble with English that made him misunderstood, a little mysterious, endearing. He had the talent: speedy skating, smooth stickhandling, rocket shot. He had the girl: tennis sex symbol Anna Kournikova. Oh, and he had the drama:

After the Wings won the '97 Cup, Kournikova waited for him in the dressing room, and she rode with him in the victory parade. His teammates took the Cup on its first trip to Russia, he didn't go with them and they criticized him for it. His contract expired, he and the Wings couldn't work out a deal, and he held out. People thought he was greedy; he wondered why the Wings didn't want him anymore.

"I took it pretty hard," he said. "It was an ocean of emotions."

In public, he said he never would play for the Wings again. In private, he wondered if he could play for anyone else. Detroit was his second hometown. He held out until the 1998 Nagano Olympics, when he signed a six-year, $38-million offer sheet with the Carolina Hurricanes. The Wings matched it so that they could keep him, he came back and they won another Cup.

"Some people got mad because of what happened," he said. "My challenge was to win some fans back."

Kournikova captured much of the fans' attention, not to mention the media's. Fedorov and Kournikova got engaged when she turned 18 in the summer of 1999. They didn't announce it, but that didn't matter. When she wasn't on tour, she often was in Detroit, at practices, at games. He endured snide comments and jokes about everything from her age to her looks to her athletic performance.

In February 2001, news broke that she had gotten engaged to Florida Panthers star Pavel Bure, who played with Fedorov when they were teenagers. He endured more than ever now, but he kept quiet, and a few days later, with Bowman's blessing, he flew to Phoenix, visited her at a tournament and straightened everything out.

"I'm not a machine; I'm a human being," he said. "It is hard to go through when somebody tries to mess up your life. Looking at all those reactions from all those people who have absolutely no idea what's going on and trying to make an opinion. . . . None of the actual people involved, at least me and Anna, said anything about it. Absolutely nothing. So I don't know how people can judge, but that tells me people sometimes are blind. They just want to take a shot."

While the Kournikova comments never stopped—*Are they married? Did they break up? Is she with Enrique Iglesias now?*—neither did the comments about his play. He had a heart: He gave millions to charities. But some said he had no heart, in the hockey sense. He often didn't perform well if he didn't feel tip-top physically. Perhaps the worst thing he ever did was dominate the

1993-94 season, scoring 56 goals and putting up 120 points, winning the Hart, the Pearson Award as the NHL Players Association's most outstanding player and the Selke Trophy as the league's best defensive forward. Although he was a great player afterward, winning the Selke once more in '96, he didn't have the Hart, and so no one was satisfied.

"I think people had reasonable expectations to think I could do it again," he said. "That's why I was very frustrated and very disappointed in myself when next season, next season, next season, I didn't do anything except just have low points in my career every season I play.

"I played so much that year"—Yzerman sat out injured for 24 games in 1993-94, allowing Fedorov to be more of The Man—"and I was really pumped for myself to play again. It was my thing: I love it, I've done it and I think I can do it again and again. But hockey is a team game, period. We have quite a few great players on this team, and it's never going to be designed for one player. . . .

"I was sad I cannot do it again. But then I settle down and look inside me and realize, 'Hey, things may not go that way. We can try something new.' It took me a while to adjust and play well again."

After the Wings' next exhibition that Tuesday night, Fedorov stood just inside the doorway of the dressing room in Montreal, spoke to a reporter and apologized publicly for his impaired driving. He later pleaded guilty and, because he had an otherwise clean record, received only a year of supervised probation and 100 hours of community service.

"Obviously, I'm very embarrassed," he said. "I just screwed around and made a bad mistake. . . . I made an error in judgment, and I'm sorry about that. I want to make sure that something like that never going to happen again. . . . The circumstances are very, very serious. . . . Off the ice, I'm going to try to take care of this matter in the best way possible. . . . On the ice, I'm going to do whatever I can for the team, make sure it doesn't affect me."

The Wings went 4-3-1-1 in exhibitions, but no one cared. The big developments were that Krupp suffered a groin injury and then a shoulder injury, rookie center Pavel Datsyuk showed he had some spectacular ability and won a roster spot, and the Wings looked as if they would have one hell of a power play.

"Do they have a lot of power? Yeah, they do," Chicago Blackhawks coach Brian Sutter said. "It doesn't take rocket science to figure that out."

Holland came close to a deal with the Rangers that would have netted center Mike York, but he never was able to trade Osgood. He had to leave him exposed for the waiver draft, and the Islanders snatched him with the first pick. Kris Draper walked into the lobby of the team hotel in Chicago that day when his cell phone rang.

"Well," Osgood said, "I'll see you five games into the season."

Draper laughed. The Wings visited Long Island on Oct. 13, then hosted the Islanders on Nov. 2. Draper grabbed another guy from the old gang, Kirk Maltby, and they gave Osgood some grief.

"Don't worry about it," they said. "You went first overall!"

Osgood laughed.

And one chapter ended so another could begin.

Chapter 4
Great Scott

Scotty Bowman turned 68 on Sept. 18. Some said he had mellowed a little, but he was still Scotty, still every bit the legend who had stood behind the bench, sucked on ice chips, jutted his jaw like a bulldog, tilted his head backward, barked at the referees, tinkered with his lines and won, won, won as long as anyone could remember.

Ahab had his whale; Bowman had his Cup. This was a man who named his son Stanley after you-know-what and maybe his son Robert after Bobby Orr, a man who dropped names like Jean Beliveau and Dickie Moore and turned casual conversations into history lessons, a man who said he had a "good time just going over the statistics that are available" on the Internet, a "Rain Man" who knew everything going on in the NHL all the time, a man who could come home from a long road trip and talk about going to a junior game that night, a man who still went to practice wearing bandy gloves given to him by fabled Russian coach Anatoli (Papa Bear) Tarasov three decades before, a man so stubborn that he overcame a blockage in his heart and a knee replacement to coach into a record fifth decade.

Hockey, he said, "never gets boring."

It was his life. He was born and raised in Montreal the son of a Scottish blacksmith. He might have made the NHL, but his playing career ended in 1951, when he was only 17. In the final minute of a junior playoff game at the Montreal Forum, he broke away, and defenseman Jean-Guy Talbot clubbed him on the head from behind. Doctors put a permanent metal plate in his skull. He stayed in the hospital for three weeks. He tried a comeback. It didn't work out. He got a job as a paint salesman. It didn't last long.

He became coach of the junior Canadiens and learned from Toe Blake, as the senior Habs had their way with the league. He rose to assistant coach of the expansion St. Louis Blues in 1967.

One night, he suggested a certain defenseman sit out a shift, coach Lynn Patrick sent the defenseman out anyway and the opposition scored. The next morning, Patrick called Bowman and said, "I think this coaching business has passed me by." The next game, Bowman was the head man. He was 34.

And he just *had* to win. He asked the woman who became his wife to attend games that season. But there was a catch: If the Blues won, she would wait for him outside the dressing room. If they lost, she should go home, because he wouldn't be in the best of moods.

"The Blues were in the middle of a long losing streak, so I never got to see him," Suella Bowman said. "Then they tied a game, and me not knowing much about the game, I thought that was a pretty good thing, because at least it wasn't a loss. So I waited for Scott."

She waited. And waited. After about two hours, she finally asked a dressing-room attendant if he was still around.

"And then, all of a sudden, he comes out and looks surprised that I was there, because they hadn't won," she said. "I found out then that there was no middle ground with Scott. If it's not a win, nothing else would be acceptable."

Now in his unprecedented 30th season, Bowman had won 1,193 regular-season games—more games than all but two men had coached. He had won 207 playoff games—84 more than the next-best man, Al Arbour. He had won the Jack Adams Award twice and had been runner-up three times. He had coached the three teams that had won the most games and earned the most points ever in a season: the 1976-77 Canadiens (132 points, 60 victories), the '95-96 Red Wings (131, 62) and the '77-78 Canadiens (129, 59).

Four seasons with the Blues. Eight seasons and five Cups with the Canadiens. Seven seasons with the Buffalo Sabres. A Cup as director of player development with the Pittsburgh Penguins, then two seasons and another Cup as coach. He had stepped out from behind the bench at times, but he always had come back, and here he was, going for his third Cup in nine seasons with the Wings.

"It's in his blood," Barry Smith said. "His energy level's still there, his passion."

In November 2000, when Bowman became the first to coach 2,000 games, his colleagues stepped back from the competition and allowed themselves to express their amazement. After all, more than 25 of his former players had coached in the NHL, several had served as general managers or in other front-office positions, and, as Brian Sutter said, every coach had adopted something from him.

"He's an elite coach at 67 years of age," Ken Hitchcock said, knowing Bowman's vitals off the top of his head. "That's 20 years from where I am now. I don't see me at 67 coaching. I think I'll be driving the equipment truck or something. I don't think anybody can come close."

"As long as he's living on this Earth," Nashville Predators coach Barry Trotz said, "he's going to be coaching."

"My status is always (evaluated) at the end of the season," Bowman said. "Things can change in a hurry: your health, your team, your goals, your desires. That's what I always have in the back of my mind. But when you do something for a long time, one of the decisions you have to make is what you do when you don't do the job you've done for a long time."

Bowman was a walking contradiction.

He was an old man, but he was a big kid. He loved model trains. He collected trading cards. When the Wings won the 1997 Cup, he strapped on his skates so he could take a victory lap, because he always had dreamed of doing it. He loved golf, and after serving as an alternate scorer at the 2000 U.S. Open, he went to the draft and showed off his souvenirs: a Tiger Woods golf ball, a final-round scorecard signed by Woods and Ernie Els, and a laminated photograph of a television set, showing Woods with him in the background.

He was old-fashioned, but he knew how and when to change. He studied video before other coaches did. His encyclopedic, calculating mind took to computers quickly. When the Wings had five talented Russians in the 1990s, he put them on one unit, the "Russian Five," to take advantage of their native, puck-possession style in a North American, dump-and-chase league. As Brendan Shanahan once pointed out to Sports Illustrated, "He started coaching guys who had summer jobs and crew cuts, and now he's coaching guys with Ferraris, earrings, blond streaks and agents."

"The thing is, Scotty's methods have stood the test of time," Hitchcock said. "Most people that are in his status, the Woody Hayeses, the Bobby Knights, the elite coaches that have won on a consistent basis with old-school techniques, have not adjusted to new-school personalities. Scotty's kept the same ideas and the same principles, but he's adjusted with the times."

He was a control freak, but he believed in fate. He was superstitious, wearing the same sport coat over his barrel chest and eating at the same restaurant when things were going well. He wouldn't stay on the 13th floor of a hotel or sleep in a room with 13 in the number—even if the numbers only added up to 13.

He was a loner, but he had a wife and five children. He had an apartment in the Detroit area, stayed at the arena all day sometimes watching out-of-town games, had a late dinner other times at a Greek restaurant that gave him a private table near a television, drank a regular cup of coffee at a car dealership, lunched most every day with an investment guy named Lenny, sat now and then by himself at baseball games. His family still lived in Buffalo, but he rarely revealed why: His son David was handicapped, born with water on the brain, and he didn't want to uproot him.

He was well-known, but few knew him well. Away from the arena, friends said, he showed a soft side, a sense of humor. He could be generous. But at the arena, he didn't let the players, press or public see much but hardness, unless, say, his team had just won the Cup.

"That's the way he likes it," Chris Osgood said. "He's Scotty Bowman. Nobody's ever going to know him, at least not completely."

The night he coached that 2,000th game, he allowed no pomp and circumstance, no syrupy ceremony. During a stoppage in play 6:07 into the first period, public address announcer Budd Lynch boomed over the loudspeakers and announced the feat.

A message flashed on the scoreboard. The fans stood. Players from both teams tapped sticks and gloves against the boards near the benches. A couple of coaches clapped, including Dave Lewis. The arena roared. And Scotty? He just stood there.

Hockey Gods

When Lynch began, Bowman talked with Smith. Then he looked down at his feet. Then he stared straight ahead. Then he looked up at the screen. Then he chewed the right corner of his lower lip. That was it. He had a game to win. When Lynch finished and the applause ebbed, Bowman looked at a player.

"Go," he said.

And the player did.

Although Sergei Fedorov gave him a 3-2 victory over the Vancouver Canucks by scoring with 27.2 seconds left, he didn't loiter on the bench. He bolted off, accepting only a pat on the back from Lewis as he headed into the tunnel.

"He'll celebrate," Smith said. "But he won't do it publicly."

Bowman received the game puck—someone wrote "2,000" in black marker on white hockey tape, then pasted the tape on the puck—and took a team picture in the privacy of a closed dressing room. When reporters approached, he hid the puck in his left jacket pocket.

"How do you feel?" someone asked.

"We've had better games, that's for sure," Bowman said. "It's just that I wish we would have played a little bit better, but those things happen."

"Aren't you going to enjoy this even a little bit?" another asked.

"Nah," he said. "What are you going to do? We're going to New York."

The Wings were leaving for the airport in a few minutes. They had a game the next night against the Islanders. He had just coached his 2,000th. Already his mind was on his 2,001st. Interviews finished, Bowman rushed out of the room, found his son Bob in the hall and sneaked him the prized puck.

"See you later," he said.

Then he was gone.

A coach Bowman once knew did his own press releases.

"He would write, 'So and so is hurt today,' or, 'Such and such's father is visiting from out West; they're going fishing,' " Bowman said. "Then he handed the reporters the news, and he was done with it."

53

Bowman couldn't do that. He didn't have command over this one area of his world. But he did his best.

He could be honest, insightful, funny and enjoyable, but he was that way much more often with the national media, whose praise could puff him up, than the local media, whose praise meant little but whose reporting might hurt his cause. He installed a curtain in the dressing room—gray, the color of iron—to shield the training room and showers. He sometimes shooed away reporters the second their allotted 30 minutes of access was up—or when he had a whim. The day the O.J. Simpson verdict came down, a group of reporters covering practice gathered around the dressing-room television. Just as the foreman rose from his chair, Bowman announced a team meeting had been called and the media had to leave at once. After Simpson was found not guilty, Bowman let the media back in.

He lied. He didn't do it all the time, but to keep his strategy a secret or protect his players or just because, he did it enough to keep everyone guessing. His injury reports were the most unreliable. Once, Shanahan sat out a morning skate at Phoenix, and a reporter asked why. Bowman said Shanahan was sick, and he even disappeared for a moment, ostensibly to check with the training staff. Shanahan played that night. Asked how he was feeling, Shanahan said something to the effect of, "Oh, I had back spasms. Had to see a specialist this morning. But I'm fine." During the 2001 playoffs, Bowman told the truth about Shanahan's broken foot, but he lied about Steve Yzerman's fractured fibula, calling it a bad ankle sprain, and Yzerman's broken finger, denying its existence. He berated a reporter for questioning him in print, and even though his statements forced others in the organization to keep up the charade, he stuck to his story.

He often spoke in what one writer called "a stream of unconsciousness." Sports Illustrated once called him "a vexing conversationalist, abandoning sentences in mid-thought, scattering non sequiturs like rose petals. He is not always a good listener." The magazine related this telling story: Gord Miller, a Canadian broadcaster, ran into Bowman after working a junior game between the Oshawa Generals and Peterborough Petes.

"Who won that?" Bowman asked.

"Oshawa won, 4-2."

JULIAN H. GONZALEZ/Detroit Free Press

Who needed a stick? Not Dominik Hasek, whose unorthodox style included, at times, dropping his lumber, hitting the deck and leading with his blocker.

In five seasons as the Red Wings' general manager, Ken Holland felt the adulation from winning the Stanley Cup and the criticism from a first-round playoff defeat.

KIRTHMON F. DOZIER/Detroit Free Press

No longer best known as "Stevie Y.," the heartthrob and scoring whiz of the '80s, Steve Yzerman became "The Captain," an embodiment of leadership.

The Ilitches had given players crystal, Rolex watches and silver sticks to mark milestone achievements. After his 100th career goal, Darren McCarty found a stick wrapped in tinfoil in his locker, courtesy of the PR staff.

Luc Robitaille received a hug from Brett Hull after scoring his 611th goal, which broke the NHL record for left wings set by Brett's father, Bobby.

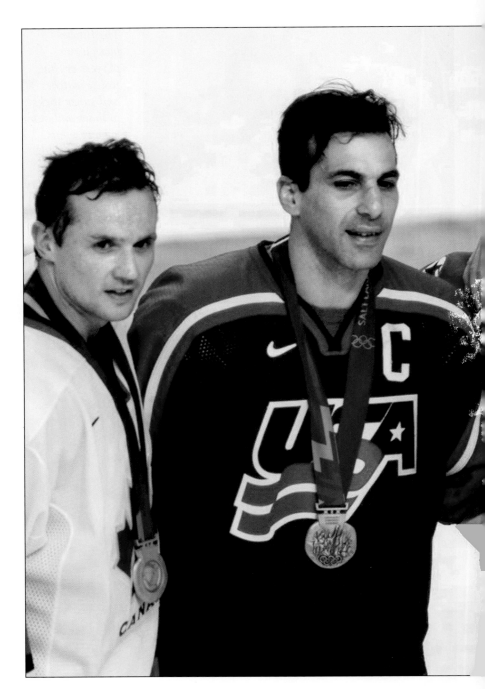

Eleven Red Wings, plus a Swedish prospect, played in the Salt Lake Olympics. On the final afternoon of the Winter Games, two Canadians – Steve Yzerman and Brendan Shanahan – posed with gold, and two Americans – Chris Chelios and Brett Hull – posed with silver.

Playing for an elite team for the first time, Dominik Hasek didn't win the Hart or the Vezina trophies, but he posted a career high of 41 victories.

Brett Hull scored 30 goals for the 12th time, but the career sniper won rave reviews for his passing, defense and teamwork — all without losing his devil-may-care grin. He called his line "Two Kids and a Goat" — with you-know-who as the oldie but goodie.

Coach Scotty Bowman felt the pain of the low point of the playoffs — a 5-2 loss to Vancouver in Game 2 of the first round. Down 0-2, Detroit won the next four.

Nicklas Lidstrom earned pats aplenty for the goal in Game 3 that turned around the Vancouver series — a 90-foot blast late in the second period.

Only in Hockeytown is the octopus a symbol of victory and fans know the Zamboni driver by name. He's Al Sobotka, who also draws thunderous cheers when he retrieves the slimy mollusks from the ice and swings them overhead.

"What's that series at?"
"Two-nothing, Oshawa."
"They're running the goalie, huh?"
"Who? Oshawa?"
"No, the college game last night at the Joe."
Baffled silence.
"What was the attendance?" Bowman asked.
"At the college game?"
"No, at Oshawa."
"Standing room only."
"Who won that?"

Everybody had a Scotty story. Some were about how weird he was. One time, he called the Wings into a semicircle at practice as if to speak to them, then turned and went off the ice without a word. Some were about how cunning he was. According to folklore, he asked players for a light, even though he didn't smoke, so he could read the matchbook covers and find out where they were going after hours. He had someone wait in a hotel lobby one night and ask players to sign a stick—in order of entry, so he would know, as one writer put it, who came in "late, later and last." He walked into a bar another night when his Blues were out past curfew. He didn't say anything. He plunked a quarter in the jukebox and left. The song? Fats Domino's "Kansas City," which just happened to be the locale of the Blues' farm team.

Many of the stories, though, were about his mind games, about how big a bully he was, mean and manipulative, ruthless and cruel. There was the time he told the Blues' Bob Plager he had traded him and to go to the airport, and when Plager called from the airport to ask where he had been traded, Bowman told him to come back. (Bowman denied it.) There was the time Buffalo News writer Jim Kelley tried to check into his hotel in Quebec and learned his room had been canceled by a "Monsieur Bowman." (Bowman denied it.) There was the time he let Smith coach the Sabres in an exhibition against the New Jersey Devils. Smith won.

"Nice job," Bowman told him on the bus to the airport.
"Thanks," Smith said.

55

"Great feeling, huh?"

"Yeah, it really is."

Bowman smiled, cleared his throat, looked out the window.

"Too bad Jersey's such a shitty team. . . ."

They go on and on. His tantrums. Supposedly having the visitors' dressing room painted before games. Sending the Sabres' Tom Barrasso to the minors after six starts, even though Barrasso had won the Vezina the season before. Scheduling practices so that his players had to drive in rush hour traffic and remember what life was like for regular people. Inciting the Penguins to have a no-holds-barred, anti-Bowman bitch session in general manager Craig Patrick's suite at the Skyline Hotel in Calgary. The time Colorado Avalanche coach Marc Crawford was going ballistic and he told him, "I knew your father before you did, and I don't think he'd be very proud of what you're doing right now." Telling the bus driver to take off early after a road game— a player's wife was in labor—even though he knew he was leaving behind Wings radio broadcaster Ken Kal. The way he liked tension, to keep people on their toes. How he often did the opposite of what people expected him to do. One writer said he seemed like Anthony Perkins when the fly landed on his hand in the final scene of "Psycho." *They think I'm going to kill that fly. Well, I'll show them. I won't touch it. I'll show them, show them I wouldn't hurt a fly.*

"If you figure him out, he's out of the game," Kris Draper said. "Scotty wants to have that edge."

One writer called him the "Evil Genius." Bowman came up with ideas no one else could and did things no one else would, from shuffling his personnel at the last minute before a big game—or during one—to telling his players to forget fundamentals and try something new. Because of who he was and what he had done, he had that latitude. Players swore at him; players swore by him.

"He was just the best I ever played for," former St. Louis goaltender Glenn Hall once said. "I never had a problem with Scotty. Other people thought he was this and that, but I found if you just played hard for him, you got no grief whatsoever."

"Scotty, you're 60 years old," former Detroit forward Shawn Burr once told him. "You play with toy trains. You use a duck call to make line changes. People call you a genius. I think there's something wrong with you."

"As a hockey coach, he's the best ever," Dino Ciccarelli once said. "But as a person? He's a jerk."

"You hated him 364 days a year," former Montreal forward Steve Shutt once said, "and on the 365th day you collected your Stanley Cup rings."

"He is not someone who is easy to like," former Montreal goaltender Ken Dryden wrote in his book, *The Game*. "He has no coach's con about him. He does not slap backs, punch arms or grab elbows. He is shy and not very friendly. ... He is complex, confusing and unclear in every way but one. He is a brilliant coach, the best of his time."

Bowman wanted to be the best; everything else seemed secondary. This was a man who lost his playing career because of that incident with Talbot—and went on to coach Talbot for three seasons in St. Louis. Hey, Talbot had given him an early start in his new career, and if he could help on the blue line. . . .

"I'm trying to get a team to believe in one another; that's what matters," Bowman once said. "It's OK if they don't like the coach. . . . But if they like one another, they got a chance."

With Bowman, these Wings had their best chance.

Chapter 5
A Fun Game

Brett Hull sat in the center of a San Jose community rink Oct. 3, surrounded by the rest of the Red Wings, leading stretching. When finished, he stood, smiled and said, "OK, fellas!" Then he tapped his stick on the ice.

"To get to play with all these unbelievable hockey players. . . ." His voice trailed off. His grin got in the way.

Training camp was a tease; the exhibition season showed only so much. The Wings practiced in split squads for the most part; their nine potential Hall of Famers played together only twice. Now, finally, the roster was set, all that talent squeezed onto one surface, the regular season a day away.

"It's cool," Luc Robitaille said. "It's about time."

It was starting to get serious.

When the Wings won Cups four out of six years in the 1950s, Jack Adams scoffed at writers who compared them to the New York Yankees: "We are not the Yankees of hockey; the Yankees are the Red Wings of baseball," he said. Jimmy Devellano wouldn't go that far now, but he didn't play down the comparison. It didn't work on all levels, of course. But both teams had tradition, glamour, some elite homegrown talent and lots of the best players money could buy. Both were winning. Both had big targets on their backs.

"We're very similar to the New York Yankees, even to the point where a lot of people get ticked off at us," Devellano said. "A lot of people get jealous, just as they're all jealous of the Yankees."

Both faced incredible expectations. The Wings set the bar so high that they left little room for success but lots for failure. The season before, their 111 points meant nothing because of their first-round loss to the Los Angeles Kings, and this time, the pressure was going to be only greater. Las Vegas had them as favorites to win the Stanley Cup—at 3-1 odds. With the buzz came the burden.

"We understand that's the nature of the beast," Devellano said. "This is a franchise people are very passionate about now. We've created that. That's a good thing. . . . Those are expectations we just have to try to live up to."

If you asked Steve Yzerman about expectations, he would say simply, "Our goal is to win." But not only did the Wings have to win, they had to win every night. If they lost, it would be news. If they lost two straight, it would be a concern. If they lost three straight, it would be a crisis. *What's wrong with the Wings?!?!* People would question their age. *A dozen regulars 30 or older, eight of them 35 or older—and that's before any birthdays?* People would wonder about their egos. *Didn't Robitaille say, "We look like an All-Star team; I just hope we don't play like an All-Star team"?* People would wait for the next blockbuster deal that would fix everything. *What's Ken Holland gonna do next?*

The NHL had many bad teams. It had many good teams that played boring hockey. The Wings wouldn't be allowed to be bad or boring. With all these stars, there had to be highlights, sweet goals, sneaky passes, spectacular saves, riveting story lines. They would be filling buildings all over North America. People would be coming out to see the best; they would demand to see it.

"If they're expecting us to win, 10-0, every game, I think they're going to wait a long time," Hull said. "But as far as excitement goes, I think any time we send a line out there you're going to have the possibility of unbelievable plays, individual skill. It's going to be a lot of fun to watch."

Darren McCarty brought up a hockey truth: "No matter how much talent you have, in order to win, you've got to have a lot of things go right for you," he said. But even if injuries or bad breaks were too much to overcome, few were going to cut the Wings any slack. *The cream rises, eh?* In the end, after all the smiles, all the superlatives, all the hype, all the money, they had to drink from that Cup. If they didn't, everyone would be left thirsty.

"When a team goes out and supplies you with this type of group to work with, it's up to the group to go out and do the job," Brendan Shanahan said. "There's going to be a lot of people hoping for us to fail. We have to realize that. It's not just enough to have a certain amount of career goals or to have played in a certain amount of All-Star Games. We have to translate it into wins.

"Otherwise, the names mean nothing."

Opening night was an omen.

Hull had scored his first goal for the Wings, Shanahan had scored twice, and they had a 3-1 lead at San Jose midway through the third period. They blew it, and 34 seconds into overtime, Sergei Fedorov cross-checked San Jose captain Owen Nolan into the boards. The Sharks had a power play; the Wings were reliving a nightmare.

But while killing the penalty, Nicklas Lidstrom fired the puck into the San Jose end. Shanahan gave chase ahead of the pack, but he couldn't touch the puck: The officials would have whistled a two-line pass. He held up a bit. Goaltender Evgeni Nabokov skated into the corner to his left. He wanted to push the puck up ice for the power-play unit: If he had frozen the puck, there would have been a face-off in the San Jose zone.

"I can't stop the game in that situation," Nabokov said later.

He fired the puck off the glass. CLANK!

"We didn't know what happened on the bench," Dave Lewis said. "We heard it, but we didn't know where the puck was. All of a sudden, Brendan's got the puck on his stick."

The puck hit a metal partition and kicked out into the San Jose zone. Luck o' the Irish. Shanahan picked up the puck, walked in alone on Nabokov, heard Nabokov swearing in Russian, made what seemed like several moves and slipped the puck over the line.

Goal. Hat trick. Victory. The Wings mobbed Shanahan. "It was a gift," Shanahan said. "Bad break for them, lucky one for us."

How excited was Hockeytown? Although the puck dropped on a Thursday night at 10:00, an average of 133,000 homes tuned in to Fox Sports Net throughout the game. It was the fourth-highest-rated program in the cable network's four-plus years, by far the highest-rated late-night telecast it ever had.

After a victory at Vancouver on Saturday night, the Wings came back from the West Coast for their home opener. But it wasn't until Wednesday night, and the fans couldn't wait.

A Fun Game

As the Detroit Lions stumbled to a 35-0 loss to the St. Louis Rams—and an 0-3 record that would become 0-11—the desperate, disappointed Silverdome crowd started chanting, "LET'S GO, RED WINGS!" "Monday Night Football" funnyman Dennis Miller wisecracked that the crowd wanted Alex Delvecchio at quarterback.

Kris Draper was watching on television.

"I was sitting there, lying in bed, and I started hearing it," Draper said. "It was as clear as day, too. I knew exactly what was going on."

The Lions were lousy. The Detroit Tigers had been terrible. The Detroit Pistons' prospects were uncertain. As much as the fans were indicting the Lions, they were saying to the Wings, "Our city turns its lonely eyes to you."

"Everybody's frustrated in a lot of ways," McCarty said. "Hopefully, we can bring them some enjoyment."

Like much of downtown, Joe Louis Arena was not a pretty sight. It was just a gray-red-and-black box by the Detroit River, mostly siding and cinderblocks. It had been around only 22 years or so, but already it was one of the oldest buildings in the league. Cracked concrete. Dingy stairwells. Few amenities.

But, Yzerman said, "from a player's perspective it's a great arena to play in. It's a simple arena. It's got a good atmosphere."

The Joe held few events other than hockey games, so it kept good ice, and the Wings took advantage of it. They went 17-0-2 in their last 19 games there the previous season, setting the franchise record for a home unbeaten streak. They put on a good show, and the place had its own little culture: Local celebrities included even Karen Newman, the anthem singer; Al Sobotka, the Zamboni driver; and Scott Stebbins, a fan known as "Mo Cheese" who danced to music in an aisle midway through games.

Robitaille had vivid memories of visiting with other teams.

"We were always so scared," he said. "We had to play our best game here."

As it turned out, the home opener was about settling into the season more than celebrating this new All-Star cast. The player introductions had no pyrotechnics, and the order wasn't scrubs first, stars last; it was numerical. The fans gave huge cheers to their favorites, of course. Yzerman and Dominik Hasek received the loudest and longest ovations. Robitaille received a "LUUUC!" But other than that, nothing special. The Wings raised a banner for their 2000-01 Central Division championship—but they did it a couple of weeks before, with no fans in the stands, with no fanfare.

A reporter asked Hull whether teams normally blew off banner-raising ceremonies like that. Hull looked at him as if he were crazy.

"Yeah," Hull said. "You don't raise a banner for a division title."

You raise one for a Cup.

"That's what we're here for," Robitaille said.

The Wings faced the Calgary Flames. Although the Flames weren't going to make the playoffs, they were young, fast, physical. The Wings ran into serious penalty trouble, fumed at the referees . . .

And lost.

The 4-2 defeat was the highest-rated show in Fox Sports Net's history. An average of 174,300 homes tuned in throughout. Between 8:00 P.M. and 8:15, 213,000 homes were tuned in. More people were watching the game than anything else on local television.

Ratings stayed strong. Over the next seven weeks, the Wings seemed to have script writers.

The Buffalo Sabres came to the Joe that Friday night with chips on their shoulders. Before the game, coach Lindy Ruff said Hasek wouldn't have won his sixth Vezina without his former teammates, and they "obviously were stung" by some of Hasek's comments after the trade. Slava Kozlov didn't appreciate Hasek's saying he told Darcy Regier not to ask for too much from the Wings because he needed "every good player." Kozlov also said he wondered how the Wings were "going to split the puck."

Lidstrom earned his 570th and 571st points, passing Reed Larson as the Wings' highest-scoring defenseman of all time. Robitaille and Fredrik Olausson scored their first goals as Wings. Unimpressed with Robitaille, Scotty Bowman had played him with rookies Pavel Datsyuk and Jason Williams until then, when he put him with Tomas Holmstrom and Igor Larionov. The crowd gave him another hearty "LUUUC!"—or a "BOOO!"

"I'm not sure," Robitaille said.

It was a "LUUUC!"

"The good thing," Robitaille said, smiling, "is that when you make a bad play, you can still say they're going, 'LUUUC!' "

Hasek handed the Sabres a loss. Afterward, Ruff referred to him only as "the goalie," and the Wings were laughing. Toward game's end, "the goalie" had made one of his trademark moves, dropping his stick, grabbing the puck in the crease with his blocker hand and throwing the puck out of danger as if it were a baseball. Problem was, he ended up throwing his blocker, too.

"It was an accident," he said.

The Wings couldn't help themselves. Draper and Shanahan were sitting next to each other on the bench, and Draper said they were "in tears."

"We'll be talking about that on the plane," Draper said.

The Wings jetted off to New York for a reunion with Chris Osgood that Saturday night. Four times, they came back from one-goal deficits against the Islanders. The last time, Robitaille scored with 10 seconds remaining in regulation. In overtime, Yzerman scored his second goal of the game and gave Osgood his first loss.

Comebacks were an early season staple. In the final minute Oct. 18, the Wings trailed the Philadelphia Flyers at the Joe, 2-1. Bowman pulled Hasek, and Fedorov tied the game with 40.1 seconds left. Bowman called a time-out, and Hull won it with 17.8 seconds left. The fans roared until the final horn. And beyond.

"That was *loud*," Hull said. "Those comebacks, they build confidence. They build great team morale."

Hull smiled.

"I think," he said, "it shows other teams that the Red Wings are never out of a game because of the people that are here."

Jeremy Roenick frowned. No sense for him to wonder, "What if?" Had he signed with the Wings, they probably wouldn't have been able to afford Hasek.

"Who knows?" Roenick said. "I don't know if I could have made the team that much better than Dominik has. So maybe it worked out better for them."

Two nights later, the Wings faced the Kings for the first time since the playoff debacle, and Robitaille faced them for the first time since leaving them. This episode had everything: laughter, tears and a happy ending.

The Robitaille family was together for the Buffalo game, but had to split afterward. Luc was off to Long Island; Stacia and the boys were going back to Los Angeles. Luc looked at his six-year-old, Jesse, but the little guy wouldn't look back. He couldn't look back: They weren't going to see each other for a month.

"He was crying, and Luc started to cry, and I thought, 'This is so hard,' " Stacia said. "It broke our hearts."

When Stacia got home, she got an idea. The L.A. game was on a Saturday night. She didn't have work. The boys didn't have school.

"How great would that be to turn around and go back?" she thought.

So they came back to Detroit for the weekend—as a surprise.

They flew out the day of the game. On the plane, Stacia's cell phone rang. It was Luc. She answered, pretending she was in L.A. Then, suddenly, without warning, she hung up on him. A flight attendant was speaking over the intercom, and Stacia didn't want to give herself away.

Luc called back. Stacia answered again, pretended again, hung up on him again. This happened three or four times. Finally, as Stacia and the boys were driving to the Joe, Luc asked what the heck was going on.

"Hon, I'm sorry," Stacia told him. "I have such a bad connection here."

He had no idea.

The horn sounded, and the teams went off for the first intermission tied, 2-2.

"Hey," someone said to Luc, "your kids are here."

"What?" Luc said. The guards let Steven and Jesse come down into the hallway outside the dressing room. So when Luc came out for the second period, they were waiting for him, his biggest fans, going, "LUUUC!"

"What a shock," Luc said.

"He just had instant tears," Stacia said.

At 15:41 of the second period, on the power play, in front of his family, Luc tipped a point shot—and scored the goal that beat the Kings.

Next?

Medical drama. Goaltender Manny Legace was on the wrong end of a collision in the crease at Nashville the following Saturday night, and he was taken off on a stretcher with his head immobilized.

"It felt like I hit my funny bone in both arms," he said.

With the television on at home, Legace's wife, Karen, had to console their crying children, Sabrina, six, and Manny, three. He was rushed to Baptist Hospital, where he underwent a battery of tests and spent the night.

Sunday, Legace flew back to Detroit. Monday, although he complained of a sore neck, shoulders and back, he wanted to practice. The doctors wouldn't clear him until he had an MRI, so the Wings scheduled one for 8:00 A.M. Tuesday. Their thinking: If he passed, he would fly to Carolina and rejoin the team for the game that night. He would dress as the backup the next night at Dallas.

Legace's alarm clock rang at 6:30 Tuesday morning. He was at Henry Ford Hospital by 8:00 for the MRI. Everything checked out. He was out of there by 9:30.

"It ended up just being a bad stinger," Legace said. "Football players get it."

Legace went home for a moment, packed, then headed to Metro Airport to catch a 1:30 flight. Of course, the flight was delayed. It took off about 2:00. He didn't try to sleep.

"Oh, no," he said. "I watched a movie on the plane. I didn't expect to be playing. I didn't even expect to dress."

He saw "Swordfish" on his portable DVD player.

"Awesome movie," he said. "Loved it."

At 4:20, he stepped out of a cab at the team hotel and ran into Barry Smith on the sidewalk. Smith told him Hasek had flu-like symptoms. They had nothing to do with the mystery virus he had over the summer, but he couldn't dress. The Wings were down to minor-leaguer Jason Elliott.

"You're starting," Smith said.

"Are you sure?" Legace asked.

"Yeah."

Legace didn't even enter the hotel. He threw his bags on the team bus, which was to depart in about 15 minutes. Then he caught a cab with Hull, Robitaille, Yzerman and Chris Chelios to get to the rink a little early, so he could have his neck, shoulders and back treated.

A little after 7:00, the puck dropped.

Of his stomach, Legace said, "Butterflies were flying around."

The Wings gave Legace a quick cushion, scoring three goals in a span of 7:09 in the first period. Legace had to work afterward. The Hurricanes scored twice in the second and outshot the Wings, 21-12, the final 40 minutes. But he won. Yzerman scored an insurance goal in the third, Draper an empty-netter.

Legace shrugged when someone noted, through all this, he improved to 13-0-2 in his past 15 decisions and 31-5-5 in his Wings career.

"Yeah, I know," he said. "It's kind of scary, huh?"

Legace started again the following night, on Halloween, and he won again. But Hull had to be the hero in his return to Dallas, didn't he?

Before the game, Hull insisted he had nothing to prove to the Stars, who had beaten the Wings the week before. He said he wasn't bitter.

"If I was still sitting at home, wondering where I was going to play, I would be bitter," he said. "I hooked up with a pretty good team . . . so bully for me."

He was so happy with the Wings that his role didn't matter.

"With this team," he said, "I'll play the tuba."

Hull scored once. Then, with the game tied, he was out for the final three minutes of regulation—or at least he seemed to be to Ken Hitchcock, who said, "He just kept circling. He was like a vulture."

A Fun Game

In overtime, he broke down the left side on a 3-on-1 against goaltender Ed Belfour. Hull said he didn't use any knowledge he had gained from practicing against Belfour the previous three seasons.

"I don't do that, especially on a guy like Eddie," Hull said. "He's such a great goalie. He doesn't have tendencies. He's good everywhere."

No matter. Hull whipped the puck between Belfour's pads, and the Wings won again. The Detroit Free Press headline the next morning read: "Hulloween: Hull tricks former team . . . Ex-Star treats Wings to 4-3 OT win."

"It's nice to come in and win, especially when they came into our building and beat us," he said.

Asked whether scoring twice at Dallas made him smile, he said, "I'd be lying—and you know I'd be lying—if I said it didn't."

The next game, a Friday night, was Osgood's return to Detroit. Beforehand, he just wanted to get it over with. Play well. Win one for the Islanders. Move on. He was glad he didn't have to come back to the Joe again that season. But by that morning, he felt different.

"Now," he said, "I'm thinking it would be nice to come back some more."

He had been tense in his first game against the Wings. He had been on Long Island for only two weeks, and it was his home opener. But now he had an 8-1-1 record, 1.85 goals-against average, .936 save percentage, two shutouts and NHL player of the month honors. His team, the league's worst the previous season, was 9-0-1-1.

"Everything's going so well," he said. "I'm not nervous. I'm just enjoying coming back."

For a while, it seemed Osgood never had left. The night before, he called Draper, his good friend, and he spent time at his Detroit-area home with his wife and child, who weren't going to join him on Long Island until later in the month. That morning, he rode down to the rink with Legace, another good friend, and he spent time in the Wings' training room with more good friends.

"We just talked about the kind of stuff you talk about with a buddy who has a new job at a new office down the hall," McCarty said, shrugging.

Eventually, Osgood made his way to that new office, the visitors' dressing room.

"I'm sure it's the first time he's ever seen that area," Draper said.

Although his uniform was blue and orange, Osgood put on the same red goalie pads he wore with the Wings, because he hadn't broken in his new ones yet. As the Islanders stretched for practice, John Wharton ribbed him from the Detroit bench.

"Cut the cord!" he yelled, smiling. "If you let us go, we'll let you go!"

Then Wharton turned back into the tunnel.

Quietly, he said, "Nah, we'll never let him go. He's the best."

Osgood realized he had to cut the cord. He felt a surge of pride when he looked up at the Wings' nine Cup banners, knowing he played a large role in winning two of them. But he put that out of his mind. This was not the time.

"When I retire and come back to Detroit, then I can reminisce about what I did in Detroit," Osgood said. "But right now, I think it would be unfair to my teammates and the coaches and people in New York if I continuously talk about what I did in Detroit and winning Cups, because now I want to win a Cup in New York."

He smiled. "I had a great time in Detroit, and now I'm having a great time in New York," he said. "So I'm pretty spoiled."

Draper's wife, Julie, and Osgood's wife, Jenna, watched the game together. They sat in Section 121, lower bowl, right on the red line. They shared popcorn. Their husbands lived together before they were married. They were roommates on the road.

The wives laughed about the first game, when Draper broke in on Osgood—and passed.

"He was taking it easy on him," Julie said.

The play led to the winning goal, but in their many phone conversations, Osgood ribbed Draper.

"Oh, I heard about it," Draper said, smiling.

Draper wanted another chance at bragging rights. Asked about all the hoopla surrounding Osgood's return, he said, "Let's get it out of the way—then fill the net on him."

A Fun Game

The Islanders scored on their first shot. But what do you know? Later in the first period, Draper stole the puck in the neutral zone, raced down the right wing and snapped a shot. Osgood got a piece of the puck with his blocker, but not enough. It dropped across the goal line, and the game was tied.

"Before the game, because he had faced him so much in practice, he was thinking about a new strategy," Julie said. "He must have found a new hole that Ozzie didn't know he knew about."

The fans used to chant, "OZ-ZIE! OZ-ZIE!"

Now they taunted, "OS-GOOOD! OS-GOOOD!"

And now what do you know? In the second period, deep in the corner to Osgood's right, defenseman Maxim Kuznetsov threw the puck in front. Draper had scored two goals in a game only once in more than three seasons, but here he held off Michael Peca, held his stick with one hand and tipped the puck past his buddy. He celebrated what turned out to be the winning goal with a big smile, throwing his arms into the air.

"OS-GOOOD! OS-GOOOD!"

"After the first goal, Kris was laughing the whole time; my Chris was mad," Jenna said before the third period. "After the second goal, my Chris was really mad."

The wives laughed.

"I told him I'd never talk to him again if he scored on my husband," Jenna said. "It's going to be a long time now."

The wives laughed again.

"After the game," Julie said, "they'll be laughing about this."

Oh, they were.

Draper, in the Detroit dressing room: "It was two good friends just going out and having fun, playing a fun hockey game. We'll laugh about it. For sure we will."

Osgood, in the New York dressing room: "I'll get a good laugh with Drapes someday. But I'll get him back. You put that in the paper: I'll get him back one day. . . . He was laughing a couple of times. But I was laughing, too, when he fumbled a breakaway (in the third period)."

Draper, back in the Detroit dressing room: "I definitely would love to have that one back. Lucky for him, or we would be talking about three goals, not two."

Hockey Gods

Osgood, back in the New York dressing room: "Our wives are sitting together. They took the kids out to Halloween the other night. Then he does that to me."

Back and forth they went. "It's all in fun," Osgood said. "We were laughing about it on the ice."

Pause. "It's kind of ironic," he said, "isn't it?"

The friends planned to catch each other on their cell phones afterward, but they didn't have to. They ran into each other on their way out of the rink.

"We both just started laughing," Draper said.

They didn't talk much about the game. Mostly, they talked about the kids' cute Halloween costumes. The Drapers' 20-month-old daughter, Kennedi, dressed up as a giraffe. The Osgoods' 6-month-old daughter, Mackenzie, dressed up as a cow.

When the Islanders scored that night, they burned Chelios and Kuznetsov. Chelios took out his frustration with a mighty tomahawk chop to the top of the net. There was only one problem: Hasek was resting an arm there.

Chelios got him good.

"I jumped," Hasek said.

Hasek whirled around and started to raise his stick.

"I thought it was one of the Islanders," Hasek said. "So I was going to slash back. Then I saw it was Cheli."

Chelios apologized immediately. Hasek said nothing.

"Not right away," Hasek said. "I know he has a very high temper: When they score a goal, if he sees something around, he tries to slash it. I knew he tried to slash the crossbar. I knew it was by accident. But at first, I was upset."

The two talked after the game, and helped by the fact the Wings won, they had a good laugh.

Later, Hasek smiled. "You know what he told me?" Hasek said. "Cheli said, 'I slashed you after they scored on the first shot, then you didn't give up any goals. So we'll have to do it again.'"

After the Wings' morning skate at Chicago two days later, Bowman walked up to Wharton, gave him a little elbow and said,

"Watch this." He went up to an unsuspecting reporter—the author of this book—in the middle of the dressing room and got in his face.

"It's always you with the words," Bowman barked, "twisting the words. . . ."

"Scotty, what are you upset about?" I asked.

"What's this 'with what Bowman called a sore wrist'? If I say it's a sore wrist, it's a sore wrist! Just say it's a sore wrist!"

Holmstrom hadn't played against the Islanders, I had asked why and Bowman had said Holmstrom had a sore wrist. To be safe, in the final paragraph of the next day's notebook, I wrote, "Forward Tomas Holmstrom sat out with what Bowman called a sore wrist."

Nose-to-nose with me, Bowman shouted, "MY WORD IS GOSPEL!"

Bowman pivoted and started to walk away, but I lost my temper.

"Your word is not gospel!"

Bowman turned around.

"What did you say?"

I reminded him of how he had lied about injuries the previous playoff run.

"When you tell the truth, then your word will be gospel!" I shouted.

"Well," Bowman said, storming off, "keep my name out of it."

After the Blackhawks beat the Wings that night, Bowman treated me as if nothing had happened. He was pleasant as could be.

In vintage style the following Friday night at Anaheim, Robitaille became the 13th NHL player to score 600 goals. First period. Detroit power play. As Shanahan sent the puck toward the net, Robitaille slipped into the low slot. He tipped the puck out of midair, about waist-high, down and past the right pad of goaltender Jean-Sebastien Giguere.

"I saw Shanny had the puck at the blue line," Robitaille said. "When he took that wrister, I just made sure I got in good position to tip it in. I've gotten many in my career like that."

Lucky Luc laughed.

"I guess it's all positioning," he said.

For once, the timing wasn't perfect. Robitaille's wife and boys weren't there. He had to say hello to them via a first-intermission television interview. They were going to the game the next night, his first at Los Angeles since he left. But that was all right.

The Wings already were the first team with three active 500-goal-scorers. Now they were the first with three active 600-goal-scorers—and they had them on one line. Bowman had put Robitaille with Hull and Yzerman. Hull led active players with 656 goals. Yzerman had 649.

The experiment didn't last long. As Robitaille later told Sports Illustrated, Hull turned to him on the bench one game and said, "This is stupid. We can't play together. No one wants to pass the damn puck. Stevie, he's not a good passer, and you, you can't pass the puck at all." But it made for a memorable moment.

Robitaille received a standing ovation and a "LUUUC!" from the Southern California crowd, which had a lot of Wings fans, as usual, and many who had appreciated him in L.A. for so long.

"I feel pretty good," Robitaille said. "I mean, I'm happy it's over with, you know? I just wanted to get it as quick as possible and get moving."

He needed 10 goals to reach the record for left wings, held by Hull's father, Bobby.

"When you think of that and then you think of being the number one left wing all-time," he said, "that's going to be pretty special."

Angry after that Nov. 10 game at Los Angeles, an overtime loss, Shanahan threw a water bottle off the bench. Most people missed it, but it started a chain of events that led to Shanahan's sitting in a car on the side of a rainy highway and getting an earful from a high-ranking NHL official.

After the Wings left the Staples Center for their red-eye flight back to Detroit, the final game summary still wasn't available. A reporter—again, the author of this book—asked an L.A. media relations official why, and he told me two penalties had to be added: a minor for throwing an object onto the ice and a 10-minute misconduct, both to Shanahan.

73

"What happened?" I asked.

"He threw a water bottle at the referees."

The Wings were off the next day. Without being able to talk to Shanahan, who later said he threw the bottle aimlessly, I noted in the final paragraph of a story inside the Detroit Free Press sports section that Shanahan had thrown the bottle "at" the referees.

A Toronto TV station read the story and made a bigger deal of the incident the next day, and so it came to the attention of NHL vice president of hockey operations Colin Campbell.

And Campbell was not pleased.

Early in the season, Shanahan had ripped the referees.

"It's ridiculous," he had said. "In the three games I've seen so far this year, it's just a joke what's happening to this league. I'm all for protecting players and eliminating dirty plays from the NHL, but you know, divers are being rewarded in this league, and without addressing it, the league is losing some of its integrity."

The night Draper scored twice on Osgood, Shanahan received a gross misconduct after the game. Why?

"I guess I was gross," Shanahan said.

The Wings took four minors in the third period against the Islanders, and Shanahan took the last for slashing with one minute left. Earlier, an errant stick had cut Shanahan's left cheek, but the referees hadn't called anything.

"They refused to believe I was cut with a stick," Shanahan said.

After the final horn, Shanahan flipped referee Shane Heyer the puck, as if giving him the game puck for a good effort. Then Shanahan clapped his gloves and smiled. Obviously, he was being sarcastic.

"It was a good game," Shanahan said. "I just thought, with two first-place teams playing tonight, we should be able to play 5-on-5 in the third period. I said some things in the end maybe I shouldn't have. But the game was over at that point. I voiced some frustration."

Shanahan was fined $1,000, the maximum allowed under the collective bargaining agreement.

After the game in L.A., Campbell asked the Kings to send him a tape of the water-bottle toss. Someone, whom he identified only as a member of the Wings organization, told him Shanahan had knocked the bottle off the bench with his stick. But the tape showed that the bottle, as he put it, "was whistled across, spiraled . . . like Brett Favre threw it." It cleared the Kings streaming off the bench and slid on the ice in the direction of the referees.

What's more, league officials felt Shanahan had been complaining about diving—and diving himself.

"That's what really pissed us off," Campbell said.

A fine wouldn't do.

"It's easy to fine a guy $1,000; it's easy for a guy to get fined $1,000," Campbell said. "It has no impact."

So Campbell came up with something novel.

"I said," Campbell recalled, " 'Look, we've had something before, you've made some comments in the paper this year, and that's enough. You've always got an excuse. Come and talk to me. We'll talk about it.' "

On an awful afternoon—rainy, foggy, misty—Shanahan had to cross the border from the United States to Canada, drive about 2½ hours on the 401 and stop at a little parking spot when he reached the Highway 19 interchange, between Woodstock and London. He had to meet Campbell, who was based in Toronto, lived in a small Ontario town and was on his way to one of his son's hockey games.

"He got out of his car and came into my car," Campbell said. "We sat there and talked for a half-hour. . . . He had some issues with the refereeing. I said, 'This is how it is: At the end of the day, calls are made. They might be right and they might be wrong. You have bad games. Well, the referees have bad games. But you can't take it into your own hands. The league's good. The league's good to you.' "

Shanahan drove back to Detroit in the dark. The league didn't have a problem with him the rest of the season.

To be sure, Shanahan's Irish temper was just part of his personality—a personality that made him one of the league's most popular players.

He read books without pictures. He watched movies without explosions. When "Jeopardy" was on the dressing-room television, he played along and did pretty well. He once used his imagination to tell tall tales about off-season exploits, like playing backup goalkeeper for Ireland in soccer's World Cup and serving as an extra in the football scene of his favorite movie, "Forrest Gump."

Frankly, he was a fun guy, and for the most part, he was good to and good for the media. He had the ability to take a step back, see things from a different angle and make an insightful, articulate comment—or a witty one.

In November 1999, Larionov showed a deep disregard for his relatively old age by scoring his fourth game-winning goal of the young season. Looking for a good quote about him, a pack of hungry reporters cornered Shanahan in the dressing room. He stood silently for a moment. Then it hit him.

"He's the Dick Clark of hockey," he said.

How can you not like that? Laughing, the reporters looked down at their notebooks, scribbling. Most missed the second part of the quote, which never appeared in the newspapers. As he watched the spectacle before him, Shanahan smiled. He knew what he had done. Meat to the wolves.

"I'm good," he whispered, winking.

On another occasion that season, a handful of reporters approached Shanahan and asked whether the Wings' new line of Shanahan, Yzerman and Pat Verbeek was the league's most accomplished. Verbeek and Yzerman each had more than 500 goals, and Shanahan had more than 400. Shanahan grinned.

"There's not too many lines in the NHL where I'd be the youngest guy," he said.

"Or the guy with the fewest goals," a reporter prodded.

"Oh, yeah. That's right, too. Yeah, so I have to go get some water and stuff like that when they're thirsty. I hang up their equipment for them. . . . Call me 'Kid.' "

Before Shanahan was "Kid," he was kid brother to Danny, Brian and Shaun, the sons of Irish immigrants growing up in the Toronto area.

"There was kind of a big age gap between me and them," said Shanahan, six years younger than his next-oldest brother. "They were always playing sports together, and I was kind of like their rink rat, their ball boy in lacrosse, their water boy, their tape-fetcher in hockey."

When he was allowed to play, he developed the sniper's creativity that he displayed in the NHL. He had to, just to survive.

"Playing against my older brothers, I always had to find a trick or two, because they were bigger and stronger," he said. "I always had to be sneaky in a way. I couldn't beat them straight up."

In 1990, while Shanahan was in his third NHL season, his father, Donal, died of Alzheimer's disease. In '97, after Shanahan won his first Cup with the Wings, he took it to his father's grave.

"The place was totally empty," Shanahan said. "I just sat there with it."

The Wings kept winning. And winning. And winning.

At Columbus on Nov. 21, Legace pitched a 38-save shutout, Robitaille scored with 42.4 seconds left in overtime, the Wings went to 19-3-0-1 and Ken Holland said their record was "way more than we could have hoped for."

"They've seemed to hit it off," Holland said. "Everybody's bought into team success . . . and everybody's getting a chance to contribute."

Two nights later, in the teams' first meeting since the Wings won the Hasek sweepstakes, the Wings beat the St. Louis Blues. Only the 1929-30 Boston Bruins, who started 20-3 (without the benefit of overtime, let alone 4-on-4 overtime), had reached 20 victories faster.

"I knew this was going to be a winning team, but to have 20 wins after 24 games, it's even for me a surprise," Hasek said. "To be honest, I don't think we can go like that for 80 games."

Pause. Smile.

"But maybe I'm wrong."

Two nights after that, the Wings blew a 3-0 lead and settled for a 4-4 tie. Still, a couple of things illustrated how well the season was going for them: While their dressing room was silent, the Blackhawks blasted a Buckcherry rock CD, and goaltender Steve Passmore was so excited that he said, "That was a solid road win." Detroit's WKBD-TV (Channel 50) recorded its highest rating of the season: An average of 221,000 homes tuned in throughout.

Hockeytown had become Boomtown. Radio ratings were up more than 100 percent on WXYT-AM (1270). Television ratings were up 62 percent on Channel 50, 116 percent on Fox Sports Net. Merchandise sales were up 30 percent. Little Caesars, Mike Ilitch's pizza company, had sold 75,000 bobblehead dolls—not of any of the potential Hall of Famers, but of the Grind Line guys: Draper, McCarty and Kirk Maltby.

"The numbers have just been spectacular," said Channel 50 executive producer Toby Cunningham, in his 27th season. "The interest in the team is as high as I've ever seen it."

TV ratings stayed steady even when the Wings played unglamorous opponents. They didn't count viewers outside the Detroit area and didn't take into account people watching in groups. As Cunningham said, "There are thousands of people watching in bars." Like the Wings' Hockeytown Café in downtown Detroit. Business was up there, too.

The Wings won yet again Nov. 30, beating the New Jersey Devils, the defending Eastern Conference champions. They were 22-3-1-1. They were 8-0-1-0 in their past nine games, 10-0-1-1 in their past dozen.

Legace, *the backup goaltender*, a just-happy-to-be-here former minor league journeyman, was 7-0, 17-0-2 in his past 19 decisions and 35-5-5 in his Wings career. He shut his eyes and smiled, then started waving his arms around as if impersonating a blind octopus. He was describing his goaltending technique.

"Just hope for the best," he joked.

He laughed. Everyone was laughing. The joke was on the rest of the league.

"Hockey's a fun game," Larionov said, smiling.

"Yeah," someone said, "but it's a lot more fun when you win all the time."

"Exactly."

Chapter 6
From A to B

After the Red Wings lost Dec. 1 at New Jersey, Scotty Bowman brought up "a security thing" as a reason.

A security thing? Bowman declined to elaborate.

"It's very confidential," he said. "I can't divulge anything. (It took) all day. I think it took our minds off the game. We couldn't focus on anything. We didn't seem to have much going for us."

Asked whether the problem had passed, he said, "Hopefully. We don't go back there."

Reporters went to Ken Holland, and he said only that the situation "did not involve a threat against the team" and "no one was in danger." And that just added to the intrigue: It was less than three months since Sept. 11, Continental Airlines Arena was just across the Hudson River from Ground Zero and "a security thing" could have meant anything. After all, Wings officials had been opening fan mail with rubber gloves, worried about anthrax.

Some investigative reporting revealed what happened: Richard Goodman, a Detroit lawyer representing the victims of that 1997 limousine accident, couldn't collect damages from the driver, Richard Gnida, or the company, Gambino Limo Service, so he was looking into whether the Wings' insurance would cover them. Process servers approached security officers at the team hotel and the arena, seeking their cooperation in handing subpoenas to members of the Wings organization. Security turned them away. They left without incident. Most of the team had no idea they had been there.

No, the Wings hadn't been distracted by "a security thing."

But they had been thrown off by something.

Four nights after that New Jersey game, Dominik Hasek had his first duel with Colorado's Patrick Roy—and looked awful. Fans who roared with playoff-like furor before the opening face-off started streaming for the exits when a whistle blew with 5:09 left. With 3:30 left, Hasek allowed what looked like a harmless shot to slip underneath his pads. By the final horn, Joe Louis Arena was nearly empty. While Roy stopped 30 of the 31 shots he faced, Hasek allowed four goals on 18 shots.

"I know," Avalanche forward Milan Hejduk said, "he can play probably better than that."

Three times in their first 27 games, the Wings had lost in regulation. Now they had done it back-to-back, by the same 4-1 score—and to teams they considered their peers among the NHL elite, the previous season's Stanley Cup finalists. Hasek wasn't the only one who had a bad night against the Avs. Steve Yzerman failed to cash in on some scoring chances and was a team-worst minus-3; he showered, dressed and departed by the time the dressing room opened to reporters. Jiri Fischer took three of the Wings' six minor penalties; he said he didn't have much to say. Brett Hull went without a shot; he took shots at himself afterward while riding a stationary bike, sweat dripping down his nose.

"There's only about three guys on this team doing anything offensively, three to five guys," Hull said. "That's not how you win. . . . You're not going to win too often with Brett Hull not even getting a shot on net. I know that."

Hasek didn't speak to reporters. He was so upset that he spent the night at the arena. The next day, he said he probably had played his "worst game this year," even though Nov. 4 at Chicago he was pulled after allowing five goals on 14 shots. He said he hadn't "proven anything here yet."

"I felt terrible, after a game like that," he said. "I gave up goal on the first shot. I gave up goal on the last shot. I gave up goal on the first power play. It's like . . . I was very disappointed with myself. What can I say? . . . I feel I could be more helpful to the team. I feel like I came here to play better than I've played until this point."

At 15-6-1, Hasek led the league in victories. But his 2.54 goals-against average and .902 save percentage were nowhere near the league leaders, and thus, they were nowhere near his high standards. He shrugged off suggestions that he had saved the team at times and that he had a history of starting slowly, only to heat up.

"I expect more from myself," he said. "I'm sort of upset."

Things got worse.

Two nights later, the Wings had a 1-0 lead with 1:05 left in the third period, when the Phoenix Coyotes pulled goaltender Sean Burke for an extra attacker. They were about to make it 2-0 seconds later, when Sergei Fedorov, one of the NHL's fastest players, streaked toward the empty net with the puck on his stick.

But two Coyotes, forward Shane Doan and defenseman Paul Mara, didn't give up. They backchecked hard, caught up to Fedorov and sandwiched him. Instead of easily going into the net, sending the Joe Louis Arena fans home happy, the puck skidded wide of the right post.

"It's not over until it's in," Doan said. "I think he thought we might quit."

Back the other way. The Coyotes dumped the puck in the Detroit zone, and Hasek decided to play it.

"Maybe I could freeze it and the face-off could be in our zone," Hasek said. "I don't know. It's tough decision."

Just off the net to his right, Hasek caught his stick on Doan's right skate—and lost it. Forward Claude Lemieux chased the puck into the corner to Hasek's left, and after a scramble, Doan emerged with it along the boards. He sent a pass into the right circle for center Daymond Langkow. Quick shot. Hasek had an open man to his right, so he couldn't challenge Langkow, and the puck went high into the net with 32.4 seconds left.

The game ended in a 1-1 tie.

"We'd better get out of here in a hurry before the cops show up," Phoenix coach Bobby Francis said. "We kind of stole one here tonight."

Hasek tried to shrug it off.

"This year, we've won so many games in the last seconds of the game," he said. "We were lucky couple times. So at least one time this season we weren't lucky. It sometimes happens."

But the mood in the dressing room was sour. Suddenly, all these superstar snipers were having trouble putting the puck in the net. The Wings had three goals in three games. After practice two days later, Hull came in and ripped off his gear. Bowman had shuffled his lines and put him with rookie Pavel Datsyuk and youngster Boyd Devereaux. Hull was frustrated by fruitless shots, several hit goalposts and a couple of disallowed goals.

"It's not really good when you're a goal-scorer and you can't score," he said.

Asked what might snap him out of it, Hull said, "If I could tell you stuff like that, I would be a genius. . . . I'm still unlucky. That's the way my career is going right now—downhill."

Yzerman had been moved from center to left wing and wasn't happy with himself, either.

"It's not even a slump," he said. "I feel pretty good. I'm skating well. I'm just not getting anything accomplished. I don't really know why. I'm kind of frustrated by the whole thing. All you can do is keep playing away and hope to get a little bit more accomplished."

Things got worse.

The Wings took a three-game trip to western Canada, they started off with a 2-0 loss at Calgary and, in his postgame comments, Bowman focused on the matchup between Fedorov and Brendan Shanahan and the Flames' Craig Conroy and Jarome Iginla.

The game was scoreless early in the third period, when Conroy slashed Shanahan across the right wrist at the Detroit blue line. Conroy stole the puck, skated in on goal and fired a shot. Hasek stopped the puck, but center Dean McAmmond threw it back on net. Iginla got his stick on it and scored, and the Saddledome fans went nuts. The Flames' other goal was an empty-netter.

"I thought the difference was Conroy and Iginla," Bowman said. "They outplayed Fedorov and Shanahan."

Bowman added that he had wanted a different matchup but couldn't do much, because the Flames had the last change.

He left practice the next day without speaking to reporters, but Fedorov and Shanahan did speak. Fiddling with his stick in the hallway, Fedorov was somewhat diplomatic, saying, "I'm not really disagreeing with what Coach said, but overall, I don't feel that my line got outplayed." Sitting in the dressing room after skating on a line with Brent Gilchrist and Kirk Maltby, Shanahan was upset.

"I'm surprised because no one said anything to me; I'm surprised I have to get the coaching from you guys," Shanahan told the Detroit beat writers. "These types of things shouldn't be played out in the press. They should be played out in the coaches' room between two men. But it's nothing new."

Shanahan was Bowman's favorite whipping boy. After a 1-0 loss to the Dallas Stars the previous season, Bowman had blamed Shanahan, pointing out how his failure to dump the puck deep before a line change led to the goal. In the 2000 playoffs against the Avs, Bowman demoted Shanahan to the fourth line during the decisive Game 5. Those are just two examples.

"No player on this team is above mistakes and above being reprimanded by the coaching staff," Shanahan said. "I just don't know why it always has to happen this way." As for the turnover that led to the Calgary goal, "I thought they were going to get a penalty. I guess I should lie down on the ice. I think I've shown in the past I don't go down. I'm not a soft player. You'd like a little support from your coach when you get a two-hander across the hands."

Although Shanahan had 34 points, first on the Wings and third in the league, he figured Bowman was down on him.

"The last four, five games, all of a sudden, I find myself not playing the power play, not killing penalties," he said. "Power play, killing penalties, that was really the key to my success early in the season, getting all that extra ice time. Playing in those key situations really keeps you very involved in the game. I thought it was going pretty well, but. . . .

"The timing is strange, but it usually happens at some point."

Was Bowman hurting Shanahan's chances of playing in the Olympics? Team Canada was soon to announce its full roster for the Salt Lake Games, and Shanahan was a candidate for one of the open spots.

"It's frustrating to see us losing games by one goal when you feel like you can do something about it," Shanahan said. "That's what's most important to me, and I hope that's all that's on anyone's mind."

Bowman shot back the next day after practice. He also announced that Shanahan already was on the Canadian Olympic team.

"They told me last week," Bowman said.

Of Shanahan, he said, "He's upset that he made a mistake. It's unfortunate. But I can't hide all the mistakes all the time. I'm not going to. We're allowed to criticize players, and we're allowed to play them—or not play them. And that won't change. And I won't criticize players unjustly. Iginla and Conroy outplay a lot of guys. Iginla is the best player in the league right now."

The Wings won at Edmonton, 2-1, and Yzerman said it was "the kind of game we all feel good about winning." But then they lost at Vancouver, 3-0. They came home and threw Manny Legace in goal against the Chicago Blackhawks: He hadn't lost in almost a year. He was on the verge of signing his first real NHL contract, a four-year extension. Maybe he could turn around their luck. Legace was outstanding, making 35 saves, but the Wings lost, 2-0, and left the ice to light boos. Three shutout losses in four games, a 1-5-1 slump and the radio waves were hot, even though the Wings were still the NHL's top team. *Told you this was too good to be true. Told you these guys were too old. Told you . . .*

Meanwhile, the Wings had a new Uwe Krupp controversy. This time, his back was fine, but his right shoulder wasn't. This time, he wanted surgery, but the Wings *didn't.*

While pursuing an iced puck Sept. 28 in an exhibition at Chicago, Krupp wedged his right arm awkwardly between an opponent and the boards. He finished the game, but he said he felt sharp pain in practice afterward whenever he opened his bottom hand to shoot or pass. The Wings gave him an MRI, and he said it revealed "frayed" cartilage.

He took a pain-killing injection and played Oct. 20 against Los Angeles. It was his first real game in almost three years, or about 34 months, or 1,034 days. All things considered, after early nerves, he did pretty well. He played 15:40 and led the team with five hits. The statisticians gave him one blocked shot, but Dave Lewis said they could have given him more.

"I haven't made a habit of not playing for three years and then coming back and knowing how it will go," Krupp said. "We'll just keep plugging away, keep the doctor with the needle ready, and off we go."

"I think he'll only get better," Bowman said. "If he can stay healthy, he can help us."

Krupp had to come out during the next game. A team doctor recommended surgery, and surgery was scheduled for Nov. 26. But Holland said the Wings "really wanted a second opinion." They sent Krupp to New York on Dec. 13 to see a highly regarded surgeon. Krupp said the surgeon needed 10 minutes to concur with the original diagnosis: torn labrum, frayed rotator cuff and a problem with the biceps tendon. "He was very clear; there's no doubt," Krupp said. "What am I going to do?"

Surgery was scheduled for 10:30 A.M. Dec. 18 at Henry Ford Hospital in Detroit. But the Wings called it off the afternoon before. All Holland said was: "Surgery has been postponed indefinitely while we weigh our medical options."

"I think we've been wasting a lot of time," Krupp said. "I don't know what is going on."

Krupp said he didn't "even want to begin to speculate what sort of agenda" the Wings might have. In short, without saying so publicly, the Wings wanted him to play hurt. Had Yzerman or Chris Chelios had the same injury, they felt, he would have been out there every night without complaint. Krupp said his shoulder was unstable and tended to lock up.

"I can poke-check," he said. "I can be a poke-checking defenseman like I am in practice, basically. But you can't play hockey like that. You're spending a lot of time with one hand on your stick and with the other hand you've got to muscle somebody. You have to be healthy for that."

Krupp said he would play as soon as the Wings figured out a way to make his shoulder "somehow work."

"I've been ready," he said. "Shoot me up. Anything. . . . However they want to do this is up to them. I'm game. Send me to a voodoo doctor."

Not until Jan. 9 did Krupp finally have surgery.

Early in the first period Dec. 19 at Joe Louis Arena, Fischer dumped the puck into the Vancouver zone along the left-wing boards, goaltender Dan Cloutier misplayed it behind the net and Hull batted it in from a bad angle.

"I think the guys saw it as a sign that we were going to get some lucky bounces," Devereaux said.

The Wings beat the Canucks, 4-1. In three periods, they scored one goal fewer than they had in their past seven *games*. For more than two weeks, the dressing room had been dead, silent. But now there was laughter, life. The Wings had called up an undrafted 21-year-old kid with a Brett Hull T-shirt in his suitcase, forward Sean Avery, to provide some energy and a much-needed mean streak, and the veterans were calling him "The Savior."

"I don't think it'll stick," Avery said.

"It's amazing," Devereaux said. "Hockey's pretty much a game of confidence. Even though we have 600-goal-scorers on the team, when the pucks aren't going in, everybody feels it, even those guys. Certainly, it was a good feeling to get some goals."

During their scoring slump, the Wings quietly tightened their defense, which few noticed was too porous during their spectacular start. They played a trapping system, directing the puck to one side of the ice, trying to force neutral-zone turnovers. When the San Jose Sharks came to town two nights later on a 9-0-1 streak, the Wings beat them, 3-0. Hasek faced only 19 shots, but he felt a lot better about himself.

"I made some saves, and that's my job," he said. "My goal is to play at the highest level. I always expect the best of myself."

Two nights later at Chicago, the Wings broke out with a 5-0 rout of the Blackhawks, who were 2-0-1 against them. With the game still in doubt, Hasek made a huge save, laying his left pad across the goal line and stoning center Steve Sullivan on a breakaway. After allowing eight goals in two games, he had allowed only six in his past seven. The Wings had earned their first back-to-back shutouts in almost four years, and they felt great going into a two-day Christmas break.

"We've got the confidence back," Igor Larionov said. "Finally, we found that balance between the defense and the offense. We play solid defensively, and we get chances and score goals. We play as a team, as a unit. Every unit is playing good hockey. That's the name of the game."

Hockey Gods

Things were looking up. Problem was, the Wings' brass was looking ahead—and worrying. The Wings had 10 men named to Olympic rosters, two more than any other NHL team. And that didn't include prospect Henrik Zetterberg, who was playing for Sweden. Shanahan and Yzerman were playing for Canada; Hasek for the Czech Republic; Fedorov and Larionov for Russia; Tomas Holmstrom, Nicklas Lidstrom and Fredrik Olausson for Sweden; Chelios and Hull for the United States.

"You've got so many Olympians," someone said. "It's great."

"Yeah," a Wings official said. "It's great for the Olympics."

What's more, the Wings knew they would have several players at the All-Star Game. Was their talent a curse in disguise? Because they had more than anyone else, might it hurt them as well as help them? The Wings were the league's oldest team, their best players were veterans, and those players would be playing more, increasing the chances of fatigue and injury.

The situation was even worse considering 18 of the Wings' final 28 games were on the road, and that stretch started in February, when the All-Star Game and Olympics would be. Plus, Bowman pointed out only a fraction of his players would return to the team in good spirits, with a gold medal.

Although Bowman could do nothing about the players' mental state, he could do a little about their physical state. He started cutting back on morning skates—the Wings hadn't had one in three games, and they had won three in a row—and said he would continue to. He said he also expected to give certain players more practices off.

As far as reducing some players' ice time or even holding them out of games to rest, that depended. The Wings wanted to keep their cushion atop the league and go on cruise control. But if they were "in a dogfight," Holland said, they were "going to have to go right to the wire."

The night after Christmas, the Wings were reminded of just how fragile their Cup quest was. Yzerman had scored two power-play goals at Minnesota when, killing a penalty midway through the second period, protecting a 2-1 lead, he took a shot off his lower left leg—between the top of the boot and the bottom of the pad, where there is no protection.

Before any official could blow his whistle, Yzerman got up and staggered off. For about two minutes, he grimaced on the bench, head down, hands gripping the top of the boards, rocking back and forth. He went down the tunnel. He came back to kill another penalty, but at the end of the shift, he glided to the bench with his leg pulled up lame, stopped at the door without putting any weight on it and put his stick in the rack.

Bowman said initial X rays were negative, but he didn't rule out a break. He said Yzerman was in "excruciating" pain, in more pain than he was the previous season, when he suffered the fracture in the same area that kept him out almost all of that playoff series with the Los Angeles Kings. Bowman said medical personnel had instructed Yzerman to stay off the leg. "Right now, it's deemed a bad bruise, but that could change," Bowman said, looking forlorn. "You just hope nothing shows up later."

Yzerman liked to say the one player the Wings could least afford to lose was Lidstrom. But, in truth, the one player they could least afford to lose was Yzerman. He wore No. 19 on his back, and he had carried the franchise on his back for 19 seasons. He was there in 1985-86, when the Wings put up only 40 points in 80 games, their lowest total since they had 38 in a 48-game schedule in '39-40. He was there in '97 and '98, when the Wings hoisted those Cups, because the team had transformed itself—and he had transformed himself.

In the late 1980s and early '90s, Yzerman scored 50 goals or more five times and more than 100 points six times. Perhaps only two players were more potent: Wayne Gretzky and Mario Lemieux. Yzerman's 155 points in '88-89 are the most ever by anyone except Gretzky or Lemieux. While Gretzky won the Hart in '89, Yzerman won the Pearson. But then Bowman arrived. The league was becoming less wide-open, the Wings were becoming more well-rounded and Bowman turned Yzerman from a one-way player into a two-way player, as he had done with the Montreal Canadiens' Jacques Lemaire in the '70s and the Pittsburgh Penguins' Ron Francis in the early '90s.

The evolution wasn't easy on Yzerman. The Wings considered trading him. His offensive production dropped. The Wings were swept by the New Jersey Devils in the 1995 Stanley Cup finals, they had that banner '95-96 regular season but lost in the Western Conference finals to the Avalanche, and he was haunted by the fact he still wasn't a winner. Once, he was on vacation in Las Vegas, and while he sat at a craps table, two guys recognized him. *Hey, it's Yzerman from the Red Wings!* They looked at the action, they looked at Yzerman and one of them whispered, "We better get away from here. There's no luck at this table." Yzerman said he "wanted to slug 'em." But he didn't.

And after his first Cup, his game wasn't the only thing that had changed. Amid the spraying champagne, he said, "They always say, 'He's a good player, but he didn't win it.' And now they can't say that anymore. No matter what, they can't say it, you know?" In '97, Yzerman finished two votes shy of winning the Conn Smythe. In '98, as he was closing on his cabin, once owned by the trophy's namesake, he did win it. In 2000, he won the Selke. In '91, he was cut from a Canada Cup team; in '98 and '02, he made Olympic teams. His stature grew more for his willingness to sacrifice than it ever had for his ability to score. He became known for his hot competitiveness, for his determination to win. He was the Wings' moral center. His teammates tried to follow his example on the ice, in the dressing room, in the weight room—and everywhere else. On the road, even if they weren't hanging out with him, they often would find out where he was going and what time he was coming back.

Yzerman didn't have the colorful personality of, say, Shanahan, one of his good friends. Yzerman's words had weight because of what he had accomplished, but also because he spoke less than most. He had a dry sense of humor. He was moody and not always approachable. But he was without question the Wings' most popular player. Alex Delvecchio and Gordie Howe were the only others to have played more than 1,000 games for the Wings, and the fans felt attached to him. With affection, having watched him since he was a teenager, a heartthrob with high cheekbones, they called him "Stevie" or "Stevie Y." With respect, having watched him grow into a man, a father of three daughters with a scarred, striking face, they called him "The Captain." He was the mayor of Hockeytown. Even after the Wings acquired Hasek, Hull and Robitaille, their top-selling sweater was No. 19.

"People are always asking me, 'Who do you think are the great hockey players of all time?' " Mike Ilitch once said. "And I say they're the guys who can skate, shoot the puck, play defense, muck it up as rough as anybody and not hang up at the blue line and cherry-pick. That's Steve Yzerman. He probably rivals Gordie Howe more than anybody I've ever seen."

Everyone exhaled the day after that Minnesota game. Yzerman was on crutches and had a lot of swelling, but an MRI was clear: He had only a bad bruise. The Wings said he would sit out one to two weeks, but he said his status was "more day-to-day."

"It's very good news," Holland said.

The Wings blew out the Columbus Blue Jackets that night at the Joe, 5-1. But two nights later at Nashville, they had yet another nightmare. They took a 2-0 lead into the final 4½ minutes of the third period, and after a rash of bad plays and bad breaks, they lost in overtime, 3-2.

Fedorov thought back to the L.A. debacle and said, "When those things happen, there is a reason. I'm sure other people think there's no red flags there, but there are some red flags there. . . . I'm hoping it's not a problem."

Two nights after that, on New Year's Eve, Bowman called Fedorov into his office about two hours before the Wings faced the Minnesota Wild. Bowman told him he was moving him to defense, at least at even strength.

"It's not my favorite position," Fedorov said, "but I've played it before."

Defense? The two-time Selke winner had the talent to excel on the blue line, but he was sensitive, and Bowman had befuddled him by using him there for a stint in 1996-97. Why would Bowman do it again? Bowman said he wanted more attack from the back, but he seemed to have more on his agenda: getting Fedorov going and perhaps muzzling him; waking up his defensemen; sending a message to everyone he wasn't happy with his defense and, thus, prodding Holland to upgrade it somehow; and just shaking things up in general. These were the dog days: The early season excitement had worn off, the playoffs were too far away yet and maybe the Wings needed something to stay on edge.

Fedorov liked a lot of ice time, and he got 22:50 that night. He made good first passes in his zone and joined the rush. The Wings won. Against the Mighty Ducks of Anaheim on Jan. 2, he sped ahead, took a pass, fired the puck—and scored his first goal in 13 games. The Wings won again. Score another one for Bowman.

"I think he's always a threat back there," Bowman said. "We're getting some goals because he's jumped up and kept a lot of pucks in. The way games are played now, you need that kind of play. . . . It seems to be easier to come up from the back. . . . We need a good balanced attack, both forwards and defense."

The Wings were one game past the halfway mark. Despite their disappointing December, they were 29-8-3-2, the class of the NHL, no contest. A reporter asked Yzerman what midterm grade they deserved.

"Honestly," he said, "a B."

If the Wings were to be champions, then they had to be perfectionists, and perfectionists aren't satisfied. The Wings led the league with 132 goals, but they wanted more offense. Their power play ranked first at 22.8 percent, but it had been inconsistent, and they dwelled on that. They ranked fifth with 92 goals against and fourth in penalty killing at 88.7 percent, but for all their skill they were soft in their zone.

No lead seemed safe with them. After that Nashville game, they took a 3-0 lead into the third period against the Wild, let it dwindle to 3-2 and then won, 4-2, thanks to an empty-netter. Then they had a 4-0 lead over the Ducks late in the second, let it slip to 4-3 and won, 5-3, thanks to a late power-play goal. In three games, they had allowed six third-period goals and an overtime goal.

Bowman shrugged off questions about the trend.

"I just look at the win column," he said. "Bottom line."

But Darren McCarty said the Wings weren't looking at just the win column.

"We know from experience that to win Cups and be successful in this league you have to play 60 minutes of hockey, and we're not doing that right now," he said. "We are winning, and that's a good thing. But we're not fooled by it. We want to be more solid. . . . We know what we have to do. It's just going out and doing it."

The Wings' toughest tests were yet to come: more matchups with top teams, the Olympics, all those road games and, most important, all-important, April and maybe May and June.

"The success of our season," Yzerman said, "will be determined by what we do in the playoffs."

Chapter 7
Fire and Ice

After the first period Jan. 9, the Vancouver Canucks had a 3-0 lead at Joe Louis Arena. After the second, it was 4-1. The Red Wings' lone goal was Luc Robitaille's 610th, which tied Bobby Hull's record for NHL left wings.

Then, on the power play early in the third, Steve Yzerman took a shot from the left circle. The puck hit Brendan Shanahan in front and went past goaltender Peter Skudra. Then, less than a minute later, Pavel Datsyuk made the prettiest play of the season: He picked up the puck in the Detroit zone. He raced up and through three Canucks, schooling star defenseman Ed Jovanovski most of all. Making it look easy, Datsyuk flicked the puck past Skudra's left pad.

"Just a beautiful goal," Yzerman said.

The arena roared, and Boyd Devereaux said the Wings had a collective thought: "All right, we've got to win this now, after something like that."

With 6½ minutes remaining in regulation, Sergei Fedorov took a shot from the left wing, Datsyuk patiently flipped the rebound across the low slot and Brett Hull banged in the puck.

This time the third period was theirs. After fumbling with so many late leads, the Wings had forced a fumble, and Kris Draper finished off a 5-4 victory by scoring in overtime. The Wings were 8-0-1-1 in their past 10 games; they were out of their doldrums. The place was jumping, and many fans were waiting for Budd Lynch to announce the three stars. Datsyuk, a rookie, a baby on what was supposed to be an old-timers' team, was number one. He took a quick spin on the ice, strolled into the dressing room—and got a big reception from his teammates.

"Big smile on his face," Devereaux said.

Those comebacks, they build confidence. They build great team morale. Hadn't Hull said that when the Wings were rallying regularly back in October? In little more than 20 minutes, against the Canucks, the Wings had used a lucky goal, a great individual play and a team effort to overcome a seemingly insurmountable deficit. This was something they could use down the road. *I think it shows other teams that the Red Wings are never out of a game because of the people that are here.* Hadn't Hull said that, too?

Datsyuk led stretching before *and* after practice the next day. The honor was his. When reporters came calling, they had to use Maxim Kuznetsov as an interpreter: Datsyuk had been in Detroit only about four months and the Russian spoke little English. Still, they found he had plenty of savvy and a sense of humor.

"What about the game?" a reporter asked.

"He's forgotten game already," Kuznetsov said. "He's preparing for next game."

"Why did he come over to the NHL?"

"He say they fire him in Russia," Kuznetsov said, smiling. "He's joking."

"Who was his favorite player?"

"Max Kuznetsov."

The Wings were laughing again.

Shanahan scored on their second shot three days later, ripping a slapper from the top of the right circle between the pads of Dallas Stars goaltender Marty Turco. Shanahan went back to the bench and sat between Robitaille and Yzerman. As Lynch announced the goal was Shanahan's 1,000th point and the fans gave him a standing ovation, Shanahan tried to be stoic.

C'mon! Robitaille and Yzerman told him. *Stand up! Wave!*

Shanahan did, and Robitaille and Yzerman turned on him.

Sit down! they scolded. *A thousand points? That's all?*

Shanahan sat down, tried to suppress another smile and gave each of them an exaggerated, mock elbow. Robitaille had 1,238 points, Yzerman 1,614—before the season even started.

"It's humbling to be in the room with the players and the coaches we have," Shanahan said. "They were teasing me. They were telling me to do something, and when I finally acknowledged the fans, they made fun of me for that."

Shanahan added two more points, a goal and an assist, and the Wings added another victory that afternoon.

Hockey Gods

In the weight room afterward, Fedorov got a shot of adrenaline. On television, the NHL announced the starters for the All-Star Game, and along with Shanahan, Dominik Hasek and Nicklas Lidstrom, he was one of them.

"I was benching 225, no problem," he said.

The writers had voted Fedorov a trophy winner and a postseason All-Star. The players had voted him a trophy winner. The league had sent him to the All-Star Game as a reserve. But the fans, who always had so many players from whom to choose at his position, never before had voted him an All-Star Game starter, as they had Hasek, Lidstrom and Shanahan multiple times each.

"It put a smile on my face," Fedorov said. "I'm really honored. It kind of came as a surprise. . . . Tonight, at home, I'm probably going to go crazy a bit, have sort of a little celebration, I guess."

The fans voted Fedorov the starting *center* for the World team, not a starting defenseman, which was funny: Scotty Bowman was coaching the World team. Bowman said he would play Fedorov at center in the All-Star Game, but as Lidstrom said, "Who knows? We'll see what Scotty's going to pull out of the hat."

"Fans think right, because I'm better offensively, I think," Fedorov said, grinning. Whatever happens, "I don't mind, as long as I'm somewhere out there on the ice. . . . Going to try and do my thing, and hopefully I fit in somewhere in between."

One day at practice, Shanahan loosened the top of a water bottle and left it on the boards at the Detroit bench. The old salt-shaker gag. Lidstrom skated over, grabbed the bottle and lifted it to his lips. Sure enough, the top popped off, and bright blue sports drink dumped down the front of his black practice sweater.

Lidstrom frowned, nothing more. Without a word, he went back to work.

Shanahan loosened the top of the bottle again; Lidstrom came over and grabbed the bottle again. But this time, Lidstrom checked the top, tightened it, foiled the prank and drank.

Let's just say Lidstrom wasn't Mr. Emotion. He was thin, blond, with ice-blue eyes, and to find something truly colorful about him, you had to go to Vasteras, Sweden, where he played before Detroit, where he lived in the summer—and where he was part-owner of an American-style sports bar, Bars and Stars.

When you thought of a Wings defenseman owning a sports bar back home, you thought of Chris Chelios, who owned Cheli's Chili Bar in Chicago. Cheli was a rabble-rouser, the kind of guy you envisioned cracking open a couple of cold ones. But Lidstrom? He never would have thought of rousing a rabble. He was the kind of guy you envisioned walking into a bar and saying, "Got milk?" Maybe he would go nuts and order a Magic, the energy drink he owned.

"Nick is relaxed, carefree," Bars and Stars employee Erik Soderlind said. "I ask him if he wants coffee, and he says, 'No. I'll get my own coffee.' I'm like, 'Sit! Sit! You're one of the best defensemen in the world!' He doesn't sit. Really, he's just a nice guy."

Bars and Stars had a drink named for his team and number, the "Red Wing No. 5." It was a mixture of booze and cranberry juice, served with an umbrella and some silver tinsel. Asked about the drink, Lidstrom said it wasn't his idea.

"I mostly drink beer," he said.

"What kind?"

"Any beer, really."

News alert: Lidstrom drinks beer!

Lidstrom was so swell that he suffered from a strange double standard. At a time when people criticized professional athletes for being too bold and too brash, people criticized him for being too bland and too boring. Some said his quiet style—on and off the ice—was the reason he had finished second for the Norris three years in a row before finally becoming the first European to win it. *If only Nick were flashier, a better quote, the reporters who vote would've noticed him more, and maybe . . .*

Because Lidstrom wouldn't draw attention to himself, Yzerman often acted as his promoter.

"He's as good a defenseman as there has been in the league since I've been here," Yzerman said. "I watch him every day and really appreciate the little things he does. The majority of people don't notice those things."

Lidstrom had offensive skills that made him one of the top-scoring defensemen every season. He played pretty much perfect positional hockey on the defensive end. He picked passes out of the air with his stick, knocked down pucks with his feet, held off opposing forwards with what seemed like no effort, avoided checks and still found ways to make tape-to-tape passes.

"If you get a chance—I always tell my friends this when they ask about the team—watch him closely," Yzerman said. "He's so good. He's so talented. He's head-and-shoulders above everybody."

So Lidstrom wasn't loud. So he didn't crash and bang, taking so few penalties that he was a three-time runner-up for the Lady Byng Trophy, awarded for "sportsmanship," "gentlemanly conduct" and "a high standard of playing ability." That didn't mean he wasn't tough. He was as durable as anyone. He played so well through injuries—a pulled groin here, a broken nose there—that few outside the organization even knew it when he did. He never had played fewer than 79 games in a full season, and he had played almost 30 minutes a game most of his career. That meant he had been on the ice for the Wings almost half the time since 1991-92, his rookie season.

"His leadership is going out and being the best player on the ice," Yzerman said. "He can go into a tough building against a physical team and still play his game, not shying away a bit. He can totally be counted on. That's what leadership is."

The Wings hardly could have valued Lidstrom more than they did. In December 2001, they signed him to a two-year extension that gave him a salary of $10 million, making him the highest-paid player in their history, the highest-paid defenseman in league history and one of the highest-paid players period. What's more, he could earn an additional $1 million in bonuses each year.

Mike Ilitch said he was paying "top dollar for the top player in the league . . . defense-wise." Ken Holland said "maybe one day" Lidstrom's No. 5 would hang from the rafters, adding, "I think he's been a real hidden secret here in Detroit, and he's finally starting to get noticed around the league." Jimmy Devellano's praise was even higher: "There is not a player in the

NHL we would trade him for. I feel that he's the best player in the NHL."

The Wings came back again Jan. 15 at Phoenix. Facing a 2-1 deficit with 2:19 remaining in regulation, Hull scored his second goal of the game, tipping a shot by defenseman Mathieu Dandenault past goaltender Robert Esche. For the first time in six games, they didn't win. But they didn't lose. They were 9-0-2-1 in their past dozen.

"This team, we don't want to lose: We feel we can win every game," Dandenault said. "If we keep pushing, keep chugging, eventually their players get tired. They play a patient game, and that's when we're at our best, because we've got so many offensive weapons. We can create a lot of havoc."

Asked whether it was a relief to get a couple of goals, Hull said, "Yeah, it really is. . . . Hopefully, that's a sign that things are going to come around, I'm gonna get a few more." Hull began to embrace playing with Datsyuk and Devereaux, eventually dubbing the line, "Two Kids and a Goat." He said he had told Shanahan he wouldn't have been able to play with two 23-year-olds four years ago.

"What do you mean by that?" a reporter asked.

"Well. . . ."

He laughed.

"My attitude's kind of changed over the last few years."

He laughed again.

He talked about how he had been too impatient, too outward with his emotions, about what he had learned with the Dallas Stars.

"It's not all about goals and points; it's about winning and doing the little things to win," he said. "It's helped me be able to not only do it but also enjoy doing it with the two young guys."

Later, he told Sports Illustrated: "I would have snapped (four years ago). I wouldn't have gotten the puck when and where I wanted it. But now it's like, 'OK, they're learning.' Before, I would have said, 'Screw it.' I wanted to score. This is what I live for.

"Shouldn't I be pissed off that I (can't score more)? Don't tell me I still couldn't get 40 or 50. But I've let the game change me into the kind of player I never wanted to be. My tongue needs stitches from biting it. I still love the same things, but when I started changing, things would fester so much, I actually couldn't play. My legs would seize up, and I'd get no spit in my mouth. I'd be so damn mad, I couldn't think right to get to the proper spot on the ice.

"I don't know how that anger escapes now, but somehow it does. It used to be you were a goal-scorer or a tough guy or a shadow, which really isn't hockey. Now you have to be a complete player. If you play strong defense and get 30 goals, you're a huge asset, even if you're a pain in the ass like me."

After the Wings' hot streak ended with a loss the next night at Dallas, an odd dispatch moved out of Moscow: The Reuters news agency translated and relayed some comments attributed to Fedorov's father, Viktor, in the Russian newspaper Sport-Express.

Apparently, Viktor didn't like Sergei's move to defense: "I believe this is the latest display of disrespect to my son by his coach and general manager. . . . I'm convinced that coaching experiments by Scotty Bowman were the only real cause of my son's drop in scoring in December, when the coach broke up an excellent line of Fedorov, Draper and Shanahan. For many years, Bowman has been reducing Sergei's playing time in favor of lesser players, which prevents Sergei from showing all his talent. Therefore, when there was talk about trading Sergei to Philadelphia for Lindros last summer, I was all in favor of it."

But the veracity of the comments was questionable: Viktor also reportedly said, "This summer, when Sergei becomes an unrestricted free agent, I urge him to change the club." Sergei wasn't scheduled to become an unrestricted free agent that summer. He was signed through 2002-03.

Bowman brushed off the whole thing.

"I don't deal with his father; I deal with Sergei," he said. "Sergei's never said that to me. . . . I talked to him about what we wanted to do, and he accepted it. He's doing well."

In seven games on defense, Fedorov had snapped that goal-scoring drought; he hadn't played less than 20 minutes in a game; the Wings had given more ice time to the developing Datsyuk, who had five goals in his past nine games; and they had gone 5-1-1.

Fedorov's most negative comment about playing defense had been that it wasn't his favorite position, and he responded to the Reuters report by saying that it wasn't an issue for him "at all" and that he had been "enjoying" himself. He blamed the media for creating a controversy. Asked whether his father knew his contract status, he said, "I certainly hope so. Of course he does." Asked whether that quotation made him wonder, he said, "It makes me wonder many things."

"It could be just hockey talk" that wasn't intended for publication, Fedorov said. "If he does pass his opinion, I guess he would be honest about it, but I don't think it's a big deal. . . . Maybe somebody try and make name for themselves. Who knows?"

Fedorov later said he had spoken to his father but hadn't asked him whether the quotations were accurate. A Sport-Express reporter said not only were the quotations accurate—Viktor had been mistaken about Sergei's contract status—but Viktor contributed regularly to the newspaper.

No matter. The next game, Jan. 18 against the Washington Capitals, Bowman moved Fedorov back to center.

And Hockeytown's attention quickly turned to someone else.

Early in the first period, Kirk Maltby fired a shot from the left point. Just off the left pad of goaltender Olaf Kolzig, just in front of defenseman Brendan Witt, his skates in the crease, Robitaille stuck out his stick, scored No. 611 and broke Bobby Hull's record.

"A typical goal by me," Robitaille said. "I just tipped it into the net."

When Lynch announced Robitaille had passed Hull—an awesome feat, even though Hull had left the NHL and scored 303 more goals in the World Hockey Association—players on both sides tapped their sticks against the boards and ice. The fans gave a standing ovation, underscoring it with what had become a common cry of Joe Louis Arena jubilation, another deep-throated "LUUUC!"

Bobby Hull sat in Section 212A, Row 12, Seat 2.

"That certainly makes it pretty special," Robitaille said. "It's going to be meaningful once I retire, but I don't want to stop here. I want to keep going and win a Cup."

The Capitals tied the game. But guess what? The Wings took a 2-1 lead, and the one who scored was . . . Brett Hull. Datsyuk made a breathtaking play, weaving through two defensemen, firing a shot. He didn't score. But seconds later, from behind the net, he sent a deft pass down low, and Brett one-timed the puck between Kolzig's pads.

And guess what else? As it turned out, the goal was the game-winner. Brett's 99th. Putting him past Bobby into third on the all-time list, behind Gordie Howe (121) and Phil Esposito (118).

Fedorov scored in the third, securing a 3-1 victory for what Washington coach Ron Wilson called a "Hall of Fame team," so with about two minutes remaining, Bobby was safe to leave his seat and head down the steps. The surrounding fans cheered. Bobby smiled. He held a forefinger to his lips, as if to say, "Shhh. . . ." It wasn't his night.

Bobby went to the dressing room.

"What are records for?" he asked.

"To be broken," someone said.

"Thank you."

Robitaille told Bobby his first pair of skates was a Bobby Hull CCM model. He asked him to pose for a picture. In a sweaty gray T-shirt, he clenched a cigar in his smile and The Puck in his hand, "611" written in black marker on white tape stuck to the rubber. Wearing a dark overcoat, Bobby held Robitaille's "610" puck.

Bobby laughed. He had given Robitaille that cigar—which Brett had given him for Christmas.

"If Luc gets the cigar," a reporter asked, "what's Brett get?"

"Well," Bobby said, "he gets my love."

Another game, another milestone.

It was overtime two nights later, when Yzerman chipped the puck into a corner, it slid behind the net, Igor Larionov made a pass, Dandenault scored, the Wings beat the Ottawa Senators and Yzerman, who grew up in the Ottawa suburb of Nepean, became the ninth NHL player to reach 1,000 assists.

"My role in the play was very minor, so it was a little anticlimactic," he said. "But the accomplishment itself was nice."

Yzerman wasn't kidding about the anticlimax: The play had to be reviewed because the net had come off its moorings, so by the time Lynch announced this one, Yzerman was already in the dressing room. He had no idea the fans were chanting, "STEV-IE!" He didn't make a curtain call.

"Nobody told me what was going on," he said. "You sit in the locker room, and you can't hear anything going on out there. Somebody from the organization should have come down and told me. Eventually (video technician) Joey Kocur did, but by that time, I was standing in T-shirt and shorts."

Oh, well.

As usual, Yzerman basically shrugged at himself.

"I have a lot of respect for the guys who have reached that," he said. "But I look at it that I've played a long time on a good team with a lot of good players, and it's slowly added up. So I don't really look at it as any great achievement. . . .

"We won the Stanley Cup, and those two blow everything else away. For the first 12, 13 years of my career, I was getting all these points, and it wasn't good enough, and I recognized that. 'We've got to win. We've got to win.' Everybody thought the same thing. We were able to do that. It's the same thing now. Winning is more exciting than the milestones."

Yzerman had a box of pucks at home: the puck from his 500th goal, scored in January 1996; the puck from his 600th, scored in November 1999; the puck from his 650th, scored in November 2001. The box was worth a fortune. The pucks were priceless.

"Every now and then," he said, "I think a little bit about what I'm going to do with them all."

But he didn't know where the box was. It had been misplaced.

Because Yzerman seemed so nonchalant, Dandenault joked that, hey, if Yzerman didn't want the puck, he would love to have it—and have it signed, "Thank you, Stevie." Sure enough, when he came to practice the next day, he found a puck in his locker. Sure enough, it was signed, "Thank you, Stevie."

Flipping the puck in the trash, Dandenault said, "We've got a lot of teasers on this team."

Larionov went to his Birmingham home late that night with no idea he was about to make another, far more important, assist. As he tried to unwind with his wife, Elena, they smelled something strange.

Smoke.

The house next door was on fire. Larionov ran out, ran to the front door, screamed, banged, rang the bell.

And woke up the Rays.

Bob, 59, and Suzanne, 55, had been sound asleep with their cats: Wild Thing, Alley Cat and Snickers. Their bedroom was way back in their ranch, and the fire had ignited out in the garage, where Bob had disposed of fireplace ashes he hadn't realized were still hot.

"Mr. Ray and his wife are very lucky people," said Tim Wangler, Birmingham assistant chief fire marshal.

The Larionovs called 911 at 12:31 A.M.

The flashing lights came, and the fire was out in 20 minutes to a half an hour. Just in time. It had started to spread from the garage to the attic, where it could have spread quickly.

"He literally saved our lives and our house," Bob said. "If it had been 15 minutes later. . . . We're very fortunate."

Left outside in his underwear, with no shoes, in the snow, Bob had nowhere to go. He and his wife couldn't go back inside. So the Larionovs took them in. Clothed them. Served them tea. Kept them company until almost dawn, when they left to stay with a relative.

"They were very hospitable," said Wangler, who interviewed the Rays at the Larionovs'. "It's the way it should be: neighbors helping neighbors."

Larionov declined to comment. Wings spokesman John Hahn said Larionov played down his actions, saying "anybody would've done it" and he was just glad he was in the right place at the right time.

Nevertheless, Wangler said, "He was instrumental in saving their lives, getting them out. It was one of those happy outcomes.

You hate to see the fire: It was devastating to the Rays. But it could have been so much worse."

The day the news broke, Larionov came to the rink and found a red, plastic, toy fireman's helmet hanging in his locker. The teasers had struck again.

The NHL put Hasek on a conference call with reporters Jan. 22. The biggest difference between the Wings and the Buffalo Sabres, he told the hockey world, was that with the Wings you could "make a mistake."

"I don't want to make a mistake," he said. "But on this team, if the guys need it, they can score four goals, maybe even five. We haven't played well every game, but we usually find a way to win. You can give up two goals, sometimes even three, and we still win these games."

Wouldn't you know it? Against the San Jose Sharks the next night, little more than a minute after allowing a goal on a power-play deflection, Hasek misplayed the puck behind the net, stumbled and got burned. And Hull bailed him out. Hull snapped a shot so powerful from the top of the right circle that his stick shaft bent like a banana. It was his second trademark goal of the game. It salvaged a 2-2 tie.

And wouldn't you know it? The Wings were on "Wednesday Night Hockey." ESPN presented its list of the top 10 scariest shots in NHL history during the telecast and Hull, along with his father, was featured.

"Timing's everything," said Hull, who was finally hot, with six goals in seven games. "I just like that they're finally starting to go in a little bit."

With a workmanlike effort two nights later, the Wings beat the Phoenix Coyotes. Afterward, they headed to the airport for a game at St. Louis and the toughest part of their season: 21 of their final 31 on the road, the All-Star Game for some, the Olympics for many. But they were loose, confident. They were 24-4-3 at the Joe, on an 11-0-1 run that would become 12-0-1. But they were 11-5-2-2 on the road.

"I don't think the road scares this team," Shanahan said. "Certainly, we're comfortable at home. Our fans give us a big boost. They give us great support. But I think we also play a very disciplined game, a good hockey game, on the road."

Hull strolled through the dressing room, a bounce in his step, a smile on his face. To no one in particular, he said, "Who has more fun than the Wings?"

The next night, as the Wings beat the Blues, Hull had a hat trick and two assists.

But then, suddenly, came some sobering news: Yzerman, who had looked fine since returning from that leg bruise, had arthroscopic surgery on his long-troublesome right knee.

In March 1988, Yzerman tore the posterior cruciate ligament, which connects the thighbone to the shinbone and provides stability. His cartilage gradually wore away over time. In October 2000, he had microfracture surgery, in which holes were drilled in his bones to stimulate cartilage growth. Unbeknownst to all but a few insiders, he noticed the knee wasn't right at training camp but pushed on.

Yzerman said he was going to be fine. He said he was still going to play in the Olympics. But it seemed he had become brittle, and the fans had seen how the Wings had suffered without him in the playoffs the previous season. As for the Olympics, they were only three weeks away.

After a trip to Edmonton and Calgary, the Wings flew home for the All-Star break—minus six players, who chipped in to charter a private jet to Los Angeles. Chelios, Fedorov, Lidstrom and Shanahan were going to the All-Star Game. Datsyuk was going to the YoungStars Game. Robitaille was going to see his family.

The NHL provided All-Star participants with first-class plane tickets. But the Wings had so many, plus Robitaille, six of them decided to go in real style—like "rock stars," Chelios said. They avoided airport hassles, enjoyed a smooth, 2½-hour flight, and got a good night's sleep at an important time in a hectic season. Fedorov, Lidstrom, Robitaille and Shanahan talked hockey in one part of the plane. In another, Datsyuk, the 23-year-old Russian rookie, and Chelios, the 40-year-old American veteran, watched a movie: "Black Rain."

Bowman and Paul Boyer, who was working with the World team, flew commercial. Hasek took the team plane back to Detroit, then chartered his own private jet to bring his family. But because of bad weather, his plane couldn't take off. He didn't arrive in L.A. until about 9:00 the next night.

"It was just a good idea to save energy," Fedorov said. "We had a good time. It was awesome."

Chelios smirked.

"Yeah," he said, "it's great if you want to waste money instead of flying first-class for free the next day."

Fedorov won the hardest shot competition, and he finished second to the Carolina Hurricanes' Sami Kapanen in the fastest skater competition, which he had won in 1992 and '94. Some of the Wings fraternized with the enemy, members of the Colorado Avalanche. Before the game, Patrick Roy approached Hasek.

"I felt someone had to break the ice," Roy said, "and it might as well be me."

They spoke for the first time ever.

"We were talking about hockey, about our futures, and he told me many things that probably reporters have never heard, and maybe I also told him some things," Hasek said. "However, it was a friendly game, and the playoffs are not friendly."

Hasek's and Roy's sons sat together. After the game, Bowman chatted with Roy in the hallway outside the dressing rooms. Joe Sakic walked past Chelios in the hall, and Chelios called out, "See ya, Joe!" Chelios traded sweaters with Rob Blake—and one of his sons was wearing the Blake sweater in the dressing room.

"He's going to get his rear kicked walking around in that," Chelios joked.

Hasek beat Roy for the first time as a Wing two nights later—and he did it in Denver. But with five games left until the Winter Games, the attention turned to a series of sideshows.

Bowman might have been the most qualified man to coach in the Olympics. Not only was he the most accomplished coach in NHL history, not only was his team leading the league by far, he had 10 players plus a prospect on Olympic rosters—no, make that *11* plus a prospect. Russia added Datsyuk at the last minute.

Bowman had international experience, having led Team Canada in the 1976 and '81 Canada Cups and the NHL All-Stars against the Soviet Union in '79.

But he was going to spend time with family in Sarasota, Fla., and run a mini-camp for his non-Olympians in Orlando. He pulled out at the last minute as Canada's coach for the 1996 World Cup, and many thought that was why Canada didn't offer him a position, although Team Canada executive director Wayne Gretzky said it wasn't. His adopted United States didn't offer him a position, either. He declined positions with Latvia and Russia, as well as an analyst job with MSNBC. Pointing out how he had gotten some rest during the Nagano Games, Bowman put a positive spin on his snubbing.

"I'm going to thank Wayne Gretzky for not getting me involved," he said. "I liked it in '98. I like to be refreshed, you know? It would be tough for me to get involved with the Olympics, too, at my age. . . . I'm an American citizen. I still have my ties in Canada. I'm just not getting involved. I'll use the time for family, which I haven't done in a while."

Asked whether pulling out in 1996 had cost him, Bowman said, "I don't know. I only made one call to (Canadian Hockey Association president) Bob Nicholson, and he deferred it to Gretzky. So I never called Wayne. They were already picked. All the coaches were picked. I wouldn't want anybody calling me (if I were picking the coaches). So that's the way it is."

Just before the Olympic break, the Wings put forward Brent Gilchrist on waivers, and the Stars picked him up. Seemingly out of nowhere, Bowman said he was "pretty sour" and went off on Devellano. To put it politely, Bowman and Devellano didn't get along. Devellano later told the Detroit News they had "no relationship." Bowman was upset Devellano had recommended the move, and he wanted to show he wasn't accountable for it.

"It wasn't explained to me," Bowman said. "I didn't expect it to be. That's the way things are."

The Wings put Gilchrist on waivers to open a roster spot, so Yzerman could come off injured reserve. Bowman said he wished the Wings had sent Sean Avery back to the minors instead.

"We're within one forward of having a rookie" in the lineup, Bowman said. "I wish I would have played him more."

Gilchrist was a great guy, but he had played only 19 games. The 34-year-old had one goal and one assist and was minus-3.

"Avery is OK, but he's a rookie," Bowman said. "Down the line, injuries . . . it's hard to get depth in the league."

Devellano shot back.

"Sean Avery is a player who can add more to our team now than Brent Gilchrist," he said. "It's about having the best players on the team. If Brent Gilchrist had been a real contributor to our team, he would have played more. . . . It's typical of (Bowman) to blame somebody else."

Then there was Yzerman. Concerned about his health, under pressure to find a way to get young Boston Bruins star Joe Thornton on Canada's Olympic roster, Gretzky asked Yzerman to disqualify himself if he wouldn't be able to contribute.

"We have a tremendous amount of confidence that if Stevie is healthy, he's going to play; if he's not healthy, he'll be honest with us and tell us," Gretzky said.

Yzerman was going to play. Remember, he once was denied a chance to play for his country, when he was cut from that Canada Cup team, and although he had two Stanley Cup rings, he had no Olympic medal. He played at Nagano, but the Canadians finished fourth. After the Wings' medical staff cleared him, he played in the Wings' final two games before the break.

"With a guy like Steve, you almost sometimes have to jump in and say, 'Hey, you can't do it. Get out of the way,' " Canada coach Pat Quinn said. "But it was his call."

Chapter 8
Still Friends

At a practice in January, the Red Wings ran a drill at one end of the ice at Joe Louis Arena. Dominik Hasek was alone at the other end, doing his thing, foiling imaginary foes. Then Brendan Shanahan had a free moment, decided to have a little fun and gave him a real shooter to face.

Almost four years before at the Nagano Olympics, the first to include NHL players, Canada and the Czech Republic met in the semifinals. After 60 minutes, they were tied, 1-1. After 10 minutes of overtime, the score was the same. The game went to a shoot-out: five Czechs, five Canadians, one penalty shot each, most goals wins. The Czechs tried four times; Patrick Roy allowed one goal. The Canadians tried four times; Hasek allowed zero. It came down to this: Shanahan vs. Hasek. If Shanahan scored, the Canadians stayed alive. If Hasek made the save, the Czechs won— and went to the gold-medal game.

"Take deep breaths," Steve Yzerman told Shanahan.

"Make a fake, draw him out, then go upstairs," Shanahan thought to himself. "Deep breaths. Deep breaths."

Shanahan picked up the puck at the red line and skated in. He faked; Hasek wasn't fooled. He went right; Hasek went with him. He shot; Hasek stoned him. He leaned forward in agony, arms on his thighs, head down; Hasek leaped forward in joy, arms in the air, head high. In the end, the Canadians lost bronze to Finland, the Czechs beat Russia for gold and Hasek's legend was cemented.

"I wanted to stick my head in the sand," Shanahan said afterward, voice flat, eyes dead.

Told the loss wasn't all his fault, that the four Canadians before him hadn't scored, either, he said: "But it came down to me. The (Czechs') shot before me, if they scored, I wouldn't even have had the opportunity to shoot. We were all pulling for Patrick, our whole team had our hopes on him and he pulled out the save."

Pause.

"And then they open the door and ask me to go out there . . ."

Swallow.

"And I didn't score . . ."

Swallow.

"And that's how I feel. . . . I let down my team and my country."

Asked whether he would like to play in another Olympics, Shanahan said, "Sure . . . in a second. . . . Hero or goat, I'd stand up and ask to take that shot again. I wanted it to be me."

At first, Shanahan wasn't invited to Team Canada's training camp for the Salt Lake Olympics. But he got to go eventually, and after a splendid start to the season, he made the team.

Now, little more than a month before the Games, the stands empty, the world unaware, but the pressure there, growing every day, Shanahan picked up a puck and skated in. He shot; Hasek stoned him. He picked up another puck and tried again; Hasek stoned him again. He picked up one more puck and tried one more time; Hasek stoned him one more time. Then he went back to what he had been doing, and Hasek did the same.

For a time, the Wings' Olympians had no trouble talking trash to each other about what was to come at Salt Lake City. The biggest target probably was Hasek, the Wings' lone Czech Olympian—and the man most able to ruin someone's medal hopes single-handedly.

"I've never seen guys try to score more in practice," Chris Chelios said. "It was all fun and games."

But when they came close to the Games, the fun stopped.

"In Detroit," Shanahan said, "we have so many Olympians, we kind of put an unofficial gag order on Olympic talk."

They acted brave around each other, but Chelios said it was just that: an act.

"Everybody's feeling the pressure. I don't care what anybody says," he said. "This is a big deal."

"Like football playoffs," Hasek said, "you play one game, you make one mistake, and Olympics are over for you. There's going to be lots of pressure on everyone. We talk about it. But I can say there isn't too much teasing."

Hockey Gods

After a victory Feb. 13 at Minnesota, the Wings went their separate ways for the NHL's 12-day break. The non-Olympians took the team plane home that night, then took off to squeeze in vacations before their mini-camp in Orlando. Most of the Olympians took morning commercial flights from Minneapolis to Salt Lake City. Yzerman got in around 1:30 P.M. local time. He had a chance to drop off his stuff at the Olympic Village and grab a bite to eat before heading to the rink.

Chelios got in around 1:30, too, but he had a more eventful trip. He took the team plane back to Detroit. He got home about 2:00 A.M., woke up at 6:30 and, at about 8:00, he and his family took off in a private plane. They had a rough ride. Strong headwinds. Stops for gas. Iowa. South Dakota. Idaho. Finally, they arrived in Utah—just in time for practice.

"It was a long day," Chelios said. "I'm tired now, but I'm excited. I'm looking forward to that first game."

Less than 48 hours after playing as teammates, Wings were playing as opponents. Canada faced Sweden, which meant Shanahan and Yzerman faced Tomas Holmstrom, Nicklas Lidstrom, Fredrik Olausson and the prospect, Henrik Zetterberg.

"That's kind of . . . bizarre," Yzerman said.

In the first period, Yzerman came down the right wing against Lidstrom.

"I knew it was him," Lidstrom said.

They ended up behind the net, their sticks locked.

"He closes on you so quick," Yzerman said. "I was thinking about doing something with the puck, but before you know it, his stick's right on you. He plays positionally on you. There was nothing I could do."

Wings kept running into each other, especially when walking to the dressing room, because the teams, trusted to keep the Olympic spirit, took the same path.

Olausson walked past Shanahan and patted him on the behind. Shanahan nodded. Shanahan walked past Zetterberg and playfully tipped up the back of Zetterberg's helmet. Zetterberg didn't see who did it.

"That was Shanahan," someone said.

"*Brendan* Shanahan?" Zetterberg asked, smiling.

Still Friends

Sergei Fedorov walked past Chelios with a water bottle and gave him a little squirt down the neck. Fedorov smiled; Chelios did not. Chelios and Igor Larionov met at center ice, exchanged flags and shook hands. Neither wore a letter on his sweater for the Wings, but the 40-year-old and 41-year-old were so respected as players and leaders that they were captains of their countries' teams—at a time when their teams needed them most.

Several Russian players weren't sure they wanted to represent the motherland at Salt Lake, upset with a Russian hockey federation still stuck in old Soviet ways. Slava Fetisov wrested power from the federation, became coach and general manager, and persuaded all but a couple of players to participate.

Fetisov made a personal appeal to Larionov. They were old friends. They had played together in and for the Soviet Union, winning all types of titles, including Olympic golds in 1984 and '88. They had rebelled together against the Soviet system. They had played together for the Wings, winning two Stanley Cups. An assistant coach with New Jersey, Fetisov visited Larionov at his Birmingham home Nov. 29, while the Devils were in Detroit. Larionov said Fetisov "put a lot of pressure" on him.

"Slava asked me, and I took some time to think about it," Larionov said, "and I couldn't refuse Slava."

When Larionov couldn't refuse, others couldn't refuse, either.

"If not for them, we wouldn't be here," said Fedorov, whom Fetisov also pressured personally. "I'm speaking for a few of the guys, not all of them, but a few, including myself."

Larionov was fiercely proud of his past. He grew up in the factory town of Voskresensk, Russia, living with his parents and brother in a one-bedroom apartment in a nine-story building. He started out playing street hockey.

"We didn't wait for winter," he wrote in his autobiography, *Larionov*. "When they sent us to a collective farm to harvest potatoes, we would grab a few nets and make goals out of them and use a tennis ball for a puck, sprinkling the pavement with sand in order to reduce friction."

In a news conference at Salt Lake, he made a comment in Russian about playing for the Soviet national team. The translator said in English, "Russian national team." Larionov corrected him quickly.

"Soviet national team," he said.

He had played his best hockey centering Vladimir Krutov and Sergei Makarov on the famed KLM line, making such intelligent, dazzling plays that Europeans considered him their counterpart to Wayne Gretzky. He was Soviet player of the year in 1988. He discussed his philosophy of playing "dispatcher"—Russian for center—in his book. Something is lost in the translation from his native language, but not everything.

"Let my club slaughter all opposition, one after the other. Let my line be considered one of the best," he wrote. "But if I myself played with no unpredictability, without cleverness or improvisation, I was not emotionally satisfied."

But Larionov also clearly remembered what was bad about the good old days. As a teenager in 1977, he began playing for his hometown team, Khimik. Four years later, he was recruited against his will for the Central Red Army—as a player and a soldier. He never fired a gun, but he rose to the rank of caption. In his book, he described a nine-month training ordeal in isolated Archangel.

"We continually stewed in our own juices, in boring surroundings, where the evening leisure time was spent in front of television, or playing cards, or shooting pool," The Professor wrote. "How could there be any aesthetic development, any cultivation of the personality?"

The players would have to beg the wife of tyrannical coach Viktor Tikhonov just to make a practice optional, even if they didn't have a game for three days. If she succeeded in convincing her husband, the players still had to tread carefully at the next practice.

"Ten o'clock on the ice, and if you step on a little sliver (and slip), the coach makes notes that you have been drunk last night because you fell on the ice," Larionov said. "That's what we lived like, under pressure all the time. . . . We didn't have any freedom."

Larionov fought for his freedom. He denounced Tikhonov in a popular magazine. At one point, Tikhonov claimed he had information about Fetisov and Larionov that could put them in prison for eight years. The players called Tikhonov's tactics Stalinist.

Still Friends

Not until 1989, thanks in large part to Mikhail Gorbachev and *glasnost*, did Larionov finally fulfill his dream of playing in the NHL. He had played hockey at the highest level for 12 seasons, he was 29—and he was a rookie. In 12 NHL seasons with the Vancouver Canucks, San Jose Sharks, Florida Panthers and Wings, his highest individual accolade was an All-Star Game appearance, in '98. Still, the Russians looked up to him more than any other active player.

At Salt Lake, he patted an opponent on the back at a news conference. He wouldn't have been able to do that years ago. Not only weren't Soviet players allowed to speak to the media, they weren't allowed to speak to anyone, especially foreigners. At the Olympics, they didn't even live in the Village. At Salt Lake, Larionov played left wing on a line with Pavel Datsyuk. He was Datsyuk's childhood hero.

The question hanging over the Americans wasn't if they would represent their country at Salt Lake, it was *how* they would do it. At Nagano, they finished sixth. Hours after elimination, some of them trashed rooms at the Olympic Village. The $3,000 in damage didn't leave as big a stain as the fact that no one came forward to accept responsibility—and that, for the first time, these were highly paid professionals, not amateurs.

Chelios had nothing to do with the incident, but he was the captain, so he cut a check to cover the cost and apologized on behalf of the team. His second Olympic experience had ended up sour like his first. In 1984 at Sarajevo, he took a shot off an ankle in the second game, he played the rest of the tournament with a stress fracture and the team finished seventh.

Herb Brooks was a huge story at Salt Lake. He had coached the Americans to the "Miracle on Ice" victory over the Soviets and gold at the 1980 Lake Placid Olympics, the last Winter Games held on American soil. Brett Hull fed the media frenzy by talking about "Herbie Brooks magic" all the time. But Brooks tried to make Chelios the story, saying Chelios had "paid the price" to be captain again.

"This is really his team," he said. "He's our guy. He's our focal point."

Chelios, son of Greek immigrants, was perhaps the greatest U.S.-born player in hockey history. In 19 seasons with the Montreal Canadiens, Chicago Blackhawks and Wings, he had won three Norrises, made 11 All-Star Game appearances—and ticked off most of the league with his constant yapping, warrior mentality and tenacious play. Sports Illustrated ran this telling anecdote: During a Canadiens-Bruins playoff series in the late 1980s, a sign written in Greek hung from the upper balcony at Boston Garden, suggesting Chelios dine on human waste. He was cartoonishly tough.

In a game for the Blackhawks in the mid-1990s, Chelios tore the anterior cruciate ligament in his left knee. He felt something pop, headed back to the bench, told the trainers—and stayed in the game.

"I literally didn't miss a shift," he said.

He just kept playing on the knee. And playing on it. And playing on it. Eventually, the torn ACL atrophied. But surgery wasn't necessary. Strong sinews and healthy cartilage stabilized the knee enough. Five years. No ACL. No problem.

Then, in a game for the Wings in October 2000, he twisted the knee and damaged some cartilage so badly that it had to be removed by arthroscopy three days later. He tried to keep playing on the knee, but enough was enough. The knee was so unstable that he felt he would be risking his career to continue the rest of the season. He decided to have surgery—reconstructive surgery. If all went well, he thought, he could be back in February or March.

He came back in February, only 95 days later. The same week as his surgery, he was walking—and walking around the Wings' training room, where he already was rehabilitating seven hours a day. Less than a month later, he was on the ice. If the training staff had any problem with him, it was that he pushed himself too hard.

"A couple of times," John Wharton said, "he threatened to beat up my assistant, Piet Van Zant, because Piet wanted to get him out of the weight room a little sooner than he wanted to."

The Wings acquired Chelios at the 1999 trade deadline to help fill the void left by Vladimir Konstantinov, who had been known—with affection in Detroit, loathing everywhere else—as "Vlad the

Impaler." Although Chelios once said he never would play in
Detroit, he became a classic Motor City guy, even tooling around
in a black 1964 Cadillac convertible. Fans who had hated him grew
to love him.

Chelios wore the "C" on his U.S. sweater less than two weeks
at Salt Lake, but he had been wearing it on his sleeve for far
longer. Throughout the summer and the NHL season, Brooks
spoke with Chelios at least once a week. They talked about
everything from on-ice systems to the Olympic ideal, and Brooks
gave Chelios a mission.

"If you see some of the guys," he said, "make sure that this is
on their mind."

Chelios did. In Chicago? He talked to his old Blackhawks
teammate Tony Amonte. Flyers in town? He talked to Jeremy
Roenick. No one around? He picked up his cell phone.

"A lot of guys on this club lead their NHL teams during the
regular season, but Cheli's a winner," said Amonte, the Hawks'
captain. "He's a guy that even guys like myself look up to."

During the Americans' first practice, Brooks consulted
Chelios as he would have an assistant coach. Before they faced
Belarus at 11:00 A.M. on a Monday, Chelios chatted away at an
8:00 A.M. breakfast to, as Amonte said, "get the boys ready."

"He wants to win—he wants to win *bad*," Amonte said.
"It's starting to rub off on the guys. We want to win. We've got a
lot to prove after '98."

Chelios didn't want to talk about being captain America.
He said only that he was doing his job, that he had learned from
Bob Gainey in Montreal, Dirk Graham in Chicago and Yzerman in
Detroit. He certainly didn't want to talk about Nagano. He said he
wouldn't answer questions about it. With a smirk, he joked,
"Maybe if I punch the first guy in the nose that asks, they won't
say anything, right?"

With the Games in North America, the tournament led up to
a fitting finale: Canada vs. the United States.

The Canadians, the favorites, started poorly. They lost to
Sweden, 5-2; squeaked past Germany, 3-2; and tied the Czechs,
3-3. The Canadian fans and media freaked out, fretting. The

normally reserved, super-polite Gretzky lashed out at everyone from Americans to the Czech team to the referee.

Yzerman looked a step slow on his surgically repaired right knee in the first two games, on a line with Shanahan and Jarome Iginla. But then Pat Quinn put him on the top line with Paul Kariya and Mario Lemieux.

"I didn't expect it," Yzerman said. "I was like, 'Whoa! I'm going to try to take advantage of this.' "

Yzerman and the Canadians came on. In the quarterfinals against Finland, Shanahan suffered a broken right thumb. But Yzerman scored the winner in a 2-1 victory—and forgot to stay his stoic self. He pumped a fist, showed a huge smile. In the semifinals against Belarus, he scored the starter of a 7-1 blowout—and couldn't help himself again. He pumped his left fist. Not once. But twice.

"I'm trying to stay calm," Yzerman said. "I don't like getting really fired up, because I think you get up there and then there's a crash a lot of times. I try to contain my emotions as much as I can. But it's pretty hard. You're pretty fired up. . . .

"I'm enjoying playing. The last Olympics was a ton of fun. This will probably be the last one for me. I don't know that I'll be playing in four years. . . . Canada wants the gold medal, and the (people) will be disappointed if we don't get it.

"I just really want to win."

The Americans started strong. They beat Finland, 6-0; tied Russia, 2-2; and blew out Belarus, 8-1.

Hull scored two big goals in round-robin play, then added an awesome third goal in a 5-0 quarterfinal rout of Germany. Mike Modano, his former Dallas Stars teammate, took a shot from the slot. It went wide left but bounced back off the end boards. At the side of the net, from a bad angle, Hull tapped the puck through his legs on his backhand. It went along the goal line and sneaked inside the far post.

"That's Brett Hull," Modano said, "the luckiest guy, I think, in the world."

"That's just stupid talent," Roenick said, "to be able to score a goal like that."

Afterward, Hull said he wasn't thinking about facing the Russians in the semis.

"I'm thinking about a nice, cold Bud Light right now," he said.

But others were thinking about the Russians, the semis—and fate. Twenty-two years before at Lake Placid, Brooks had coached the Americans to victory over West Germany on Wednesday, Feb. 20. They faced the Soviet Union on Friday, Feb. 22. Now at Salt Lake, Brooks was back behind the bench, the points in the tournament were the same, the opponents were the same, the days of the week were the same and the dates were the same.

"Hopefully, that's a sign," Chelios said. "We've got to believe it. Herb's been there. He did something that was magical. Hopefully, he's got a lot of that magic left in him."

As fate would have it, the Americans survived a frantic third period and beat the Russians, 3-2. Fetisov charged the referees and the tournament itself with having a pro-North American bias, but the Americans and Canadians didn't care.

"It's almost too good to be true," Chelios said.

Televisions would be tuned in to the final from coast to coast.

"The streets are going to be pretty empty," Shanahan said, "unless you've got a car with a satellite dish on it."

In the end, the Canadians beat the Americans convincingly. Iginla gave them a 4-2 lead with 3:59 left. He took a shot from the left wing. Goaltender Mike Richter got a piece of the puck with his glove, but not enough. It fluttered in the air and fell inside the far post. Yzerman, who earned an assist on the play, leapt into Iginla's arms.

Joe Sakic iced the 5-2 victory with 1:20 left. He broke in on Richter and beat his right pad. Shanahan jumped on top of Sakic in a pile along the boards. Yzerman jumped to his feet on the bench and hugged a couple of teammates. In the stands, Canadian fans broke out in song. And not just any song. They sang "O Canada" loud and proud. *God keep our land glorious and free . . .*

"It gave us chills," Shanahan said.

Then the buzzer sounded, and it was over, the game, the tournament, the torment. As Quinn had said, Canadians feel they invented hockey, developed hockey, taught hockey to the world.

Now they had the Olympic men's hockey gold medal. For the first time in half a century.

"It's a huge victory," Yzerman said. "Hockey, it's the number one sport in Canada, the most popular sport. So we're thrilled to be Olympic champions."

While the Canadians celebrated, the Americans watched. They had failed to finish the fairy tale. But after a few minutes, Chelios led the team to center ice. The players raised their sticks to the crowd in unison, and the American fans cheered. In a sense, they hadn't lost gold as much as they had won silver. The medal was the United States' first of any color in men's hockey since 1980.

The teams lined up and shook hands. Shanahan and Yzerman hugged Chelios and Hull. The Americans congratulated the Canadians; the Canadians consoled the Americans.

"You know, it doesn't prove that Canada's the best," Yzerman said. "We're just Olympic champions, that's all."

The Americans received their silver medals. Chelios frowned after his went around his neck; Hull winked and sort of smiled. Then the Canadians received their gold medals. As soon as his went around his neck, Shanahan looked down, took it in his left hand and examined it.

"It's nice and heavy," he said.

Then he stepped back, waved to his family in the stands and held it up.

"I did the best I could on painkillers and adrenaline," he said, his right thumb wrapped in a bandage. "Nagano was such a disappointment. When I wasn't initially invited to try out for the team, I just thought, 'Well, I guess that's it for my Olympic experience.' So to be sitting here today with a gold medal, I feel like a pretty lucky man."

Yzerman grabbed Owen Nolan's video camera and taped Nolan as he received his medal, then Yzerman gave the camera back and received his medal with a big smile.

"It's a great moment," he said.

After the Canadian anthem was played, Shanahan and Yzerman posed for a picture on the ice with Chelios and Hull.

"We talked about it before the tournament, thinking this was what North America wanted, a Canada-USA final," Chelios said.

"And then, when it got to be that, we didn't know if we really wanted that. It was wild, the look we gave each other in the cafeteria" at the Olympic Village.

Chelios said he meant no disrespect toward the other Wings who played at Salt Lake. Datsyuk, Fedorov and Larionov won bronze. Lidstrom, Holmstrom, Olausson and Zetterberg lost in the quarterfinals, as Hasek did. But, Chelios said, he had a special bond with Shanahan and Yzerman, a "North American thing."

"Shanny and Stevie, I've been growing up with those guys," he said. "I've been through the wars with those guys. I'm proud of those guys. I'm happy for them. I'm happy for us, and I'm just as happy for them."

The next day, they would be teammates again. The Canadians were sure to give it to the Americans a little bit. But that was all right, Chelios said.

"We'll just give it to Dominik and Nick."

Chapter 9
Waiting Games

The Red Wings reconvened in Florida in late February and had fun beating two dregs of the NHL, the Tampa Bay Lightning and Florida Panthers. They were a team again.

The Olympic break had disrupted their defensive cohesion, but in a way, that was good. Dominik Hasek wanted a lot of work. He *needed* a lot of work.

"It helps me forget the failure in Salt Lake City," he said.

Hasek made 34 saves against the Lightning, and one of them was a comical confidence-booster. Kris Draper hauled down Dan Boyle on a breakaway, and a referee called for a penalty shot.

A penalty shot? Dan Boyle?

"I didn't know who he was," Hasek said. "The ref came to me and said, 'He is a defenseman.' So I thought, 'OK, so maybe he is not the best stickhandler.' "

Boyle picked up the puck at the red line and skated in.

"I think he lost the puck twice before he shot, first at the blue line and again in front of me," Hasek said.

Hasek stopped Boyle so easily that it was embarrassing. Despite his broken right thumb, Brendan Shanahan scored his second goal of the game in overtime. The Detroit Free Press headline the next day was "Two thumbs up!"

At Florida, Luc Robitaille rallied the Wings from a 2-0 deficit, scoring his second goal of the game—and third in the two games—with 2:13 remaining in regulation.

Robitaille had wanted to play for Canada at Salt Lake, and he had a good relationship with Wayne Gretzky, a former linemate on the Los Angeles Kings. But his subpar skating would have been magnified on the larger, international ice sheet, and he wasn't even mentioned as a candidate for the team. He was the only one of the Wings' nine potential Hall of Famers who wasn't an Olympian.

He spent most of the break at his place in Aspen, Colo. He relaxed with his wife and boys, going sledding, even skiing.

"I was careful," said Robitaille, who rented short skis that seemed like skates. "I just kind of followed my six-year-old, going, 'Don't break anything, you little weasel.'"

But he also watched some hockey, including the gold-medal game, and worked hard. He woke up early and did his regular off-ice training regimen: squats, box jumps, bike rides.

"For me, the big thing was, I wanted to come back and play strong," said Robitaille, who had only four goals in 17 games before the break. "I want to raise that Cup. That would be the thing for me, you know?"

The Wings pumped so many shots on the Panthers that goaltender Roberto Luongo set a franchise record with 57 saves. The public address announcer informed the crowd of the feat—with 1:07 left in overtime.

"They should wait until the game is over," Hasek said.

Luongo had made nine of his saves on Brett Hull, and with 48.5 seconds left, Hull got his revenge with a goal.

"The P.A. announcer," Hull said, "should be slapped."

There was one problem: Steve Yzerman didn't make the trip. After the Olympics, he had an MRI on his right knee, it didn't look good and he took the first of three injections to ease the grinding of bone on bone. He held a news conference at Joe Louis Arena and said he expected to be out about 2½ weeks.

Yzerman received sympathy from fans, but he also received a little criticism—and with him, a little criticism was a lot. Some didn't like it when he said team doctor David Collon had wanted him to sit out a month, but he elected to have the arthroscopic surgery that kept him out little more than two weeks, allowing him to play in the Olympics. Some didn't like it when he said the knee had become "puffy and sore" after his third game at Salt Lake, but "once you're in the tournament you stick with it."

Here he was wearing a maroon, Canadian Olympic jacket in the heart of a blue-collar American city, where he played, where he made millions upon millions of dollars, where he became a U.S. citizen. Here he was breaking up the monotony of the medical questions with that dry sense of humor, flashing the prize he had won by beating the United States, smiling and saying, "By the way, Canada won a gold medal in men's hockey." A few fans—not many, but a few—voiced displeasure on the radio and in the newspapers.

At practice March 7, a reporter asked Hasek whether he could remember his last loss, not including the Olympics.

"I don't remember," he said. "Maybe if I think about it deeply, I would find out. But I don't know right now. It probably was a long time ago."

It had been more than seven weeks, since Jan. 16 at Dallas. He was 12-0-2 in his past 14 games, 17-1-2 in his past 20.

"I think," Shanahan said, "he was getting geared up for the Olympics, and he was really intense during the Olympics, and he's carried that over since he's been back."

The Wings went to St. Louis for a Saturday matinee. Hasek extended his unbeaten streak to 15 games, a career best. The Wings won their eighth straight, one short of the franchise record; won their eighth straight on the road, a franchise record; and reached 100 points, before anyone else had reached *84*. The Wings were flying. What in the world could keep them from getting where they wanted to go?

Well, the weather, for starters. That night, the Wings took off for Buffalo for a Sunday matinee, but they couldn't land because of high winds. After circling, they were diverted to Cleveland, where they spent the night at the Airport Marriott. They made it to Buffalo in the morning but didn't arrive at HSBC Arena until 1:05 P.M. The game was at 3:00.

Scotty Bowman said he thought he would rest Hasek. Manny Legace hadn't played in more than a month, and the game was the second of a back-to-back set. But Hasek hadn't played at Buffalo since leaving the Sabres, and he made it clear he wanted to start, perhaps even dropping a subtle hint about his future, which he said he wouldn't consider until after the playoffs.

"I'm not the coach; I don't make the decisions," Hasek said. "But I hope I'm going to play in Buffalo. . . . I'm excited to go back and play one more game in that building."

Hasek started, received a mixed response from the fans—and allowed four goals on the first 12 shots he faced. Goal number one came during a two-man advantage, number two during a power play, number three on a breakaway. Number four? Hasek dived to his left, trying too hard, anticipating a move that never was made. From the left wing, Chris Gratton shot the puck into an open net.

"I just guessed, and I made a funny move," Hasek said. "I don't know why. It was the worst goal I've ever given up."

Hasek was pulled after two periods. Instead of sitting on the bench in the third, he rode an exercise bike. The Wings lost, 5-1. They hadn't lost by as many as four goals since Nov. 3, 2000, when they lost to the Chicago Blackhawks, 6-1.

"I was a little bit nervous before I stepped on the ice," Hasek said. "It was a weird feeling. I'm glad it's over. . . . It wasn't my day or the team's."

It went from bad to worse.

While the Wings flew back to Detroit, Hasek stayed behind. He went to a bar after the game—and someone stole his black, leather NHL Players Association jacket from the back of his seat. He spent most of Monday with Hasek's Heroes, the hockey program for underprivileged children he had started in Buffalo with a $1-million donation. After flying back to Detroit, he discovered he had left a bag behind—and it contained his car keys. He had to take a taxi home.

Draper, who lived in Hasek's suburban subdivision, gave him a ride to practice Tuesday. "Car's still at the airport," Hasek said.

Yzerman went for a light skate March 13 and said the knee felt tender but "way better" than it had at the end of the Olympics. He said he expected to return soon.

"I've responded without any difficulty to anything," he said, "so I don't see this being a problem in another week."

Two days later, the knee felt bad again. Three days after that, he went to see specialist William Clancy in Birmingham, Ala., and Clancy told him to stay off skates for 10 days to two weeks. It was less than a month until the playoffs, the city was starting to get antsy and Yzerman opened up to Detroit News columnist Bob Wojnowski.

"I have my concerns," he said. "I have since . . . it first bothered me. I'm not to the point where I'm real nervous. I will be playing, no question, whether it's six games before the playoffs or whatever. There's no new damage. It was just sore, and we want to be cautious. . . . The doctors described it like a scab, and if you keep picking at it, it never heals. Because of where we are in the standings, there isn't pressure to come back and play right now. It actually feels pretty good. I do have to change the way I train. I can't put much stress on it. I mean, the best thing for my knee, for anyone's knee, is to never play again and retire."

Pause.

"But I'm not going to do that."

Yzerman defended his decision to play in the Olympics. He said the knee "wasn't sore at all" after the Wings' last game before the break.

"I felt fine," he said. "How could I not go? I have no regret whatsoever. I absolutely made the right decision. I made the decision any player would have made. If my knee hurt at all, I wouldn't have gone."

That said . . .

"If you had told me a month ago, before the Olympics, that if I played I'd miss 12 games, I would've reconsidered," he said. "If I'd known what I know now, it would have been much more difficult to go. . . . I can't deny what my body is facing. I've had problems off and on since the knee surgery 14 years ago. I've worked through it, and I'll work through this. It's just the wear and tear. Slowly, it takes its toll."

The trade deadline was 3:00 P.M. March 19. Ken Holland hadn't made a major deadline deal since 1999, but the fans remembered that year, when he brought in Chris Chelios, Wendel Clark, Bill Ranford and Ulf Samuelsson. After the splash Holland made in the summer, the fans were hopeful for another.

If the Wings had needs, they were grit and defense, and there was a gritty defenseman on the market: Pittsburgh's Darius Kasparaitis. Problem was, the Penguins wanted Jiri Fischer for him. Fischer was the Wings' first-round pick in 1998. He was 21, 6-feet-5, 225 pounds. He was smart and skilled. He was paired with Chelios, and Chelios had taken him under his wing.

"Chris understands the game . . . when to go, when not to go; when to stand up; whom to challenge, whom not to challenge; timing of it," Dave Lewis said. "He knows the opponent, he knows how to play, he plays with an edge and I think all those things have rubbed off on Jiri. If you have a veteran willing to teach, there's nothing better as far as a tool for teaching a young player how to play."

Fischer was blossoming. No way were the Wings going to give him up. The Wings looked at several other options—the Columbus Blue Jackets' Lyle Odelein, the Panthers' Jeff Norton, the Washington Capitals' Ken Klee and Frantisek Kucera—but couldn't find a fit. They didn't want to part with any of the players on their roster or their top prospects.

Kasparaitis went to the worst place possible from a Detroit perspective: Colorado. The Avalanche sent the Penguins two decent young players, defenseman Rick Berry and forward Ville Nieminen, even though Kasparaitis was scheduled to become an unrestricted free agent July 1. The Avs had added Rob Blake the year before, Ray Bourque the year before that. Kasparaitis wasn't in their class, but once again, to Wings fans' chagrin, the Avs had acquired the best defenseman available.

"He's going to make them much stronger," Holland said. "They're the defending Stanley Cup champions, and in my mind, the defending champions are always the team to beat. So you know that they're one of the favorites, if not the favorite, going into the playoffs."

The Wings knew the Avs were after the Atlanta Thrashers' Jiri Slegr, too. They had scouted Slegr, 30, heavily and weren't impressed: He wasn't the gritty guy they wanted; they weren't even sure he was as good an offensive threat as what they already had in Steve Duchesne and Fredrik Olausson. But they had liked him in the past, he had the experience Maxim Kuznetsov and Jesse Wallin lacked, and they felt he might perform better on a first-place team than a last-place team. They decided to try to keep him from Colorado, thinking, at worst, he would give them some more depth. They convinced Atlanta general manager Don Waddell, a former Wings assistant GM, the minor-leaguer they were offering was better than the minor-leaguer the Avs were offering. About 2:45, they had a deal: Slegr for forward Yuri Butsayev, who had no future with the Wings, anyway, and a third-round pick in the 2002 draft.

"He's capable of playing a lot of minutes if he needs to," Holland said of Slegr. "In the event that we do have some injuries, or depending on who he fits in with, we think he can play a lot of minutes and bring a lot of things to our hockey club."

After their bad day in Buffalo, the Wings beat the Edmonton Oilers. But they blew a 2-0 lead in the third period, then a 3-2 lead with 15.4 seconds remaining in regulation. Chelios had to smirk afterward, because he had scored the first regular-season overtime goal of his long career.

"C'mon," he said. "I could've sworn I had one. . . ."

But his smirk didn't last long.

"We have to realize teams are fighting for playoff spots now, and they're going to raise the level like it's a playoff level, and we have to do the same thing," he said. "We're just lackadaisical out there."

The Wings lost at Boston. They won at New York—but barely: The Rangers scored, but the officials disallowed the goal, and Darren McCarty scored the winner with 2:08 left. On trade deadline day, Anaheim coach Bryan Murray called the Wings the favorites to win the Cup, saying, "I don't know that there's a team that should beat them." That night, Paul Kariya scored twice, and the Mighty Ducks, the second-worst team in the Western Conference, beat them, 2-1.

"To lose against a team like that, it's very frustrating," Hasek said. "It seems we weren't focused mentally. We just thought we were going to beat them easily, because they have maybe one player, Kariya, and that's it. . . . The way we competed I don't think is the way we can be Stanley Cup contenders. We've got to wake up and do the things we should do."

The Wings beat the Blue Jackets, the worst team in the West, but only because Fedorov took advantage of a couple of lucky bounces, forcing overtime with 4:47 remaining and scoring again 25 seconds into overtime. That they had clinched the

Central Division wasn't even mentioned in the next day's newspapers. That they could clinch the Western Conference in their next game, March 23 at Colorado, didn't matter to Hull.

"It's going to happen sooner or later," he said.

Asked whether the Wings needed a game against the Avs to inspire them, Hull said they weren't "very professional" if they did.

"But I guess we need something to give our head a shake," he said. "We're doing a lot of good things, then just go brain-dead, and that's what kills us. We're just doing stupid things."

Shanahan was stuck on 499 goals. After he scored March 2, his next shot hit the crossbar. Then he dribbled one wide of an empty net. Then he said No. 500 didn't matter to him.

"I think I jinxed myself," he said.

Eight games: no goals. Oh, he had chances. Glorious chances. But the puck always slipped off his stick, struck iron or found a path with a dead end.

"It's just strange to have so many good chances where these goalies are, like, diving across the net, swiping them out of the air," he said. "Like, I'm getting great wood on them."

Thirty-eight shots on net: nothing. So many spoiled story lines: Shanahan could have scored his 500th against Toronto, his hometown team, but didn't. He could have done it at St. Louis, where he scored 156 goals in four seasons, but didn't. He could have done it on St. Patrick's Day, as a tribute to his Irish heritage, but didn't—even though he put green tape on the knob of his stick.

He smiled and spoke of evil spirits screwing him up. He had to laugh. What else could he do? He wasn't playing poorly. Eight games: eight assists.

"Usually when you're not scoring, you're really frustrated and you want to change things and you're down," he said. "But any time I look at a guy on the team, he says, 'Don't change a thing.' You can't. A lot of the shots I take, they're the shots that have gotten my 499 goals. I'm not changing anything."

In the third period at Colorado, while the Wings had a two-man advantage, Nicklas Lidstrom sent a pass from the point to the left circle, and Shanahan broke his drought and a scoreless tie in signature style. He one-timed the puck past Patrick Roy.

"I don't know how many of those I've gotten from Nick in my career here," Shanahan said. "I'm just glad it came against a great goalie, in a big game, and it helped us win a game. That makes it more meaningful."

The Wings beat the Avs, 2-0, and won the season series, 3-1. But afterward, people didn't talk about that, or the conference title, or Shanahan's 500th, or how Hasek was first among active players with 61 shutouts—and Roy was second with 60.

Shortly after Shanahan scored, defenseman Martin Skoula pushed Kirk Maltby into the Colorado net. Maltby fell into Roy, and Roy thought Maltby had run into him intentionally.

"What I didn't like is that he tried to take my knee off," Roy said. "It was clear to me, because normally a guy will hit me in front, and he tried to hit me on top. . . . I really think he tried to hurt me."

Roy went after Maltby.

"He was getting eye-gouges in there," Maltby said. "It felt like a wrestling match."

Brawl. With six Avs on five Wings, Hasek left his crease and bolted down the ice, fiddling with his glove and blocker to get them off as he went. As the Wings and their fans watched the present, their minds flashed back to the past and forward to the future. In 1997, Mike Vernon fought Roy. In '98, Chris Osgood fought Roy. But Hasek was brought in to beat Roy, not beat him up; the playoffs were 3½ weeks away and if Hasek got hurt . . .

As Hasek closed in, he slipped on Roy's discarded stick and tumbled. The brawl became a blooper. Hasek got up, but before he and Roy could throw down, the officials separated them.

"I was pretty upset at the moment," Hasek said. "The referee grabbed me. I want to be involved. It's part of the game."

"He was probably trying to prove something; I don't know what it was," Roy told the Denver Post. "I think it would have been more interesting if the ref had not been there."

"I respect Patrick Roy," Hasek said. "However, if something like that happens, I am ready any time. I know there is tradition in Detroit that every time a goalie is involved in a fight with Patrick Roy, Detroit wins the Stanley Cup."

Shanahan thanked God that Hasek hadn't fought Roy. Hull said what Hasek and Roy had done was "idiotic." Bowman said Hasek had scored points with his teammates and, most important, hadn't gotten hurt. As it turned out, Hasek had a minor back injury, the first of his career, giving everyone a little scare. He said he didn't know if he suffered it going after Roy or in a collision with Mike Keane afterward. But he sat out only one game.

Two nights later at Nashville, the Predators poked fun at the Wings on the scoreboard screen. They showed a bunch of old men dressed in Detroit sweaters hunched on the bench, sucking oxygen, holding diapers.

"I thought it was funny," Hull said. "Almost accurate."

The Wings had the last laugh. Twice. Shanahan scored with 1:59 remaining in regulation, and the teams tied, 3-3. Three nights later at Joe Louis Arena, Shanahan scored with 2:05 remaining in regulation, and again, the teams tied, 3-3.

The two points gave the Wings the Presidents' Trophy as the NHL's top regular-season team for the third time in eight years, but Bowman said, "I don't think anybody's excited about the Presidents' Trophy right now."

For weeks, the Wings had been waiting for the only thing that mattered: the playoffs. Now it was official—they had nothing for which to play—and there were still eight games left. Draper said the Wings had to motivate themselves somehow, but they were fighting human nature, and frankly, winning wasn't their top priority anymore.

Bowman gave players practices, games and road trips off. The Wings had worried about the impact of their age, the All-Star Game, the Olympics and their road-heavy schedule down the stretch. Well, they had earned the opportunity to rest, and they were going to take advantage of it.

Some teams complained. Edmonton general manager Kevin Lowe and Vancouver Canucks GM Brian Burke spoke to Holland and league officials. They were fighting for playoff spots, and they worried their competition would have an easier time against a weaker Wings lineup. Teams were obligated to dress the best lineups they could.

NHL spokesman Frank Brown said the Wings could act in their best interests as long as they did so "within reason," and the Wings made an effort to dress decent lineups against teams still in the hunt. Still, Bowman suddenly became unusually forthcoming about injuries, showing he was taking care of nagging injuries, not just fatigue. He revealed Duchesne had a sore shoulder, Lidstrom a sore groin and hip flexor, Shanahan a sore wrist, etc. One day, Hull didn't practice, and Bowman said he had an injury that was "tough to diagnose. It's between his hip and his groin."

"We're not going to play guys that can't go 100 percent," he said. "We're just being careful."

"Rest is like preventative rehabilitation," John Wharton said. "It isn't just giving guys a vacation."

Meanwhile, Uwe Krupp came back from his shoulder injury April 3 at Anaheim. "I've always come back from injuries and done everything I've needed to do to come back," he said. "This has not been any different, regardless of what you heard."

He played the final six games. Despite everything—the injuries, the controversies, the hard feelings, the multimillion-dollar arbitration case still pending—he won a spot in the playoff lineup over Kuznetsov, Olausson, Slegr and Wallin.

"He's proven he's ready to play," Lewis said. "He's played in key situations, and he's been effective."

As for Yzerman, he didn't do much to alleviate the fans' fears. He played only once, April 10 against the Blackhawks: 18:15, minus-1, no shots. He said he was "saving it for the playoffs, basically." He didn't practice afterward.

"If you're going to irritate it, you might as well irritate it in the games," Wharton said. "We're at the point now where those games are all that matters. He can jump in and play 16, 20 minutes without practicing. He's been around a while."

There were light moments: Draper smashed a pie in McCarty's face on his birthday—April Fools' Day. ("Figure that one out," Draper said.) McCarty scored his 100th career goal, and the team's public relations staff presented him a stick wrapped in tinfoil. ("Silver for 500 goals . . . 100 is tinfoil," McCarty said.) But mostly, there were moments like this: A defenseman sat still at his locker after a road game, a blank expression on his face. ("Are we there yet?" he said.)

The Wings were the NHL's best team by far, finishing with 116 points, 15 more than the next best, the Boston Bruins. Detroit's high-profile acquisitions had panned out perfectly: Hasek had a career-best 41 victories; Hull and Robitaille each had 30 goals, even though Hull had some rotten luck, Robitaille a reduced role. Shanahan led the team with 37 goals and 75 points; Fedorov was right behind with 31 and 68. Chelios led the league with a plus-40 rating; Lidstrom led league defensemen with 59 points, along with the Capitals' Sergei Gonchar. Chelios and Lidstrom were clearly the top candidates for the Norris Trophy.

"They could go 1-2," Bowman said.

"They probably deserve to share it," Holland said.

But the Wings made it hard for the fans to keep the faith. In the end, they went 5-6-4-2 after reaching 100 points. They went 1-3-4-2 in their final 10 games, their only victory over Atlanta, the NHL's worst team.

Players often criticized themselves publicly. After a 6-3 loss April 6 at San Jose, Hull said their effort was "embarrassing."

"It's not that you lose," he told the Associated Press. "It's how you lose: lack of effort, a lack of commitment to the system, stupid plays that are not indicative of the attitude this organization has. We've got to show some pride, no matter what, and it's not there. It's not a red flag, but . . . it's time now. Enough's enough. We've got three games left. Let's play them the way they're supposed to be played."

But nothing changed, words or deeds. After the finale, a 5-3 loss to the St. Louis Blues, Chelios said, "Obviously, defensively we were horrible the last 10 games—no one paying attention, no one doing their job, sometimes a lack of effort, sometimes a lack of thinking. It's not one or two guys. It's the whole team. You don't mind losing. It's how you lose. And this is embarrassing."

Bowman brushed off the slump. In 1997, the Wings went into the playoffs 7-7-6 and won the Cup. In 2001, of course, they went into the playoffs 20-4-5 and lost in the first round.

Hockey Gods

"We've done it every which way over the last few years," he said. "We were determined to make sure our injured guys got over their injuries. I think we did that. Sure, you're going to lose some games because of it, and that's what you have to do. You weigh both sides. . . . We've said it all along: The regular season is the regular season; the playoffs are the playoffs."

Asked whether the slump mattered, Chelios said, "We'll see."

"Yeah, it would have been great if we had come out with some momentum, but we didn't, and it's in the past," he said. "Now we've got to go out and play great playoff hockey. For the first three quarters of the season, we played great. We've got to get back to that level, and we can if we want to do it. We've got a group of veterans here, and we've got to bear down."

Chapter 10
Captain Courageous

While expectations were no higher than usual as the playoffs opened—they couldn't get higher than the Stanley Cup, unless people wanted 16 straight shutouts or something—the stakes were as tied to the Red Wings as the skates.

So much would be affected: Mike Ilitch's ledger, Ken Holland's reputation, Scotty Bowman's legacy, Steve Yzerman's popularity and more. Dominik Hasek and Luc Robitaille never had won the Cup, of course, but neither had Steve Duchesne, Fredrik Olausson and others. Chris Chelios hadn't won the Cup since 1986, he didn't have a contract for next season and . . .

"You don't get many opportunities like this," Chelios said. "I don't take it for granted. I know I've got to go out and have a great playoff. Not knowing what's in the future, I've just got to go out and hope this is our year."

The list went on and on, right down to the young players, who had to take advantage of this chance to accomplish something with these superstar veterans.

"You know the window of opportunity doesn't stay open all that long," Mathieu Dandenault said. "The door will shut eventually, because we do have an older team, Stevie with his knee. . . ."

The fans and media put pressure on the Wings. ESPN The Magazine took a picture of the nine potential Hall of Famers huddled together in their red road uniforms and put it on the cover: "CODE RED . . . WHY THE WINGS ARE THE BEST TEAM—EVER."

But the Wings put pressure on themselves. John Wharton printed up T-shirts for the team, and you might say they made a fashion statement: On the front, they had "16," the Winged Wheel and "nothing less." On the back, they had a blank four-round slate.

"It's obvious that it's 16 wins to the Stanley Cup, and we feel the same way everyone else does in this town: Anything less is not what we're looking for," Wharton said. "Each round, the guys get to fill in with a Sharpie on the other guy's T-shirt. It's kind of an interactive T-shirt."

Pressure was part of the deal.

"I like that we have to perform in the playoffs," Robitaille said. "I love that we come in here and it's like, 'We want to win the Cup.' There's never been talk about making the playoffs. If we don't win the Cup, it's not a good year, and I love that. That's why I came here."

The Wings knew how to handle it.

"Obviously, the intensity of the game, the speed of the game, whatever it is, you elevate that way," Brett Hull said. "But you still have to play your own game. You see so many guys struggle because they try to play a different game than they're used to. That's what kills you. . . . You can't let that get to you. Just go out and play.

"I've never felt so much pressure individually as my first year in Dallas, when I was supposedly the missing piece of the puzzle to win them the Cup. First playoff series, I couldn't even breathe, because I'm going, 'Well, I got to do it all, because I'm here and I'm the reason they're supposed to win the Cup.'

"If everyone does their job, we should be fine."

Presumably, the Wings would check off Vancouver in the first round. They were 16-1-4 in their past 21 games against the Canucks; they hadn't lost to them at Joe Louis Arena since Feb. 24, 1997. But they hadn't seen them since Jan. 9, and the Canucks were the NHL's hottest team. After a horrid start, the Canucks were torrid, 28-9-3-3 after Christmas and unbeaten in their final nine games. They scored a league-leading 254 goals, three more than the Wings. They had the league's number two and number three scorers, the brainy Markus Naslund and the brawny Todd Bertuzzi. They were young. They were fast.

Hull turned serious for a moment.

"It doesn't always work out the way you plan," he said.

Then he smiled.

"But sometimes it does."

Yzerman kept his promise. He had to endure endless exercise and treatment, including zipping himself into a sort of air cast for 30 minutes three times a day to work the swelling out of his bum right knee. He had to take pain-killing injections in his butt 40 minutes before warm-ups. He had to wear a special brace. He often had to play wing instead of center to lessen his wear and tear. He had to use his stick as a crutch to get up when he fell. He had to sit out practices and morning skates. But he came back for the playoffs.

And the Wings needed him more than ever before.

Everything seemed fine at first. When Yzerman stepped on the ice in Game 1, he appeared in his 155th playoff game as a Wing, breaking Gordie Howe's record. When he chipped the puck ahead late in the first period, Robitaille took it, skated in and scored. The Wings had a 1-0 lead, and the Joe Louis Arena crowd went crazy.

"LUUUC!"

But the Wings lost in overtime, 4-3.

The Wings didn't get the breaks: They fired two pucks off iron; the Canucks fired two pucks in off Wings. In the second period, Chelios' stick inadvertently deflected the puck behind Hasek, and Chelios chopped a goalpost with the stick. In overtime, the puck went off Igor Larionov's pants and past Hasek's left shoulder, and Hasek said, "They got lucky, but it's part of the game."

The Wings made mistakes: They took three leads, and they coughed up three leads. The last time, Dandenault tried to pass out of his zone in traffic instead of banking the puck off the boards. The puck hit a shin pad, stayed in and ended up in the net. Dandenault said, "I didn't get it out. If I make the safe play there. . . . The puck's got to get out. That's the bottom line."

Hasek felt the heat the following day. He had gone 0-3-3 down the stretch, playing especially poorly in the regular-season-ending home-and-home series with the St. Louis Blues. Now he had allowed four goals in his first playoff game for the Wings. *Everybody is going to be looking at it and saying, "I don't want to play Hasek in the first round."* Hadn't Yzerman said that when Hasek was introduced July 2? Well, what was going on? Hasek sat at his locker after practice, sweating through all his gear on a hot and muggy afternoon, wiping himself with a towel.

"I know I have to play better if we want to beat Vancouver, because they are a good team," he said. "I don't see any problems with the pressure. I like it. I believe I can play better."

Captain Courageous

Hasek allowed four goals again in Game 2, and the Wings lost, 5-2. Again, the Wings didn't get the breaks: They fired another puck off iron; the Canucks fired another puck in off a Wing. Again, the Wings made mistakes. After allowing three goals on the first 10 shots he faced, Hasek thought to himself, "What did I do wrong?"

"It's not a good feeling," he said.

There was panic in Detroit. *See? They're too old! They ran out of gas! See? They shouldn't have rested down the stretch! You can't just flip a switch and turn it on!* After Hasek put the Wings in a 2-0 hole by allowing bad goals—one puck handcuffed him, the other was deflected between his pads—the fans started to fret vocally. They rode Hasek as they used to ride Chris Osgood, cheering sarcastically the next time he stopped the puck. As the Wings kept passing the puck, trying to make the perfect play, the fans grew more frustrated. They pleaded with them as they hadn't in recent memory. They shouted. It seemed the whole arena shouted.

"SHOOT THE PUCK! SHOOT THE PUCK!"

Midway through the third period, facing a 3-1 deficit, on the power play, Yzerman stickhandled toward the net, waited patiently and fired the puck in off the chest of goaltender Dan Cloutier. Yzerman slammed his stick into the glass behind the net.

"Just excited," he said.

The fans went into a frenzy, and so did the Wings. Robitaille had a chance. Yzerman threw a hit.

"SHOOT THE PUCK! SHOOT THE PUCK!"

But the Canucks iced the game and added an empty-netter, and at the final horn, the fans booed the Wings off the ice.

"That was pretty rare," Vancouver's Trevor Letowski said. "You don't expect that when you go into Joe Louis, that's for sure. I think we were kind of proud of ourselves for doing that. You know it's not every day they get booed out of that rink."

The Wings had outshot the Canucks in the series, 71-46, but they hadn't won in almost three weeks, and they hadn't beaten anyone other than the Atlanta Thrashers in almost a month. They had lost six straight playoff games and 10 of their past 13, dating to 2000. After all the off-season moves and regular-season drama,

138

were the Wings going to end up right back where they started, with another bitter, bizarre first-round loss? The next day, above a picture of a puck flying past Hasek, the Detroit Free Press exclaimed in a headline, "This can't be happening!"

Yzerman quickly stripped off his gear, showered, dressed in his street clothes and made himself available for interviews, drawing reporters to himself and away from his teammates.

He was calm.

"I don't think we've been outplayed in either of the two games we've lost, but we're just not quite there," he said. "Our power play isn't there. Maybe we're not as sharp as we should be, not as cohesive as we should be. I don't know if that's because of the stretch run or not."

He was diplomatic.

"People here, they want the team to win; they want the team to do well," he said. "I've been through it before. There's high expectations. So I'm not really concerned about it. The thing is, we know when to shoot the puck. You want to shoot the puck, but you can't shoot it into three people."

He was defiant.

"Before the series is over, you're going to say, 'That Dom, he's an unbelievable goalie. He played fantastic for Detroit,'" he said. "I'm not concerned about goaltending at all. He's a fantastic goalie and will prove it."

Asked whether he expected the series to go the distance, Yzerman lowered his eyebrows.

"Maybe not," he said, firmly.

Pause.

"Doesn't mean we're going to lose, either."

The Wings had a quiet trip across the continent that night. They arrived in Vancouver and went from the team plane to the team bus about 2:00 A.M. local time.

But as the bus pulled out onto the main road to town, it came upon a bunch of fans waiting in cars, and the fans started following the bus, honking horns, hooting and hollering.

"It was like a wedding," said WXYT radio host Art Regner, who traveled with the team.

At first, the fans thought the Wings were the Canucks. But soon, they figured out they weren't. It got ugly.

"FUCK YOU!"

"SWEEP!"

"OVERRATED!"

It always was a long ride from the airport to the city center, but this was a *long* ride, and when the Wings finally arrived at the Pan Pacific Hotel, more fans were waiting. And this time, the fans knew who the Wings were from the start.

"GO, CANUCKS, GO!"

"SWEEP!"

"OVERRRATED!"

The Wings kept taking the taunts as they stepped off the bus and unloaded their bags—until Yzerman appeared. Suddenly, the fans started applauding. It was like a wedding again.

"THANK YOU, STEVIE!"

"GOLD MEDAL!"

"TEAM CANADA!"

Red-faced, the Wings went to their rooms and went to sleep.

"That bus ride, I think it was a humbling experience for them, an angry experience," Regner said.

Funny those fans should cheer Yzerman for what he had done in the Olympics. The Canadians were loaded with talent and under crushing pressure as heavy favorites. They started slowly and got grief from the fans and media. But with Yzerman standing out despite his bum knee, they stuck together, came back and won the ultimate prize. Yzerman could draw from that experience against the Canucks.

Before practice the next afternoon, the captain stood up in the dressing room and spoke for three or four minutes as if reading from a cue card.

"We just had a brief little meeting," Yzerman said.

Asked what he told the team, Yzerman said, "I thought despite losing the first two we did a lot of good things. The thing we couldn't do was beat ourselves up. So again it was, 'Let's just relax. We'll be ready for the game. Go out and play hockey. . . .'

"At some point in the playoffs—unfortunately it was after two games—you're faced with a must-win game. It's how you respond in that one. Either you respond and play well, or you go home. Been through it before.

"So we're comfortable that, 'Hey, if we just win, we're all right. We're in good shape. It's not the end of the world.' Coming in here down, 2-zip, we felt pretty good about ourselves and our chances of winning this series."

Yzerman said his speech "wasn't anything brilliant."

Kris Draper agreed, saying, "He just said the things we all knew. I mean, that's it. Game 1, we had that slip away. We realized that. We knew we just had to be better and get better."

But, Draper added, "He's the kind of guy, when he steps up the whole room just listens. He picks his spots. That's why he's such a great leader. A guy can say things, but he goes out and backs everything up."

After practice, Hull ripped the fans—not the fans who had gotten on the Wings in Vancouver, but the fans who had gotten on them in Detroit.

"I guess they pay the money so they can do whatever they want, but as a group we're disappointed in that," Hull said, according to the Associated Press. "Those are the people you need the most and . . . expect to be with you. When they turn on you it's just kind of like, 'OK, we'll stick it up theirs.'

"It's really disappointing especially when they get on Dom, who has played so fantastic for them all year. . . . Hopefully we can come in and take a couple here and go back home . . . and we won't listen to them then, either."

Everything changed in Game 3.

Out went Uwe Krupp, who was minus-5. In went Olausson, who had been out of favor the entire second half of the season. Bowman stopped trying to match Chelios and Nicklas Lidstrom against the Canucks' top line of Bertuzzi, Naslund and Brendan Morrison. Basically, the Wings went back to familiar, proven combinations.

Yzerman played with Sergei Fedorov and Brendan Shanahan. Hull played with Pavel Datsyuk and Boyd Devereaux, as he had done so successfully during the regular season. Draper, Kirk Maltby and Darren McCarty reunited as the Grind Line, the popular playoff staple. Larionov centered Robitaille and Tomas Holmstrom. On defense, Lidstrom went back with Olausson, Chelios back with Jiri Fischer, Dandenault back with Duchesne.

The first period was the Wings' best period in a month. The General Motors Place fans taunted Hasek, and Hasek later admitted he was more nervous than usual. But the Wings gave him time to settle down, outshooting the Canucks, 13-4.

"The veteran presence on our team is probably why we didn't panic," Shanahan said. "We came out with a very solid, controlled, calm, hardworking effort."

An Yzerman effort.

Yzerman drew a penalty midway through the period. On the ensuing power play, he grabbed the puck behind the net, wrapped around the left post, fought through two checks, stuffed it in and gave the Wings a 1-0 lead. Then, with all his 185 pounds, he laid a hit on Bertuzzi, the 235-pound behemoth.

"There's not too many guys that can compete and battle like him in this league," Morrison said. "I think a lot of guys in here, including myself, have a lot of admiration for him. Basically, he's on one leg out there. . . . He's been incredible."

Yzerman lost a draw in the second period, and Bertuzzi burned him by scoring. Then Bertuzzi rammed Chelios into the end boards, sending his helmet flying. But Chelios got right back up, Hasek started to play like Hasek, the Canucks hit a post and the Wings got a break—the kind of break that turns a series.

As the period wound down, Lidstrom carried the puck up ice. He knew Cloutier had been allowing big rebounds. He knew Hull was racing up the right wing.

"So," Lidstrom said, "I just wanted to get it low for a rebound."

He fired a 90-foot shot. Instead of striking Cloutier and skipping to Hull, the puck went underneath Cloutier's glove and into the net. The Wings had a 2-1 lead. There were 24.6 seconds left.

Early in the third, Fedorov and Yzerman won a battle for the puck in a corner, and Shanahan scored. Then Hasek held on for a 3-1 victory. With 9:06 left, he stopped a sharp Naslund shot from the left circle. With 4:35 left, after stopping the initial shot, he scrambled to his left and robbed Ed Jovanovski on a rebound chance.

"I just stretch my legs, and I think he hit my knee," Hasek said. "I didn't even know where the puck was."

Finally, with 3:06 left, Lidstrom hauled down Bertuzzi on a breakaway, and a referee called for a penalty shot. Bertuzzi picked up the puck at the red line and skated in. Hasek gave him the five hole. Bertuzzi went for it. Hasek closed it in time.

"I don't think he had any hole there," Hasek said.

When the final horn sounded, Hasek had his first victory since March 23, when he had his near-brawl with Patrick Roy.

"He maybe didn't win us the game, but he certainly preserved the win for us in the third," Yzerman said. "He's an experienced guy, been through a lot, and I don't think he's going to be fazed by the two losses that we had.

"There were some strange goals that went in on him. Everybody was kind of, 'What's wrong with Dom?' or, 'He's not playing his best.' But it's difficult for a goalie on redirections and deflections. You just hope you're in the right spot. Unfortunately in the first two games, every deflection went right in the corner."

As soon as the dressing-room door opened, reporters rushed around the corner and up to Hasek.

"How did you feel coming off the ice after what happened late in the third?" a reporter asked.

"What happened late in the third?" Hasek said softly.

"The three big saves, including the penalty shot."

"Oh," Hasek said, almost whispering, "yeah."

Maybe Hasek was just mentally drained. Then again, maybe, just maybe, he wanted the media to acknowledge what he had done well, having picked apart everything he had done poorly. He had his competitor's cockiness back.

"Well," Hasek continued, "it feels great to win a game again. I don't remember when I won my last game, so at least it feels better, and that's all I can say about it."

Asked whether he had done anything differently in Game 3, Hasek said, "I didn't do anything differently. I think overall we played a better game, and myself . . ."

He smiled for the first time. "At least no bad bounces."

Everything evened out in Game 4.

The Canucks didn't get the breaks: The Wings took a quick 2-0 lead when Fischer fired a puck in off a Canuck and Chelios—

shortly after enduring chants of "CHELIOS SUCKS!" for his battles with Bertuzzi—fired another in through traffic.

The Canucks made mistakes: After they tied the game with 31.6 seconds left in the second period, defenseman Mattias Ohlund fell in the right-wing corner and turned over the puck early in the third. Shanahan threw it into the circle, Fedorov sent it down low and Yzerman scored the winner, avoiding a Cloutier poke-check and sliding it over the line.

The goal gave Yzerman seven points in the series and 159 in his playoff career, one more than Howe, making him the Wings' all-time leading playoff scorer. What's more, he announced his knee felt better than it had all series, saying, "I'm encouraged that maybe I got over the hump."

"Our captain, he's pretty amazing," Dandenault said. "I'll tell you what: We wouldn't be here if he wasn't playing. He's a great leader, and the team picks up on it. Everybody's pushing in the same direction."

"He's played like a lion," Barry Smith said. "He's played as large as any player I've seen with the injury he has. We weren't sure if he could skate. We weren't sure if he could play half a game. We weren't sure if he could play 10 minutes. He ends up playing 18 minutes, and he's the best guy on the ice."

The Wings won, 4-2.

"The last month of the season, we definitely lost something," Yzerman said, "and I feel we've regained it now."

The series was tied, 2-2, but it was over.

Brian Burke, Vancouver's general manager, went off in a news conference. Although he once oversaw the officiating for the NHL, he blasted the officials. His best line: "Todd Bertuzzi does not play for Detroit; it just looks like that because he is wearing two or three red sweaters all the time." Although he was an American, Burke said, "We pay the same dues to the National Hockey League that Detroit pays, and even though we're just a little Canadian team, we deserve a level playing field." Because the Canucks' payroll was about half the Wings', he added, "The respect gap here now is as absurd as the payroll gap is." He took a sarcastic swipe at Hasek by saying Cloutier was "the goaltender on the ice that does not dive when he gets brushed." The league later fined Burke $30,000.

The Wings just laughed. They took three penalties in a row in the first period of Game 5, but Hasek was a wall, and with four seconds left in the last penalty, they took a 2-0 lead. After the Wings took a 3-0 lead, the Canucks pulled Cloutier. When Peter Skudra made his first save, the Joe Louis Arena crowd cheered sarcastically, as it had done to Hasek less than a week before. Then Hull came down the left-wing boards on the rush and flipped a pass in front. With one hand, Fedorov swiped the puck into the net.

"It seems like we're getting more and more confident as the series is going on," Duchesne said. "This is great right now. We've got to keep going."

A fan held up a yellow sign with black letters:
BURKE
■ SHUT UP
■ LOSE
■ GO HOME

The Wings cruised to a 4-0 victory. As the clock counted down the final minute, the fans roared.

"It's a great feeling to win at home," Hasek said, "and not be booed like last time."

When the Wings' team bus pulled out of the Vancouver airport early the next morning, no one was waiting for them.

"Where's our escort?" McCarty yelled out.

The Vancouver visitors' room became the scene of another Scotty story after the Wings' next practice.

The room was divided into a changing room, where the players changed into and out of their street clothes, and a dressing room, where the players put on and took off their equipment. Under NHL rules, both areas were open to the media.

The morning of Game 4, a reporter—the author of this book—was the only member of the media in the changing room. Bowman walked in, I said hello and Bowman told me to leave because the room was being used for medical reasons. I reminded Bowman that the room was open to the media and that the Wings already had a medical room.

"What? Do you like to watch guys change?" Bowman said. "How would you like people watch you change?"

Bowman held the door open and gestured for me to get out. I left. After Game 4 that night, while most media members were in the changing room conducting interviews, Bowman saw me in there and warned me that he would close the room in the future.

"What? Didn't believe me?" he said. "You'll see. Game 6."

Now, the day before Game 6 in Vancouver, Bowman held his normal playoff news conference. Toward the tail end, after most of the media had gone, I asked Bowman whether Fischer had cracked ribs. I had known about Fischer's injury and hadn't pursued the story because Fischer was still in the lineup, but Fischer hadn't skated that day.

Bowman blurted out, "What would you ask that for?" He said no, that he never had a player play with cracked ribs. When there were no further questions, I said, "Thank you." As Bowman walked out of the room, he called me a snoop and "Cot-sa-sneak-a." I tried to laugh off the comments as Scotty being Scotty.

"So," I said, "that's what you're calling me behind my back now."

"No," Bowman said, "that's what I've always called you."

A few minutes later, Bowman walked into the changing room and closed the door behind him. Shortly after, because there were few players available in the dressing room, I opened the door and started to step into the changing room. Bowman was waiting. With an open hand, he pushed me in the chest. He didn't shove me. He didn't punch me. But he pushed me, crossing a major line and causing a distraction at a critical time for his team.

"It's a medical room," Bowman said. "Get out of here!"

"Don't touch me!" I yelled. "Don't put your fucking hands on me!" Bowman pushed me again. I yelled again—with more profanity, admittedly—and told Bowman to apologize or I would report the incident to the league. Bowman bent down in a blocking stance, sticking out a forearm, and said he was sorry in a mocking manner. I told him he had made a big mistake and walked away.

Shortly after, Bowman walked into the dressing room, passed me and called me names again. I lost my cool and yelled a couple of expletives, regrettably.

Later, I called New York Post columnist Larry Brooks, the president of the Professional Hockey Writers' Association, to ask what I should do. Brooks called the league.

The incident was discussed on the "Hockey Night in Canada" broadcast of Game 6, then became news in Detroit, although I gave a brief account only to my paper, the Detroit Free Press, and Bowman and the Wings declined to comment.

The league interviewed the parties. I never asked the NHL to fine or suspend Bowman, only that Bowman never touch me or verbally attack me again. The writers association pushed for a fine and suspension. Bowman admitted he had made contact with me and the league fined him $10,000. The league also fined the Wings $25,000 for violating media regulations.

Bowman never apologized, but afterward he treated me no differently than he treated anyone else.

The Wings finished off the Canucks with a wild, 6-4 victory in Game 6. They took a quick 2-0 lead, and again the Canucks pulled Cloutier, who never looked the same after allowing that long-range Lidstrom goal. The Canucks tied the game, but Bowman called a time-out, and the Wings took control again. Larionov had a goal and three assists. Chelios had four assists, and after the final horn and the handshakes, he threw up his arms at the GM Place fans who had booed him like a villain. After failing to score earlier in the series, Hull had a good time scoring the first playoff hat trick of his career.

"There's nothing more fun than scoring," he said.

Pause.

"Well, there's a couple things," he said, "but they're not involved in hockey."

Looking back, the Wings were *glad* they had fallen behind in the series, 2-0. The Canucks had snapped them back to attention. Shanahan pointed out that in 1999 and 2000, the Wings swept their first-round series and lost in the second round.

"So this was a good character-builder for our team," he said. "It's certainly a nice tune-up."

"It turned out to be a really good series for us, something to really build on," Yzerman said. "It was encouraging the way we played. The intensity was really good. Really a lot of good things to take out of it: in our play, our enthusiasm, energy."

"We had to really fight for the wins we got," Lidstrom said. "I think it helped playing a team like this, that we had to really battle. You've got to battle and win those little battles to win games. That's what playoffs are all about."

Chapter 11
Signature Work

S t. Louis was a step toward bigger and better things for these Red Wings. Individually, Scotty Bowman, Brett Hull and Brendan Shanahan spent great years there, then moved on and won their Stanley Cups elsewhere.

Dominik Hasek, of course, considered going there before accepting less money to come to Detroit. As it turned out, Hull was interested in going back, but the Blues weren't interested in him, and so he ended up in Detroit, too.

As a team, the Wings had turned the Gateway to the West into the Gateway to the Western Conference finals. The Wings went through the Blues to get to the conference finals in 1996, '97 and '98—in the second round, first round and second round. Now they had to go through them in the second round again.

The Blues were a bit sensitive about how they stacked up to the Wings, fighting off an inferiority complex ingrained in the St. Louis fans, the St. Louis media and, perhaps, themselves. They had their share of scoring stars: Pavol Demitra, Keith Tkachuk and Doug Weight. They had their own pair of Norris-winning defensemen: Al MacInnis and Chris Pronger. They had their own goaltender with a connection to Detroit hockey immortality: Brent Johnson, grandson of the late Wings great Sid Abel. Still, the Wings were the Wings. As forward Scott Young told the St. Louis Post-Dispatch, "You just get that sense . . . they feel they're a better team."

The Wings *did* feel they were a better team. That season-ending home-and-home series the Blues swept meant nothing to them: They were 7-0-3 in their previous 10 games against the Blues. Having survived the Canucks, the Wings were golden again, confident, loose. Hull, who wasn't as accessible to reporters as his loquaciousness suggested, had fun holding court with them at his locker two days before the series began.

149

Signature Work

How did you think you'd fit in when you signed with the Wings?

"I didn't come here thinking, 'Boy, I wonder if I'm going to fit in,' " he said.

"I'm here to play hockey. You can count on one hand the number of bad guys there are in hockey. So you know you're always going to get along with everybody."

Did the Wings initiate you?

"After a thousand games," he said, "you don't get initiated."

Are you impressed with how the Wings' superstars have worked together?

"When you come in, you sit there, and you think, 'How in the hell are all these guys going to keep everything in check? Someone's not going to play. Someone's going to get more ice time,' " he said, before crediting Ken Holland to the coaches to every player. "You couldn't put together a group of (these kinds of) people in another sport and have it go this smooth."

What's it like to play with Steve Yzerman?

"If you can imagine a guy like me looking forward to playing with a guy . . . it's like me playing with Wayne Gretzky," said Hull, who played with Gretzky in St. Louis in 1996. "He's been one of my favorite players, if not my favorite player, since I broke in the league."

What's it like to practice with Yzerman?

"Stevie, one of the best players ever to play the game, might be the worst practice player in the history of the game," he said.

Do you remember Yzerman's rocket-shot goal in the second overtime of Game 7 of the 1996 Detroit-St. Louis series?

"Sure do," he said. "Very well. It was a good series. Again, it's just one of those things that we always talk about: You don't want to give up that last goal. And they got it. Or *we* got it."

Are the Blues stronger now than when you played for them?

"Of course not," he said. "Geez."

Hull had six points against the Blues in the regular season, second on the team to linemate Pavel Datsyuk, who had seven.

For the first time since 1999, the downtown Spirit of Detroit statue — the unofficial patron saint of championship runs — donned its size-360 Wings jersey.

Bruce Haralson, left, the Wings' western scout, and Jim Nill, the assistant GM, checked their notes during an overseas scouting mission. This trip to Sweden in 2001 helped convince the Wings to bring Pavel Datsyuk to Detroit.

NICHOLAS J. COTSONIKA/Detroit Free Press

JULIAN H. GONZALEZ/Detroit Free Press

Whether playing center or, on occasion, defense, Sergei Fedorov still had all the moves. For the first time in 2002, he was voted to start in an All-Star Game.

JULIAN H. GONZALEZ/Detroit Free Press

*After 114 minutes and 47 seconds in Game 3 against the Hurricanes,
the third-longest Stanley Cup finals game ever, Igor Larionov, left,
scored the winning goal and celebrated with Mathieu Dandenault.*

*At 36, Luc Robitaille finally got to hold the Stanley Cup. And he shared
his joy on the Joe Louis Arena ice with his family, whom he had left behind
in Los Angeles during the season to pursue his championship dreams in Detroit.*

Brett Hull, a latecomer to the virtues of the all-around game, slowed Carolina's Bret Hedican in Game 2 of the finals, a 3-1 Detroit victory that tied the series.

Brendan Shanahan beat Arturs Irbe at 14:43 of the third period in Game 4 for the final goal in a 3-0 victory. Shanahan then scored twice in Game 5.

*As Scotty Bowman prepared to embrace Mike Ilitch after the Cup clincher,
the coach announced his retirement in a whisper: "Mike, it's time. It's time to go."*

*During the
Wings' playoff
run, all eyes
were on
defenseman
Nicklas Lidstrom,
who averaged
more than 30
minutes a game.
He became the
first European
to win the Conn
Smythe Trophy.*

KIRTHMON F. DOZIER/Detroit Free Press

JULIAN H. GONZALEZ/Detroit Free Press

Steve Yzerman skated with the Stanley Cup for the third time in six seasons — but for the first time with daughter Isabella. Stanley left Joe Louis Arena in the backseat of The Captain's Range Rover.

Sure enough, he and Datsyuk led the Wings to a 2-0 victory in Game 1.

In the first period, Hull finished a check on defenseman Jeff Finley along the right-wing boards, and the puck squirted into the right circle. Datsyuk, who had been scratched the past two games, having looked overwhelmed in his first NHL playoff experience, displayed his breathtaking puckhandling skills again. He made a quick move to avoid defenseman Bryce Salvador. As Salvador grabbed him and another defender closed in, he whipped the puck past Johnson's glove.

Killing a penalty in the second, Yzerman blocked a point shot. Hull picked up the puck and took off down the left wing, 2-on-1 with Yzerman against Weight. Hull shot, Johnson let the rebound sit just off his left pad and Hull poked it in. He had four goals in his past two games—and two of them were shorthanded. Hull, who rarely killed penalties before coming to Detroit, had two shorthanded goals in his previous *169* playoff games. This one came with 55.7 seconds left.

"Any time you give up a shorthanded goal late in the period," Finley said, "it really deflates you."

Truth be told, the whole game was as deflated as a regular-season affair—until the final minute. Hasek tried to poke the puck along the end boards, when Tkachuk came barreling in. A split-second later, Hasek was on the ice, holding his head. Had Tkachuk hit him? A host of Wings—Chris Chelios, Kris Draper, Darren McCarty—mixed it up with a bunch of Blues in a corner. Penalties were called. The crowd roared. Play resumed. Another scrum. More penalties. More noise.

Hasek called Tkachuk's check a "cheap shot." The Blues called Hasek a flop artist, Pronger saying that Tkachuk never touched him and that "he went down like he was dead and got up immediately after. We've seen it time and time again. It's nothing new." Yzerman was diplomatic again, saying, "We thought clearly that he got hit. Every goalie in the league, whenever they get touched, they all go down like they're dead. So you never really know." Who was right and who was wrong didn't matter. We had a controversy.

It was supposed to spill bad blood into Game 2, but it didn't have a chance to. Early in the first period, Johnson misplayed the puck behind the net. It skipped out to Sergei Fedorov, Fedorov sent it to Yzerman and Yzerman scored. Johnson muttered in his mask. After allowing the Wings' second shot past him in Game 1, he had allowed their first shot past him in Game 2.

Hull scored later in the period, and in the second, Yzerman made perhaps his bravest move of the playoffs. Grinding on a bum right knee is one thing; lying in front of a MacInnis slap shot—the scariest in the league—is another. But that's what Yzerman did.

"When you see a guy like that doing it, everybody wants to get on board," said MacInnis, a teammate of Yzerman's at Salt Lake. "He's the heart and soul of the team.

"Playing with him in the Olympics, you knew his knee wasn't anywhere near 100 percent, and you saw how he played there. So the way he's rested and come back and played the way he has is not a surprise to anybody. Anybody that knows Steve knows if there's any chance he can play and play at that level, he's going to do it."

Luc Robitaille scored in the second, and the Wings went into the third ahead, 3-0. Their hearts skipped a beat when Pronger upended Yzerman, and they almost blew another late lead: Forward Scott Mellanby scored 47 seconds into the period and with 39.1 seconds left. But Yzerman got up, and they held on for a 3-2 victory.

The next day, a St. Louis reporter asked Mellanby whether the Blues basically had to play perfectly to beat the Wings. Mellanby bristled.

"I think that's bull," he said. "I don't think there's anybody on this team that cares who they have. You guys are the ones who keep writing about how they're all Hall of Famers and that we respect them too much. Maybe we don't respect them enough. . . .

"We have things in our own media about how we're close to asking them for autographs after a game. I think that's bull. I don't think we over-respect this team at all. I think maybe you guys do. I think we believe in here they're a great hockey team, but we're a great hockey team. . . . We're certainly not intimidated, and I think you guys have to stop blowing smoke up their asses."

Tkachuk scored on the Blues' second shot of Game 3, and the Wings trailed for the first time in seven games. Datsyuk responded 27 seconds later, but Mellanby scored on a two-man advantage late in the first period. And Tkachuk scored on a power play late in the second period. And Tkachuk scored again early in the third.

Play had resumed by the time Tkachuk's third goal was announced, but the Savvis Center fans didn't care. They celebrated the hat trick by throwing hats onto the ice, along with yellow, foam "Bleed Blue" sticks that had been placed on their seats before the game. The officials stopped play, and the fans roared as the ice was cleared.

The Wings had three straight power plays, including 15 seconds with a two-man advantage, but instead of scoring, they allowed a shorthanded goal to Demitra. Five goals on 16 shots. Bowman pulled Hasek.

"It was just one of those nights," Hasek said. "Every third shot of theirs went in. I didn't see that many shots, but they just found a way to get by me. It's not that they did anything different. They were just able to score."

"I think it sets everybody's mind at ease," Pronger said. "We can score on him."

Manny Legace made his NHL playoff debut, forward Jamal Mayers gave him a rude welcome and the Blues won, 6-1. After six straight victories, the Wings suffered their most lopsided playoff loss in almost five years, since a 6-0 loss at Colorado on May 24, 1997. The Wings were ticked at the referees, but they admitted their effort was poor.

"I'm sure everybody could see that we were maybe a step behind everything," Jiri Fischer said. "It's something that shouldn't happen. . . . This is a huge wake-up call. When you keep winning and winning and winning, you get used to it. We have to work for it. Nothing is going to come easy."

The Wings' 2-0 series lead was now 2-1, and two out of the last three times the Wings had a 2-0 series lead they had lost in six games. The Wings did it in 1999 against the Colorado Avalanche as well as in 2001 to the Los Angeles Kings. There wasn't panic in

Detroit, but there was worry. *Will they collapse again? Have they already started?*

And it carried right through to the end of Game 4, a test of survival.

First, the Wings had to survive an early Blues barrage. The Wings took three penalties, Young gave the Blues a 1-0 lead on a two-man advantage and the Blues took a 10-0 lead in shots.

Second, Yzerman had to survive a take-out attempt. As the Blues killed a penalty of their own midway through the first period, Pronger tried to drill Yzerman once again. Yzerman ducked quickly. Pronger went into Yzerman awkwardly and fell. He got up, and he was able to take a cross-checking penalty. But when he left the ice, he left the ice for good. In trying to hit the Wings' captain, who had a bum right knee, the Blues' captain had suffered a torn anterior cruciate ligament in his right knee.

Finally, the Wings had to survive yet another near nightmare.

Shanahan scored. Fischer scored. Tomas Holmstrom scored. Yzerman got a goal as a gift on his 37th birthday: Johnson tried to clear the puck. It hit Yzerman's stomach, bounced off a defender's foot and went in. The Wings had a 4-1 third-period lead.

Then the L.A. debacle almost repeated itself. So many similarities: The Wings had a 2-1 series lead. They had a three-goal lead late in the third period. They took a penalty. Their opponent pulled their goaltender.

"When you got a lead like that, and you get a penalty with three-something to go, and you get the goalie out," Bowman said with a laugh, "I mean, it's a Chinese fire drill from there."

The Blues put the puck in the net three times—but got only two goals. Mellanby fired the puck past Hasek with 2:54 left, but it bounced out as if it had hit a post or the crossbar, and no one knew whether it had gone in. The officials couldn't review video until play stopped 21 seconds later—when Mellanby put the puck past Hasek again. When the officials found the first shot had gone in, they counted it as a goal and rewound the clock, making the second shot moot.

Tkachuk then scored with 1:30 left.

"We sort of stopped playing, thinking we were just going to be able to let the clock run out," Kirk Maltby said. "With a 4-1 lead, you tend to get a little too content out there. I think we got a lot content, and they didn't quit."

The Wings held on and won, 4-3, but they didn't celebrate— not even the birthday boy.

"Actually," Yzerman said, "the only thought I gave to my birthday was that, when I came into the league, the Wings had just acquired Brad Park, and I had always looked up to Brad Park. But he was 37 at the time. I thought, 'Wow. He's 37. He's got a wife and family. He's an *old* guy.' And now that's me. . . .

"But then, I have consolation: Igor is 41, and Chelios is 40. So I'm not the old man. I've got my own little peer group."

The next day, a St. Louis reporter asked Pronger to describe the play on which he was injured. Pronger bristled.

"What I saw or what I read in the paper?" he barked.

A St. Louis Post-Dispatch columnist had described the play as a "lapse of discipline" and called Pronger a "knucklehead."

"It was a lack of discipline apparently on my part, trying to finish my check," Pronger said. "I apologize for that lack of discipline. You apparently show too much respect for a team, you get worked over in the media about it, and then you go and hit somebody and you get worked over in the media about it. So I don't know where our team is going to stand with the lack of respect or respect for that team. It's a lose-lose situation for us."

That it was. When the Blues lost their captain, and couldn't complete their comeback late in the third period, they lost the series.

"Chris is our best player," Tkachuk said. "When you miss your best player, it's very difficult."

The Wings watched video of the end of Game 4 and talked about playing with the lead, their Achilles' heel. But they had no problem chasing away the Blues with a 4-0 Game 5 victory.

"They weren't the same team as early in the series," Hasek said. "You could tell they were missing Pronger."

Hasek earned his third shutout. Shanahan had two goals, including an empty-netter, and two assists. But this was a chance for others to shine, and the Wings did have others besides their nine potential Hall of Famers. To illustrate the point, someone cut out the others' mug shots, added them to that ESPN The Magazine cover with all the hotshots and pasted it on the dressing-room wall.

Fischer scored his third goal of the playoffs; he had three goals in 187 regular-season games. Holmstrom scored his fourth goal of the playoffs, and he did it typically, deflecting a shot on the power play. When he heard someone mention he had eight goals in 69 games during the regular season, his head popped up.

"Nine goals, right?" he said. "Was it just eight?"

"Eight," he was told.

"I thought it was nine," he said, frowning.

The Wings plucked Holmstrom from the Swedish country above the Arctic Circle with their 10th-round pick in the 1994 draft. He had a goofy grin. The guys called him Homer. He hardly could skate at the NHL level. But with extra padding on his back and the backs of his legs, he was willing to take a beating in front of the net, especially on the power play. His playing time and production suffered during the regular season partly because of the acquisitions of Hull and Robitaille, but Holmstrom always scored at double the pace in the playoffs. In 1998, he broke out with seven goals in 22 playoff games, and the Wings won the Cup. This year, he and the Wings were on pace to match that.

"I play the same way," Holmstrom said. "I don't know. Playoff hockey just fits me."

Maltby didn't score in Game 5, but that wasn't his job. He was the son of a tool-and-die company man. He was a grinder, a guy who got his hands dirty, who fittingly wore the same grubby old gloves all season. And his name was the one the fans chanted. He drew two penalties. The first time, Maltby sprayed snow in Johnson's face, and when Johnson retaliated by sticking his glove in Maltby's face, Maltby snapped his head back. He lost his stick while killing a penalty but didn't give up. He challenged the point man, positioned like a goalie, crouched, hands out. He blocked a shot with his body. Then another.

"MALT-BY! MALT-BY!"

"I was flattered," said Maltby, a laid-back, aw-shucks kind of guy off the ice. "I was just out there trying to do my job. . . . The equipment is pretty good these days."

Hockey Gods

Asked how many times the crowd had chanted his name in his career, he smiled.

"Let's see," he said. "One."

"It's fantastic to see a guy do that," Hasek said. "I think it helped everybody's emotions. We were a very disciplined team. Everyone—everyone—was focused."

Including the fans. They had heard Mellanby's and Pronger's comments. They knew the Blues' mood. One woman held up a sign: GET YOUR AUTOGRAPHS AND GO HOME.

Chapter 12
Apocalypse Now

As the Red Wings waited for their next opponent, the winner of the Colorado Avalanche-San Jose Sharks series, Kris Draper said something shocking: The Wings were rooting for the Avs.

"Believe it or not," he said, grinning.

They had a good reason: The Avs faced a 3-2 deficit, the series had been tough and a seventh game would take a toll on whoever emerged. Still, it was hard to imagine any Wing rooting for the Avs under any circumstances.

Draper especially.

After the Wings won their record 62 games in 1995-96, they were odds-on favorites to win the Stanley Cup. In the Western Conference finals, they met this new team, the Avs, who had been the Nordiques before moving to Denver from Quebec that season. In a stunning upset, the Wings lost in six games.

And the Avs added injury to insult. In the first period of Game 6, Claude Lemieux hit Draper from behind into the boards in front of the Detroit bench. Draper suffered a broken jaw and nose, displaced teeth and a concussion. He needed 30 stitches to mend his mouth. For 16 days, he drank his meals through a straw.

A straw? Well, that was the last straw.

Detroit-Colorado, as Darren McCarty said, became "one of the premier rivalries in sports."

"Lucky me," Draper said. "I got to have my face rearranged to start a rivalry."

At first, it was defined by ugly insults, violence. Forward Mike Keane called the Wings gutless, said they had no heart. Marc Crawford made fun of the metal plate in Scotty Bowman's head. Benches emptied in brazen brawls. The goaltenders, of course, fought, too. On March 26, 1997, in one of Detroit's most famous sports moments, Lemieux retreated into the turtle position as McCarty avenged the Draper incident, dumping a hailstorm of punches upon him.

As time passed, so did some of the animosity. Crawford and Lemieux left Denver. Keane left, too, before coming back. But the hot, hard-hitting hockey remained.

"It's important to focus when you play Colorado," Sergei Fedorov said. "Otherwise . . ."

He smiled.

"You might get smashed into the boards."

These teams were always trying to keep up with each other. The Wings beat the Avs in the 1997 conference finals, 4-2; the Avs beat the Wings in the second round in '99, 4-2, and 2000, 4-1. The Avs won the Cup in '96; the Wings won the Cup in '97 and '98; the Avs won the Cup in '01. The Avs added Theo Fleury, Ray Bourque, Rob Blake and Darius Kasparaitis; the Wings added Chris Chelios, Dominik Hasek, Brett Hull and Luc Robitaille.

These teams were the league's best. In the regular season, the Wings went 3-1 against the Avs and blew them away in the standings along with everyone else. But Colorado superstar Peter Forsberg sat out the entire schedule to recover from injuries, and now he was back, better than ever before, leading the league in playoff scoring.

So when the Avs came back, beat the Sharks in seven and advanced to face the Wings, people were thrilled.

The TV people especially.

"It's what you live for, what we wait for all year," ABC/ESPN analyst Darren Pang said. "We're trying to sell Tampa Bay against Anaheim during the regular season. So we absolutely get excited about this."

This was Steve Yzerman vs. Joe Sakic as Conn Smythe-winning, No. 19-wearing, British Columbia-born captains; Fedorov vs. Forsberg as supremely talented European centers; Hull, Robitaille and Brendan Shanahan vs. Chris Drury, Milan Hejduk and Alex Tanguay as sharpshooters; Chelios and Nicklas Lidstrom vs. Blake and Adam Foote as top-shelf defensemen; and, of course, Hasek vs. Patrick Roy as all-time great goaltenders.

"I'm excited to go against Patrick," Hasek said. "I've never faced him in the playoffs, and his record in the playoffs is outstanding. Four Cups, there's not too many goalies who have made it. . . . For me, there is something to prove, because in the playoffs, his record is much better. I think the pressure is on both goalies, but I never won the Cup, so maybe it puts more pressure on me."

This wasn't just for the Western Conference title.

This was for the Cup.

Game 1 was something out of a Disney movie. Joe Louis Arena was rocking.

"LET'S GO, RED WINGS!"

"HA-SEK'S BET-TER!"

In the third period, Yzerman's bum right knee gave out on him as he followed through on a shot from the right circle. He went into the corner boards hard, and John Wharton iced Yzerman's right shoulder on the bench. Shortly afterward, the knee gave out on him again in the neutral zone. The Captain was in trouble. As the cliché goes, someone else had to step up.

And someone did.

McCarty ripped a shot from the top of the left circle. Foote bent down to block it, but the puck whizzed past his head, past Roy's glove and into the net. The Wings led, 3-2. McCarty threw up his arms and gave a missing-tooth grin.

It was a great story: McCarty was one of the Wings' most popular players. Part of the reason was his role in this rivalry: A fan held up a neon orange sign: WE STILL HATE LEMIEUX! Part of the reason was that McCarty was an affable, lunch-bucket guy from across the Detroit River in Leamington, Ontario, who endured all kinds of pain to play. He was Mr. Freak Injury. In October 1999, a skate blade sliced off a nickel-sized chunk of his face near his left eye, his teammates found it on the ice, team doctor John Finley reattached it with 40 stitches or so, and McCarty finished the game—while complaining about having to wear a visor. In the 2001-02 season alone, he endured an injured shoulder, an injured knee and an infected finger that needed surgery. He had missed practice time before the series because of a bruised thigh—suffered when he tripped over his dog at home.

About 10 minutes after his goal, McCarty raced down the right wing, ripped a shot past Roy's left shoulder and scored again. The Wings led, 4-2. McCarty raised his stick. He screamed, "Woo!" He nodded his head to say, "Aw, yeah."

The great story became fantastic: McCarty had five goals and 12 points in the regular season, tying his career lows. He hadn't scored through the first two rounds of the playoffs. As it turned out, before the game, Robitaille had looked over at him in the dressing room.

"You've got to stop with that shaving sticks and everything," Robitaille said. "There was a stick you had about a month ago. You picked every corner. I think you should use that."

"I'm going with it," McCarty said.

McCarty went and got the stick Robitaille wanted him to use, his usual Hespeler, but with a flatter lie.

"A lot of blade touching the ice," Robitaille said. "It grabs a lot of puck when he shoots. He's got a great shot. For some reason, the way that lie lays on the ice for him, he picks the corner every time."

McCarty gave the stick to Joe Kocur, and Kocur banged it on the floor, putting what McCarty called a "voodoo hex" on it.

Finally, a few minutes after McCarty's second goal, Roy tried to clear the puck. Kirk Maltby knocked it down and took a quick shot. Roy scrambled and stopped it, but McCarty gathered the rebound, waited patiently and roofed it. The Wings led, 5-2. McCarty leapt into the air and about tackled Maltby in joy.

The fantastic story became a classic: McCarty had his first hat trick in his 650 games, regular season and playoffs. Bowman wasn't big on compliments, but he said, "It's a wonderful effort from a guy that gives his all every game. They were all great goals against one of the greatest goaltenders who ever played the game. There wasn't anything lucky about any of them."

The Wings won, 5-3, and as they came off the ice, McCarty's son was waiting in the hallway.

"Griffin," Chelios said, smiling, "what'd your daddy eat for breakfast?"

McCarty grabbed Griffin in a big bear hug and gave him the puck—as a present for his upcoming sixth birthday.

"He put a lot of pressure on me," McCarty said. "He wanted a goal."

He got three.

Asked whether he would use the same stick in Game 2, McCarty said, "You bet."

Then he smiled.

"We'll see what Griffin has to say."

Soon afterward, the Wings' media relations officials brought McCarty to a conference room to meet with reporters.

"I've always heard about this room," McCarty said. "I've just never been in it."

Then he settled in.

"You've all read the Bible and heard of the Apocalypse?" he said. "Look out."

The Wings had won nine of their past 10 games. But this was Colorado, and this was going to be a long series, complete with subplots. The day after Game 1, Colorado coach Bob Hartley sat on his bench and watched the Wings practice.

"I try to stay up to date with what's going on out there," Hartley said. "I'm looking for little details that could be useful to us in the future games."

Sitting on the bench to watch the opposing team's practice was considered bad form, but Hartley had beaten Bowman twice in the playoffs, and he always seemed to relish trying his hand against the mind-game master. When the Avs arrived at Joe Louis Arena during the 1999 series, workers were painting steps in the stands, and Hartley, in his French-Canadian accent, had a little fun with it in a news conference.

"Thanks to Scotty for the great smell in the locker room," he said. "Scotty always has surprises waiting for you. He didn't call me for my color, but he probably knows my taste."

Bowman brushed off Benchgate, saying Hartley was a "friendly guy" and "not uptight." But a Detroit Free Press photographer caught him giving Hartley a look from the ice. Asked whether Bowman had said anything to him, Hartley said, "Oh, he just said, 'Hi.' Like, we're close friends." Asked whether Bowman offered him coffee and doughnuts or something then, Hartley joked, "Maybe some fried octopus."

Roy was 8-0 since 1996 after allowing five or more goals in a playoff game. He went to 9-0 in Game 2. Tied at 3, the game went to overtime. A couple of minutes in, Forsberg fired a shot from the right wing, Hasek stopped it and forward Steven Reinprecht grabbed the rebound, with Drury lurking across the slot.

"Looked like he was going to pass to Drury right away," Chelios said. "We tried to take away the one-timer. Drury just skated right by me."

Reinprecht then passed to Drury.

"He was wide open," Hasek said.

The Avs had a 3-on-1. Jiri Fischer went down. Drury stickhandled around him and in on Hasek.

"I expect him to shoot, and he sort of make a nice move to his forehand and put it in the open net," Hasek said.

The Wings lost, 4-3. In the dressing room afterward, Chelios watched the replay on a big-screen television tucked along the wall by the exercise bikes. Then he trudged toward the showers—arms crossed, face frowning—and muttered the bottom line.

"Bad coverage," he said.

Hasek said the Wings "played a bad game overall," but Yzerman disagreed.

"I guess I'm disappointed how we played in overtime: It ended pretty quickly," he said. "But I'm not shocked (the series is) 1-1. We're playing what I feel is the best team in the league, and we're going to have to play hard and win any way we can. Whether we get down in a game or lose a game, we've got to come right back and play well the next one. You can't fall apart or get rattled by one game."

After Game 2, Bowman was blunt.

"Our big guys got to get going," he said.

The Wings weren't leaning on their stars: When Maltby burned Roy for clearing a puck poorly in Game 2, he became the 16th Wing to score in the playoffs. But Bowman thought the Wings were taking their balanced scoring too far: Although they had eight goals in the series, six were from what you might call unexpected sources—Maltby, McCarty, Tomas Holmstrom and Boyd Devereaux—and another was pure luck. In Game 2, Lidstrom fired wide left. The puck came off the end boards, and Roy, on his knees, knocked it in accidentally with the back of his right skate.

Bowman said that the Wings had to be more "swashbuckling" in their attack, that they had to bring the defensemen into the offense, that he was going to shuffle his lines. He said they were passing up too many shots; Hull disagreed, pointing out that they had taken 63 in the two games. Hull was the Wings' lone star forward who had scored in the series, and when a reporter asked him why Bowman would make such comments, he said, "How long have you been covering sports? What do coaches do?"

As promised, Bowman shuffled a couple of his lines in Game 3. He made one move perhaps no other coach would have in such a situation, putting Jason Williams—a rookie who spent much of the season in the minors, who had played sparingly in the playoffs—between Shanahan and Yzerman. Williams didn't find out until the Wings held their pregame meetings. The coaches didn't call him in with his usual linemates, Holmstrom and Robitaille.

"Then I went into my meeting, and I was in there with Shanny and Stevie and stuff," Williams said. "So I figured I might be with those guys. I just talked to Stevie a little bit. I asked him who was playing wing or if he wanted to play center. He said he wanted me to play center."

Williams played well, and so did the rest of the Wings. They outshot the Avs through three periods, 34-16. But they were lucky the game went to overtime, tied at 1-1. Early in the third period, Fedorov fired from the left circle. Roy allowed a rebound to his left. Defenseman Greg de Vries batted down the puck with his right glove, and it nicked Robitaille's right skate.

"I wasn't even sure it hit me," Robitaille said.

As Roy dived and stretched out his glove, the puck slid into the net.

Then, about 12 minutes into overtime, perhaps the least likely Wing to be considered a "big guy" got going. With the teams skating 4-on-4, the puck came to Hasek, and the Avs went for a line change.

"Maybe," Hasek said, smiling, "they didn't expect the European goalie can pass to the red line."

Hasek threw the puck up to Yzerman in the neutral zone. Yzerman fed Fredrik Olausson, the 35-year-old forgotten off-season acquisition, the guy who had been playing in

Switzerland, the guy who had his spleen removed little more than a year before, the guy who hardly had played the second half of the season. Olausson streaked into the slot and fired. The puck glanced off the outside of a skate blade.

"I was going for the corner," Olausson said, "but it might not have ended up where I wanted it."

No matter. It went in. Olausson became the 17th Wing to score in the playoffs and got his first playoff goal since April 18, 1992, when he played for the Winnipeg Jets, a team that now had a new city and a new name, the Phoenix Coyotes. The Wings won, 2-1. They led the series, 2-1. Olausson forgot for a moment he was an understated Swede, jumping for joy as his teammates mobbed him. But then he remembered. Asked how he felt, he said, "I was pretty happy."

The Wings were loose. Draper turned 31 two days later, and at practice, McCarty tried to get him back for that pie in the face April 1. McCarty lunged with a towel full of shaving cream; Draper escaped. But the Wings weren't loose for long.

Through the first 40 minutes of Game 4, they led in shots, 25-12. The Pepsi Center fans were so frustrated that they started screaming for the Avs to shoot the puck.

"Once again, we saw why the Detroit Red Wings were by far the best team in the regular season," Hartley said. "They were flying."

But the game was tied, 1-1, and when Sakic took a pass, sped into the Detroit zone and scored 45 seconds into the third period, the Avs came alive. Drury scored with 3:17 left. The Wings pulled Hasek with 2:52 left and went at Roy with everything they had, but they failed to beat him until Hull scored with only 2.7 seconds remaining. They lost, 3-2. The series was tied, 2-2.

In Game 5, Yzerman scored 54 seconds into the third period, making it 1-1. He held the puck behind the line to Roy's right. He had no play. So he skated in and shot the puck off Roy's right side. The puck dropped inside the post. Roy slid his left pad across to hide it, but after a second or so, referee Kevin Pollock spotted it and pointed repeatedly. The Joe Louis Arena fans roared. Yzerman showed rare emotion. No one knew that goal would be Yzerman's last of the playoffs—and the Wings' last of the game.

With about 1:40 left in the period, Shanahan stickhandled past Blake and drew Roy out toward the right circle. Shanahan was on a sharp angle, but he had an open net. He shot. Forsberg touched the puck with the toe of his stick blade—barely, but just enough to put it off the right post. Shanahan went to the bench, balled his fists and hit himself in the head. Then he looked skyward.

"I'll have a nightmare about that one tonight," he said. "I was shocked it didn't go in, because I saw the empty net. I waited and waited till everyone went down. I didn't know how it didn't go in. I was about to turn and put my arms up in the air. . . .

"Those ones really hurt."

So do these ones: Little more than six minutes into overtime, Foote knocked Draper's stick out of his hands, and Draper didn't get the puck deep in the Colorado zone. Kasparaitis made a quick pass up ice, catching Hull and Maltby heading to the bench. Forward Brian Willsie, in his second career playoff game, got away with being a step offside, because linesman Brian Murphy was held up by the changing players and out of position. Willsie sent a pass for Drury, Drury tried to shoot but fanned, and the puck went between his legs—right to a wide-open Forsberg, who finished the strange chain of events by finishing the game. As the Avs celebrated, hundreds of fans sat and stood still in stunned silence. The Wings lost, 2-1. They trailed the series, 3-2.

"After the game, our locker room was as angry as I've seen it all year," Shanahan said. "We were angry because we felt we deserved to win. We were angry because we had them back on their heels. We were angry because we had all kinds of chances in their end, and then they get one rush, one lucky pass that isn't even meant for the guy, one great chance, and they score."

He sighed.

"And now we have to forget about it."

The Wings were dead serious now. As they headed back to the Pepsi Center, they knew they had a history of fizzling out: They had lost four straight games when facing elimination, three of them to Colorado, two in Denver. They hadn't rallied from a 3-2 deficit and won a series since 1996, when they did it in the second round against the St. Louis Blues.

"There have been a lot of great things this season, starting with the development of the team last summer," Shanahan said. "This is a challenge to all of us, individually and as a team, to see what we do here."

The Wings concentrated on how the series had been close— "very close," Yzerman said. Of the 321 minutes of hockey so far, there were only 10 in which either team led by two goals or more. Each team had 13 goals. The Wings had come back from one-goal deficits eight times in the series—and they had come back from a two-*game* deficit in their first series, hadn't they? They had to stay calm.

"We can't press; we can't worry," Shanahan said. "We can't be thinking, 'Man, what happens if we lose?' "

A list of reminders was written in black marker on the white eraserboard in the dressing room for Game 6, stuff like "backcheck" and "stay up" and "support the puck." This was the first item: "To accomplish great things, we must not only act, but also dream; not only plan, but also believe!" This was the last item: "No pressure, no diamonds."

To win a ring, you have to go through the wringer, and the Wings went out to do it. As the first period wound down, Yzerman had a chance in front. Blake tied up his stick before he could get off a backhand shot. The puck went around the left-wing boards to Lidstrom, who threw it at the net. Yzerman gloved the puck, put it down and cut across the low slot. Roy dived to his left. Yzerman fired. Roy made a spectacular save.

Then made a spectacular mistake.

Roy stood up and raised his left arm to show off.

"I thought I had it in my glove," Roy said.

The puck fell into the crease.

"Fortunately, the referees didn't blow the whistle right away," Yzerman said.

As the puck rolled toward the goal line, Shanahan gave it a shove. First, Lidstrom's 90-footer against the Vancouver Canucks. Next, Yzerman's duck on Chris Pronger against St. Louis. Now this. Shanahan had his first goal of the series. The Wings had their first 1-0 lead of the series. Roy buried his head in his hands.

"I just charged to the net, hoped that there was some garbage waiting there for me; when I got there, there was," Shanahan said. "It was big. We've been talking about playing from behind the whole series, and we wanted to see what we could do when we had the lead early on."

In the second, McCarty beat Roy again, giving the Wings a 2-0 lead, and Hasek thwarted the Avs. First, a Drury shot went off his helmet and the left post. Then, while the Avs were on a power play, they challenged the legality of his stick, hoping to steal a two-man advantage.

Hartley said the Avs had "information that Hasek was playing with an illegal stick." Hasek said the information must have come from a stick he gave Hartley earlier in the season—for his son, a young goaltender. While Hartley denied having one of Hasek's sticks, Roy said he had one of them. But he wouldn't say when, where or why he got it. *At the All-Star Game, perhaps?*

"Mine's right on the line," Roy said, "and his is a little bit over."

Whatever. Stickgate smacked of desperation, and it backfired. The referees found the stick was fine, Hasek motioned for them to give it back to him, the Avs took a penalty for delay of game . . .

And that was it. Hasek held on for his fourth shutout of the playoffs, tying the NHL record. The Wings won, 2-0. The series was tied, 3-3.

"We all understood the consequences if we didn't come through: Everything that we've aimed for since the start of training camp would have come to a disappointing end," Maltby said. "But we've bought ourselves one more game."

"There's no sigh of relief," Shanahan said. "Our backs were against the wall tonight; our backs are against the wall in Game 7. The difference is: So are theirs."

Roy was the one you wanted in goal for Game 7.

"He's been proven the best in this situation over the years," Sakic said. "We've had two Game 7s already in these playoffs, and Patty didn't give up a goal in either one. That tells you right there what you need to know about the guy."

Roy was 6-5 in Game 7s, but Hasek was 0-2, and the Avs had won their past six elimination games—with Roy posting a

0.50 goals-against average and .980 save percentage—including their past four Game 7s. The Wings hadn't played a Game 7 since that 1996 series with St. Louis. They hadn't played a Game 7 this important since the 1964 finals, which they lost to the Toronto Maple Leafs.

The fans showed up early, some standing outside, holding homemade signs, to greet the players as they arrived at the Joe. Yzerman strolled in calmly, as if this were Nashville on a Monday night in November, coffee cup in his left hand, black leather coat slung over his right shoulder.

As the Wings dressed for warm-ups, Bowman walked around the center of the room. He had barked at them when they led the series, 2-1. He had backed off when they trailed the series, 3-2. Now he told them stories. This was his ninth Game 7, tying him for the NHL record with one of his proteges, Mike Keenan. Here were all those potential Hall of Famers, listening like little kids, listening as they would to perhaps no other coach.

What other coach could talk about the old days when lower-level teams played best-of-*nine* series instead of best-of-seven series, because they needed the money? What other coach could recall a series that went *10* games, because overtime went so long in the ninth game that the game was stopped and replayed? Bowman told the team about a player who scored a crucial goal in that series. He turned to Draper. Now, he had promoted Draper from checking line center to right wing with Fedorov and Shanahan much of the season, and Draper had responded by posting career highs in goals (15), points (30) and plus-minus (plus-26). Still, Draper had little scoring touch: It seemed he couldn't score on a breakaway to save his life. Bowman said that player from the old days had stone hands.

"Kind of like you, Drapes."

The Wings broke up in laughter.

Bowman told them the game would be memorable no matter what happened, to just go out and play.

"He doesn't come in and give big speeches," Shanahan said. "But certainly in big games and big moments, when you've got a guy that's been coaching as long as he has and can draw off his successes and experience, it can exude confidence to the players.

I think he's one of those guys that if he believes it'll happen, that can rub off."

As Karen Newman concluded the national anthem, a huge octopus hit the ice. Out came Pete Cusimano, the man who, in 1952, started the Detroit playoff tradition of throwing octopuses, their eight legs representing the victories needed to win the Cup in those days. He picked this one up. He held it over his head. The rink roared.

Then came the unthinkable.

Holmstrom scored on the Wings' first shot, deflecting the puck past Roy's glove. Fedorov scored on their second shot, firing from the left wing. The puck hit a stick and fluttered between Roy's right arm and his body. Holmstrom's goal was forgivable. This one . . . well, Roy usually stopped shots like that in his sleep. The fans taunted him.

"PAAA-TRIIICK!"

Robitaille scored on the Wings' fifth shot. Igor Larionov, who left Game 3 of the St. Louis series with a sprained knee, who came back in Game 4 of this one, flipped a backhand pass past an Av. Robitaille eluded his man, skated into the open down low and put the puck through Roy's pads. As Robitaille celebrated, Roy kicked the puck in disgust.

The Avs called a time-out. Roy skated to the bench and took a drink.

"Do you want to come out?" Hartley asked.

"No. I'm staying in."

Roy went back to his net, and Holmstrom scored again, this time on the Wings' eighth shot, this time on a rebound. Roy, who had played 240 playoff games, more than any other goaltender, allowed four goals in a playoff period for the first time.

Hull scored on the Wings' 11th shot, their first of the second period. Devereaux intercepted a pass behind the line to Roy's left and threw the puck into the circle. Hull fired it past Roy's glove. Yzerman said the Avs, depleted by injuries, worn out from so much hockey, came into the period looking to get going, but Hull's goal kind of took "the life right out of them."

Then Olausson scored on the Wings' 16th shot, firing the puck into the upper left corner.

"PAAA-TRIIICK!"

The Wings had a 6-0 lead just 6:28 into the second period. They had heaped an avalanche on the Avalanche, two goals on their nemesis for each of their playoff series losses since the rivalry began. *You've all read the Bible and heard of the Apocalypse? Look out.* Hadn't McCarty said that after Game 1?

"You imagine and pray for something like this, but you don't realistically think it's going to happen," Hull said. "A couple of us talked on the bench. We just said, 'We keep looking up at the clock in disbelief at the score.' "

Here came the hook.

"I felt that after six goals," Hartley said, "I have a responsibility to protect my goalie."

As Roy skated off, his teammates tapped their sticks on his pads, their gloves on his back. Roy took his helmet off, sat down and put a towel around his neck. He smirked, then frowned. Television cameras caught Mike and Marian Ilitch in their suite, Mike with his palms up, Marian with her arms up. The Detroit Free Press prepared its headline for the next day: "Au Rev-Roy!"

"HA-SEK'S BET-TER!"

Datsyuk added an exclamation point against backup David Aebischer with 3:51 left in the third period. With 3:10 left, the crazy crowd sang along to Neil Diamond's "Sweet Caroline." The Wings were going to the finals to face the Carolina Hurricanes.

In the most lopsided Game 7 ever, the Wings won, 7-0. They won the series, 4-3. Not only had Hasek beaten Roy, as he was acquired to do, as he set out to do, he had earned back-to-back shutouts. Although he had to make only 19 saves on this night, this shutout was his fifth of the playoffs, an NHL record.

What about the record? the reporters asked afterward.

"It's nice," Hasek said. "But I have different goal, and it's not about shutouts."

How did you feel when Roy was pulled?

"To be honest, I felt good," Hasek said. "It was a relief for me. I wasn't going to see him anymore."

Chapter 13
Clash of the Titans

D etroit's Hockeytown claim was questionable. People from Toronto to Montreal to Moscow begged to differ, pointing out they lived and died with the sport, not just the local team. People in Sault Ste. Marie, Mich., said they came up with the concept first. But the city strengthened its case in the Stanley Cup finals—and not just because the Spirit of Detroit statue downtown wore a size-360 Red Wings sweater, as it had in past playoff runs.

The Carolina Hurricanes had Detroit connections from player to coach to general manager to owner. They had Aaron Ward, the defenseman the Wings shipped out in the off-season because he didn't get along with Scotty Bowman. They had Paul Maurice, the coach who played junior hockey across the Detroit River in Windsor, coached junior hockey in the Detroit suburbs, then coached the Detroit Junior Red Wings of the Ontario Hockey League. They had Jim Rutherford, the general manager who played 10 seasons in goal with the Wings, after they took him with their first pick in the 1969 draft. Finally, they had Peter Karmanos, the owner who was raised in Detroit, lived in the Detroit suburbs—and had season tickets in the third row of the lower bowl at Joe Louis Arena.

"As a young kid growing up in Detroit, you played baseball in the summer and you played basketball in the winter, and you watched hockey on TV," Karmanos said. "You watched people like Gordie Howe and Ted Lindsay and Terry Sawchuk, and if you had any sense of the sport at all, you realized you were watching something special, and that generated an interest in hockey that has never died for me. I like playing the other sports, but I love watching hockey. . . . I always root for the Red Wings—except when they play the Hurricanes."

Karmanos and Mike Ilitch had much in common. Ilitch, 72, was the son of Macedonian immigrants, grew up on Detroit's west side, graduated from Cooley High and rebelled against his father. With his wife, he started Little Caesars in 1959 and made a fortune in the pizza business. In the late '80s, he moved his headquarters from suburban Farmington Hills to downtown Detroit, and mayor Coleman Young hailed him as a civic-minded savior. Karmanos, 59, was the son of Greek immigrants, grew up on Detroit's west side, graduated from Henry Ford High and rebelled against his teachers. With two partners, he started Compuware in 1973 and made a fortune in the computer business. In the late '90s, he decided to move his headquarters from Farmington Hills to downtown Detroit, and mayor Dennis Archer hugged him and said, "Welcome, my brother." Ilitch was bald (but wore a toupee); Karmanos was bald. Ilitch had two heart bypasses, Karmanos one. Both gave millions to charity. The similarities went on and on.

Which was the problem.

As his children grew up in the late 1960s and early '70s, Ilitch began sponsoring youth hockey. Little Caesars became a power. As his children grew up a decade later, Karmanos began sponsoring youth hockey, too. Compuware courted coaches and players aggressively—paying the coaches—and surpassed many Little Caesars teams in the early '80s.

In a 1995 interview with the Hartford Courant, Karmanos said: "Basically, our little kids' hockey teams beat his little kid teams, and he didn't like it. Mike's a very competitive guy. We are unfriendly rivals. He doesn't like me at all." In a 2002 interview with the Detroit Free Press, longtime Little Caesars hockey leader Chris Coury said: "They hate each other."

Karmanos became an NHL owner in 1994 by buying the Hartford Whalers. He also owned the Junior Wings, and after the senior Wings were swept by the New Jersey Devils in the '95 finals, Ilitch kicked the Junior Wings, the OHL champions, out of the Joe, where they had played for five years. Ilitch said he wanted to use the arena for other things; Karmanos said Ilitch was just bitter.

"The Red Wings are just so embarrassed," Karmanos told the Courant. "New Jersey kicked their butts. I think they are angry at everybody and everything. . . . There's nothing I'd rather see than the Whalers just whip the Detroit Red Wings. That would be fun.

Having the Whalers win the Stanley Cup before the Red Wings, I'd love that."

Karmanos moved the Junior Wings to suburban Plymouth and renamed them the Whalers. He moved his NHL team to North Carolina in 1997 and, along with changing its name, changed its colors from blue and green. Although the Hurricanes' dominant color was red so they would match that of North Carolina State, their fellow Entertainment and Sports Arena tenant, Karmanos admitted it was no coincidence their uniforms resembled the Wings'. Karmanos struck back at Ilitch in '98 when the Hurricanes signed Sergei Fedorov to that six-year, $38-million offer sheet, which broke down like this: $2-million annual salary, $14-million signing bonus and another $12-million bonus if Fedorov's team made the conference finals. The Hurricanes weren't going to make the playoffs, and they were trying to dissuade the Wings from matching the offer. Ilitch was livid, but the Wings did match the offer, rather than give up Fedorov for the NHL-mandated five first-round draft picks. So, because they won the Cup, they had to pay Fedorov a cool $28 million in virtually one lump sum.

Ilitch, who never spoke about Karmanos publicly, didn't attend a media reception before the finals; Karmanos not only attended but stayed until the bitter end. At one point, he said that there was no animosity between them and that he planned to eat Little Caesars pizza during the series. At another point, he said: "If there's acrimony, we share it equally." He smiled and said he would have the same number of conversations with Ilitch as he had with the owners of the Hurricanes' three previous playoff opponents.

"Which is zero."

The Hurricanes were such heavy underdogs that Maurice played along and called his players "mongrels." Until they beat the Devils, Montreal Canadiens and Toronto Maple Leafs and advanced to the finals, the franchise had won only one playoff series in 21 years. The Hurricanes were the Eastern Conference's third seed, but only because they won the Southeast Division, better known as the "Southleast Division." Their 91 points were seventh-most in the East. Not only would they have failed to make the playoffs in the Western Conference, they would have finished 10th. They hadn't won at Joe Louis Arena since Nov. 14, 1989, when the Whalers beat the Wings, 3-0.

People were making fun of them. They started with how North Carolina was known for NASCAR, how it wasn't exactly a hockey hotbed. *It's the rednecks against the Red Wings! It's Mayberry vs. Hockeytown! Does Opie have any offense?* They continued with the franchise's history. ESPN broadcasters, based in Bristol, Conn., used to call the Hartford Whalers "The Whale" with affectionate disrespect, and they started calling the Hurricanes "The Whale" before Raleigh, N.C., mayor Charles Meeker protested. After the Wings eliminated the Colorado Avalanche, Brett Hull talked about how he and Steve Yzerman had watched a few Carolina playoff games together.

"We both looked at each other and said, 'These guys are a whale of a team.' "

Everyone laughed. Realizing what he had done, Hull had to smile, too. But he quickly turned serious.

"Pardon the pun," he said, "but they're a heck of a team."

The Wings tried to sound a Hurricane warning. They insisted Carolina was no laughing matter, even if they expected to have the last laugh. They pointed out how the Hurricanes played a trapping defensive style—and still had scored enough to beat three excellent goaltenders: Martin Brodeur, Jose Theodore and Curtis Joseph. They pointed out how the Hurricanes had Arturs Irbe, who was in goal for San Jose when the Sharks upset them in 1994. They brought up the 2002 Super Bowl, in which the New England Patriots shocked the St. Louis Rams, although the National Football League championship was decided by one game and the NHL championship was decided by a best-of-seven series. When reporters told Hull the experts had tabbed Detroit-Colorado the real finals, he snapped, "Well, that's why you guys aren't experts."

The Hurricanes, Hull said, "are young. They're fast. They're strong. They're enthusiastic. They're very disciplined. They're great on face-offs. There's no gimmes."

"They're playing hungry," Yzerman said. "They've got something special going on with that team right now, and that makes them dangerous. . . . We recognize we're playing a great opponent, and all this favorite stuff is irrelevant. It means nothing, because the teams haven't played against each other enough for anybody to really judge how they match up."

"Everybody's going to say how good we are and stuff like that, but we're not going to hear anything about it," Mathieu Dandenault said. "This is for the Cup, and that's it."

But the city still considered Carolina hardly an obstacle to winning the Cup—the radio station that carried Wings games ran promo ads touting itself as the "home of the next Stanley Cup champions"—and the Wings were flat emotionally. They had beaten their archrival in a long, intense, emotional series, a series Hull said was "the best you'll ever see," a series that ended with a Game 7 watched by some 700,000 Detroit households, according to the combined rating of ESPN and Windsor's CBC station that carried it. Although this was for the Cup, the Detroit-Carolina rivalry was in the owners' suites, not on the ice.

With some 791,800 households watching now, the Wings, in Bowman's words, were "off-kilter" in Game 1. They passed poorly, made bad line changes, failed to clear their end well enough. The ice was bad, and the referees were whistle-happy, but those weren't excuses.

"I didn't like our entire game," said Brendan Shanahan, who called the Hurricanes "patient" and the Wings "stupid." "We were sloppy. They played the kind of game you have to play in the Stanley Cup finals, and we didn't."

Twice, the Wings took a lead. Twice, the Hurricanes came back. After two periods, the game was tied, 2-2, and the shots were even, 20-20. After three, the game was still tied at 2 and the shots were still even, this time at 25. The Wings failed to score on a power play in the final 1:41 of regulation and first 19 seconds of overtime. Then, 58 seconds into OT, the Hurricanes' lone answer to the Wings' nine potential Hall of Famers, Ron Francis, redirected a pass. The red light flashed behind Dominik Hasek, and the irony was rich: Red lights had flashed behind him that morning, when he was ticketed for going 65 in a 45-m.p.h. construction zone on the Lodge Freeway.

"All of a sudden, the puck was in the net," Hasek said. "I don't even know how it happened. It was so fast."

The Wings lost, 3-2, and fell behind in yet another series. So much for the talk of a sweep. The Detroit Free Press headline the next day was: "Hold the parade." Asked whether he had said anything to his former teammates, Ward said: "I didn't say a word. The last thing we want to do is make this team mad." The Wings often were sparse in the dressing room after games, especially after losses, but this time there were so few players there that the NHL fined the team $50,000 for violating media regulations.

Not until late in the third period of Game 2 could the Wings and their fans exhale a little bit. The Wings were better despite more bad ice and more penalties, but shot after shot after shot hit a Hurricane or missed the net or found its way into Irbe. They almost doubled the Hurricanes in shots on goal, 30-17. They tripled them in shots attempted (shots on goal, missed shots and shots blocked), 75-25. But the game was tied late in the third period. Kirk Maltby had the Wings' only goal, and it was shorthanded, giving them seven shorties for the playoffs, one more than the rest of the league combined.

One side of the Joe yelled, "GO!"

The other yelled, "WINGS!"

Then the whole rink chanted, "LET'S GO, RED WINGS!"

"There were a couple of comments made on the bench about how loud it was," Kris Draper said. "These fans want it just as bad as we do."

Then, on a power play, with the Wings 1-for-13 in the series, Nicklas Lidstrom ripped a one-timer past Irbe's glove and into the upper right corner with 5:08 left. He shouted. He pumped his arms. He kicked his right leg like a Rockette.

Nicklas Lidstrom!?!?

"Some of the guys were teasing me," he said. "They said, 'Hey, Nick. You actually showed some emotion there.' "

A leg kick?

"Well," he said, "I was happy."

Then, before the fans found their seats, Lidstrom sent a pass up to Draper, and Draper beat Irbe's glove from the right circle with 4:55 left. The Grind Line had another goal, prompting Maurice to say, "I don't know if you can call them a defensive line anymore. They are on fire, scoring left and right." The Wings won, 3-1. The series was tied, 1-1. Darren McCarty grabbed Draper in a big bear hug.

"Felt good," Draper said.

Game 3 was a thriller.

With less than two minutes left in the third period at Carolina, the Wings trailed, 2-1. Their karma was bad: Yzerman had hit the left post midway through the first, and Steve Duchesne had hit the right post early in the third. But they were confident.

"You have got so many great players and so many guys that can score goals, you never feel like you are out of it," Hull said.

The officials whistled for a face-off in the Carolina zone. Bowman didn't pull Hasek, but he put out a power-play-type unit—Fedorov, Hull, Lidstrom, Shanahan and Yzerman—searching for yet another late-game goal. Yzerman beat Rod Brind'Amour, a fellow face-off expert, and drew the puck back to the right point. Fedorov sent it along the blue line. Lidstrom fired a wrist shot, and Hull, holding out his stick in the slot, tipped the puck out of midair past Irbe. The game was tied, 2-2.

One minute, 14 seconds remained.

Hull said the play was "dumb luck," but Shanahan said Hull had such awesome hand-eye coordination that it was "not an accident he got his stick on it."

Lidstrom hit the left post with 50 seconds left. Yzerman cut in on goal with one second left.

The horn sounded.

Overtime.

The Wings' history was bad: They were 1-4 in OT in the playoffs, the Hurricanes 7-1. But the Wings were confident.

They kept getting chances. At about 8:35, Pavel Datsyuk made Gretzky-esque moves, stickhandling past forward Sami Kapanen, then defenseman Marek Malik. But Irbe got his left pad on the puck. At about 12:45, one-timing a pass from Fedorov on a 2-on-1, Shanahan fired wide left of a yawning net by inches.

Shanahan shook his head on the bench. This, after putting that shot off the post with an open net in Game 5 of the Colorado series. This, when he had one goal in his past 10 games, that tap-in after Patrick Roy's glove gaffe in Game 6.

"Good thing I didn't have a knife," Shanahan said, "or I would've slit my throat."

At about 15:35, Fredrik Olausson hit the crossbar.

"You start to wonder if it's ever going to go in," Olausson said.

The horn blew.

Overtime II.

The Hurricanes killed a penalty. The Wings killed a penalty—while Hasek fell, displaying his biggest weakness: wandering from the net.

"Sometimes I think he gets bored," McCarty said.

"With Dom," Yzerman said, "we leave him alone and assume he knows what he's doing."

At about 16:40, at the end of a pretty passing play, Shanahan sent the puck from the right wing across the slot. Yzerman put it on net, but Kapanen got his stick on it, and Irbe dived and snagged it with his glove. Yzerman rolled head over heels, then appeared to swear and say, "I don't believe it!"

Shanahan sighed.

"I was thinking," he said, " 'Well, at least I'm not the only guy.' "

The horn went. Overtime III.

In the Carolina dressing room, players were taking fluids intravenously. In the Detroit dressing room, things were relatively routine.

"When you are in a tight situation, you come in between periods, and Steve Yzerman is talking like he's about to fall asleep," Hull said. "He's so calm, but his words just ring loud."

Some guys kept most of their equipment on; some guys stripped to their underwear. Some taped sticks; some sharpened skates. Some guys stretched; some guys got massages. Some guys changed gloves (Hull went through eight pairs); some guys didn't (Shanahan used the same pair the whole game). Although many players changed T-shirts, no one asked for a new sweater.

"You try to dry everything off as much as possible, so you're going out there a little bit lighter," Shanahan said.

The Wings downed water, energy drinks and Pedialyte, designed for sick children but great for professional athletes because it had a lot of electrolytes and a fast rate of absorption.

"I've given it to my little girl when she's gotten sick, and now we've found another use for it," Draper said. "It's strange how these things work out, but if we should win the Stanley Cup, maybe we should pour Pedialyte in there before any champagne."

The game had started shortly after 8:00 P.M., and it was well past midnight. The Wings hadn't had a meal since 1:30 P.M. or a snack since 4:30, so they ate bananas, sliced oranges and energy bars.

"You try to eat what you can," Draper said. "You don't want to think about getting tired. You don't want your mind to start wandering in that direction. All we kept saying was, 'Look at where we are, how close we are to our ultimate goal. If you're tired at all, just think of that. Think of the big picture, not that we're going into a third overtime or whatever.' "

Carolina forward Jaroslav Svoboda had a chance early.

"I was kind of holding my breath a little bit," Yzerman said.

Both teams tried to catch their breath.

"Everybody was feeling it a little bit," Yzerman said. "It was basically one burst of energy and head right to the bench."

Duchesne took a puck in the mouth. He was missing six teeth—two natural, four from a bridge—but he missed only one shift.

"I've still got my bottom teeth, so I figure I'm all right," he said. "Besides, guys said I looked better than I did before."

Then Igor Larionov, the 41-year-old, the NHL's oldest player, the Dick Clark of hockey, who chewed on fruits and vegetables, who eschewed red meat, who said his secret was two glasses of wine every night, took a pass from Tomas Holmstrom. He stickhandled past diving defender Bates Battaglia. With Dandenault in front, Larionov backhanded the puck over Irbe and into the roof of the net at 14:47, scoring his second goal of the game, ending the third-longest finals game ever, giving the Wings a 3-2 victory and 2-1 series lead. He was the oldest player ever to score in the finals.

It was about 1:15 A.M.

"I think this is the biggest goal of my career," said Larionov, who never had scored a playoff overtime goal before. "It's obviously huge for me."

"I have always thought that youth and enthusiasm will take you only so far," Hull said. "I said to Iggy after the game, 'I'd rather be old and smart than young and dumb any day.' "

181

"We're the oldest team in the league, and we had the oldest player go out and dance around a couple of guys like it was the first shift of the game," Shanahan said. "It's just a big relief to our entire team. We had so many chances that I think relief was part of the feeling."

First, Lidstrom's 90-footer against the Vancouver Canucks. Second, Yzerman's duck on Chris Pronger against the St. Louis Blues. Third, Roy's glove gaffe. Now this. The Wings celebrated. The Hurricanes deflated.

"There's no question that they're a great team, but . . . but it just looks like they have a way of getting the right break at the right time," Carolina forward Jeff O'Neill said. "Just when you think you might have them—bam. They get what they need. I mean, we were a minute or so away from leading this series, 2-1, and then . . ."

Bam.

The full impact of fatigue didn't hit the Wings until they were on the bus or back at the hotel. They had a meal about 2:00 A.M.

"We weren't even sure if the hotel was going to keep the food for us, but they did," Draper said.

There was pasta, pizza, chicken, salads—all kinds of stuff.

"The food was meant to be eaten about two or three hours earlier," Maltby said. "It was actually not bad. The chicken parm was pretty good. To their credit, they kept the food warm. It didn't go stale."

How was the atmosphere?

"Pretty quiet," Draper said.

"And content," Olausson said.

One by one, the players went to their rooms and tried to unwind. Many watched some World Cup soccer.

"Some guys I'm sure had a beer," Maltby said.

Maltby turned off his television, and although he was exhausted, he tossed and turned for a half-hour or 45 minutes before falling asleep between 4:30 and 5:00.

"Your mind is racing," he said. "You're thinking about all the things that happened in the course of the game. It's hard to get to sleep when you're thinking about that kind of stuff. You're telling yourself to sleep, sleep, sleep. But every time you try to stop thinking about it, you just think about it more."

Needless to say, after playing 114 minutes and 47 seconds of hockey, neither team practiced the next day. Some players slept in as late as 1:00 P.M.

Although he wasn't a big coffee drinker, when Lidstrom walked into an afternoon news conference, the first thing he did was grab a cup.

Decaf?

"No way," he said.

The Hurricanes had the two best chances in the first period of Game 4. With about 5:40 left, defenseman Niclas Wallin fired a shot from the right point through traffic. It hit the right post. With about 40 seconds left, forward Erik Cole raced up the left wing. He went around a stumbling Chris Chelios—and ran into a surprise. Hasek came out into the circle, dived and poked the puck off his stick.

Hull scored 6:32 into the second. From the right-wing boards, Olausson passed the puck along the Carolina blue line. Boyd Devereaux picked it up with speed and charged to the right circle. He sent the puck across the slot. Hull dropped to his right knee, bent back his stick with the force of his shot and one-timed the puck off the near post and into the open net. The goal was Hull's league-leading 10th of the playoffs, and it made him the fourth player to score 100 playoff goals, joining Wayne Gretzky (122), Mark Messier (109) and Jari Kurri (106).

"There was a time," Hull said, "when there was talk that you could never win in the playoffs with Brett Hull . . ."

"Did you just refer to yourself in the third person?" Shanahan asked.

Laughter.

"I am trying to give myself a pat on the back," Hull said.

"A hundred playoff goals, you can do that," Shanahan said.

Laughter.

"I think," Hull continued, "it makes people look and maybe think a little differently about that."

The Hurricanes had a golden opportunity to tie the game on a power play midway through the period. O'Neill sent a pass across to the right side of the low slot. Francis tried to tap in the puck.

Hasek dived to his left. The puck went under Hasek's left arm, but it went off the far post, ricocheted back into the crease and ended up underneath Hasek as he rolled on his stomach.

"I was standing right there, and it was just a big relief seeing that hit the post," Yzerman said. "I just assumed it was going in. . . . That's a huge break for us."

With about 5:26 left, the Hurricanes came close again. Defenseman Bret Hedican fired from the point. The puck went wide right, but it bounced off the end boards and, as players scrambled, it sat against the outside of the right post. Hasek, as he was known to do, dropped his stick and covered the puck with his blocker hand.

In the series' first three games, the third period began in a tie. This time, it didn't, and at 3:43, Larionov gave the Wings a 2-0 lead. Jiri Fischer pinched up the left-wing boards in the Carolina zone and fired the puck—it looked like a shot, but it was a pass—to the weak-side doorstep. Alone, Larionov tapped the puck into an open net.

Shanahan put the game away at 14:43. Fedorov flew up the left wing, cut into the high slot and threw the puck ahead. Shanahan redirected it past Irbe for only his second goal in 11 games.

"I'm sure it was a relief for him," Yzerman said. "He's pretty motivated and playing with a lot of desire. So despite not scoring, he's played pretty darn well. (But) no matter how much you are doing other things well, you still feel like you have got to put the puck in the net."

The Wings had won, 3-0. They had taken a 3-1 series lead. Bowman had his record 35th finals victory, one more than Toe Blake. Hasek had his sixth shutout, extending his record. As the clock wound down, the Carolina fans saluted their Cinderellas as if they appreciated their surprising playoff run but didn't expect to see them again until next season. After the final horn, the public address announcer bellowed, "Let's hear it for your Hurricanes!"

As the Wings were about to fly back to Detroit, Bowman felt the need to address the team. They had an eternal two-day break before Game 5, and he wanted to make sure they stayed away from "the hoopla" created by their families, their friends, the fans and the media. The series wasn't over, they still had a job to do and . . .

Yzerman, on the tarmac, near the team plane, already had gathered everyone together to tell them that very thing.

"We can't lose our edge, lose any kind of focus and expect that it will be an easy game," Yzerman said. "Each game at this point for the most part has really gone down to the wire late in the third period or into overtime. I would expect the fifth game will go that way as well. As long as we're prepared to play a tough game, we will be OK."

Bowman smiled.

"It was like having another coach," he said.

One last subplot: Fischer cross-checked forward Tommy Westlund in the face in the third period of Game 4. Westlund lost a tooth cap and took five stitches. Referees Paul Devorski and Don Koharski didn't see the play and didn't give Fischer a penalty, but Colin Campbell, the NHL vice president of hockey operations, saw the replay and gave Fischer a one-game suspension.

And so, after blossoming into the Wings' best defenseman besides their Norris finalists, after averaging almost 20 minutes a game in the playoffs, the 21-year-old wouldn't have the chance to play for the Cup. He would have to sit in the stands with his parents, visiting from the Czech Republic, or watch the game on television in the dressing room.

"It's extremely frustrating," said Fischer, the first player ever suspended for a finals game for an incident in the series. "All playoffs long, you really want to leave your heart out there every game. Just one stupid thing that happened keeps you out of the lineup. I think for me it's even worse than being injured. . . . I would love to take it back, but unfortunately I can't."

And so, for the first time since the third game of the playoffs, Bowman was going to put in a different defenseman. Who would it be? Maxim Kuznetsov or Jesse Wallin? No, they never had appeared in a playoff game. It had to be Uwe Krupp, who had come back amid all that controversy, who was minus-5 in the first two playoff games, or Jiri Slegr, whom the Wings had acquired 15 minutes before the trade deadline, who had played seven games after arriving, sat out one night, played another game, then sat out for good.

To Krupp's consternation, Bowman went with Slegr.

For two months, Slegr had sat in the shadows as if he didn't even exist. A couple of days before the finals, McCarty was talking about the Wings who never had won the Cup.

"You got Dom. You got Luc. You got Duke. . . ."

"You got Slegi," Slegr interrupted, smiling.

"You got Slegs. You got Freddy O. . . ."

Slegr was angry. He had been excited to come to Detroit, because he thought he was going to play for a Cup contender, not come along for the ride. He had seen his wife, Katerina, and their three-year-old daughter, Jessi, only four times since the trade. He had been home to Atlanta once. But he never said anything, and he wasn't going to say much now.

"It doesn't matter," he said. "It's in the past. I have to look forward to the future. . . . I'm ready to go."

Hockeytown was ready to go, too. To Detroiters, there was only one way for this story to end: with the Wings hoisting the Cup in front of their fans at Joe Louis Arena, right now, that night. The "DETROIT RED WINGS 2002 STANLEY CUP CHAMPIONS" hats and T-shirts were sitting in boxes, waiting to be opened. The police had plans to close the freeways leading into the city in the event of a victory. The crowd was loud as the team came onto the ice, waiting to be satisfied.

"LET'S GO, RED WINGS!"

About 5½ minutes into the first period, the Wings came within inches of scoring. Twice. Olausson fired from the right circle. The puck disappeared into Irbe, then trickled between Irbe's legs and reappeared. It rolled on end just wide of the right post. Larionov picked up the puck and threw it in the slot. Robitaille fired. Irbe dived to his right. The puck pinged off the post. Hasek had to make a sharp right pad save at about the 10-minute mark. But then the Wings had more chances. Yzerman. Fedorov. Maltby.

The game scoreless, the crowd was quiet at the start of the second. Some fans were chanting, but they just drew attention to those who weren't. The teams traded chances. Then Holmstrom woke up the joint at 4:07. From the corner to Irbe's left, Larionov threw the puck into the slot. Charging ahead of a defender, lunging with one hand on his stick, Holmstrom deflected the puck between Irbe's legs. Holmstrom crashed into the end boards. As he lay on his back, he pumped his fists skyward. The goal was his eighth of the playoffs, tying him for fourth in the NHL. This, after he had eight goals the entire regular season.

"LET'S GO, RED WINGS!"

Slegr took a holding penalty at the six-minute mark. The Wings killed it. But Hasek had to make a huge save seconds later. From behind the net, Brind'Amour threw the puck past Draper into the slot. Battaglia one-timed it, aiming for the lower right corner. Hasek put his left pad on the puck. After Robitaille had a chance at the other end, the fans showed their appreciation in a brief burst.

"HA-SEK! HA-SEK!"

Shanahan gave the Wings a 2-0 lead on the power play at 14:04. Low in the right circle, he one-timed a pass from Fedorov off Irbe and high into the net. Whenever he scored, the Joe's disc jockey played an Irish jig. It blared now. The fans danced.

"LET'S GO, RED WINGS!"

The crowd grew even louder after the Hurricanes took another penalty. But during the power play, Shanahan went off for hooking. The teams traded chances. Then, at 18:50, O'Neill cut the Wings' lead on the power play. With Cole in front of Hasek, who held a teammate's stick because he had lost his own, O'Neill fired a shot from the left wing. The puck hit the back of the net and bounced out so quickly, the officials needed a lengthy delay to review the video and confirm the goal.

"Obviously it gives them a great boost going into the third period," Shanahan said on television during the intermission. "We have to respond, and we know we can."

Fedorov went off for cross-checking 5:23 into the third, after leveling Svoboda into the boards in the Detroit zone. The Wings killed the penalty, and the fans started to sense Stanley. They chanted some more. They cheered some more at 8:12, when Carolina center Josef Vasicek went off for interference—and the DJ played the whistling theme to the "Andy Griffith Show."

With 9:19 left, TV cameras caught white-gloved men taking the Cup out of its crate backstage. The Wings kept skating, banging, chipping the puck out of their zone, chipping it ahead, waiting to exhale.

"LET'S GO, RED WINGS!"

With about 7:35 left, Yzerman nearly beat Irbe. With about 7:15 left, Holmstrom had a chance. With 4:43 left, an octopus hit the ice ahead of Hasek. The fans roared.

And roared.

And roared.

Holmstrom had a chance. Then Fedorov.

The fans roared some more.

"WE WANT THE CUP! WE WANT THE CUP!"

With 44.5 seconds left, they had it. From just across the red line, right in front of the Carolina bench, Shanahan fired the puck into an empty net. He leapt into Yzerman so hard that they crashed into the ice. When they got up, Yzerman's nose was bleeding.

"What happened?" Shanahan asked. "Did you get high-sticked?"

"No," Yzerman said. "I think you broke my nose when you hugged me."

No matter. No pain now—not in the nose, not in the knee, nowhere. All season, the Wings had said they wouldn't celebrate until their job was done. Now it was.

"We were too old, too slow, too rich—fat cats," Barry Smith said. "That's what we were told, and these guys were unbelievable. They sacrificed an awful lot, each one of these guys. They sacrificed ice time. They sacrificed personal power plays. They sacrificed a lot of things to make this a team.

"They fought hard all season. They won the Presidents' Trophy as the best team all year, and they won the Stanley Cup. What else can you ask for?

"There's nothing else to win. They won it all."

Chapter 14
Into the Sunset

S cotty Bowman left the bench as the clock counted down. He went to put on his skates. Then the final horn sounded, the confetti fell and as his players leapt into a happy heap around Dominik Hasek, celebrating the 3-1 victory that brought them the Stanley Cup, he skated out to join them, as he had done in 1997.

He had nothing more to accomplish. The Red Wings had 10 Cups—more than all but two teams, the Montreal Canadiens and Toronto Maple Leafs—and so did he. He had one in the front office, and he had a record nine behind the bench, one more than his mentor, Toe Blake—who had won seven of his eight when you had to survive only two playoff rounds, not four. He held every important coaching record by far: five different decades, 30 seasons, 2,141 regular-season games, 1,244 regular-season victories, 353 playoff games, 223 playoff victories and . . . and on and on.

And so he found Mike Ilitch amid the throng, gave him a hug and whispered in his ear.

"Mike, it's time. The time is right now. It's time to go."

Ilitch was surprised. Bowman was 68, but he was in great shape and showed no signs of slowing down. Sure, Bowman had dropped hints during the finals: In a news conference before Game 3, a reporter asked whether he would take some time after the series to think about his future, and Bowman said he already had made a decision—refusing to elaborate. In another news conference, a reporter asked about the possible labor stoppage in 2004, and Bowman said he wouldn't be around then. But if Bowman was anything, he was unpredictable. He had dropped hints in years past and still come back.

Between Games 1 and 2 of the 1997 finals, Bowman called Jimmy Devellano in his Philadelphia hotel room and told him he was retiring after the series. Devellano said he was sorry to hear that: He would be hard to replace. Bowman asked him to go to bat for Barry Smith. Devellano said if the Wings were to promote from within he would want Dave Lewis. Annoyed, Bowman hung up. After the Wings swept the Flyers, Bowman went to Ilitch's home unannounced, told him he was retiring and said he wanted Smith to succeed him. When Ilitch said Smith wouldn't succeed him, Bowman said fine, then he was coming back, and left.

Standing on the ice five years later, the fans still roaring, some confetti still fluttering in the air, Marian Ilitch said to Bowman, "Wait. We have to talk about this." But there was nothing to talk about. When the Wings broke in the middle of their long season for the Olympics, Bowman and his family went to Florida. They spent time in the sun. Cold drinks, but no cold rinks. No practices. No games. No media. No pressure. And it was nice.

"I knew it would be four more years, the next Olympics, before I'd get to do that again, take time for myself in February, and that's when I decided," Bowman said. "I wasn't up to doing it anymore."

Bowman said he told maybe two or three people he could trust, because he didn't want to cause a distraction. He told his wife, Suella, of course. He even told New York Yankees manager Joe Torre and Yankees Hall of Famer Yogi Berra, whom he visited at spring training during the break. He didn't tell Ilitch or Ken Holland, leaving them unprepared for his departure, leaving them with few candidates to replace him. But few criticized him for it, and just a few criticized him for upstaging the team's ultimate moment.

The morning of Game 5, Bowman broke the news to his summertime neighbor in suburban Buffalo, CBC analyst and former coach Harry Neale. "I'm retiring," Bowman told him, according to Sports Illustrated. "All the other times I considered it, I *thought* I knew I was ready. Now I *know* I know it."

"So what now?" Neale asked.

"Consultant," said Bowman, whose contract called for him to serve as one for three years after stepping down as coach. "Now I can go to the games and I don't have to win them."

Bowman told Smith before the game. Suella was sworn to secrecy, and she was under the impression the gag order wouldn't be lifted for a few days. But then the game ended, and Bowman told Ilitch. And Holland. And Steve Yzerman. And Brendan Shanahan. And Sergei Fedorov. And even Aaron Ward, who had become a Hurricane because they hadn't gotten along. Bowman didn't get to everyone, but word spread quickly.

"I get down to the ice, and I find out that Scott had already told everyone," Suella said. "So when I find him, I ask him if I can finally answer questions now about this, and he said it was fine. I'm very happy for Scott, but I'm even happier for us and our family because now we'll have more time together to explore more things in life."

"My first reaction was probably shock," Yzerman said. "And then, just as quickly, I found myself to be very happy—happy for him because he's leaving on his own terms, having won the Stanley Cup in his last game. How can you have a better ending than that?"

"I was shocked," Shanahan said. "He's been so involved and so excited throughout the whole playoffs that I just thought, the way he was responding, 'This guy's going to go forever.' But I guess it makes sense now. He knew it was his last playoff, and that's why he soaked it all up."

"It's bittersweet," Brett Hull said. "To go out like this and to have the success he's had is so wonderful, but then to have it end is so sad. I feel as fortunate as anybody alive to say that he was my coach."

"I had a great conversation with the coach, finally," Fedorov said. "I said, 'It wasn't an easy road, but it was fun playing for you.'

"At times, it was very, very hard, but as long as we stick with the winning, that was the main goal. At times, he was asking more and more, and I have to adjust and do whatever Coach wants, and sometimes it didn't happen. But I think positive experience happen more than negative. The way Scotty is, he's not really like that outside of the hockey circuit. I think he is a much, much better and wonderful person. I sense that. Be he was a strong and tough coach. . . . He is the best coach ever. He can go out however he wants. He has nine championships."

191

Fedorov smiled.

"Maybe they should call it the Scotty Cup."

After the post-series handshakes, NHL commissioner Gary Bettman came out to present the Conn Smythe Trophy, and it became clear just how much of a *team* this really was. All the parts had fit together—"from the top line to the Grind Line to the bottom line," in the words of Bob Wojnowski, the Detroit News columnist—and that's why the Wings were here, while other high-payroll teams like the Dallas Stars, New York Rangers and Washington Capitals never even made the playoffs.

The Wings ran away with the regular season, and they had nine potential Hall of Famers, but they didn't have a Hart candidate. They won the Cup, but they had no fewer than five legitimate Conn Smythe candidates, and no one was sure who would win. How about Hull? He led the league with 10 playoff goals. How about Hasek? He had a record six shutouts.

Fedorov? He had only five goals, but his 19 points tied him for second on the team with Shanahan, and he didn't float. He skated his butt off at both ends. No less an authority than Yzerman talked about how hard Fedorov had played. Asked why he had been so determined, Fedorov brought up his impaired-driving arrest from September and the criticism he had received in the past.

"I had an embarrassing incident happen not too long ago, when I run too close to the law," he said. "It was my goal to be the best I could every night, because I heard before some people would say that it wasn't the case. . . . I prove it the most important part of the year, the playoffs, night in and night out."

Yzerman? His production declined as the playoffs progressed. Still, he led the Wings on the ice with 23 points—and led them in the dressing room and the training room and everywhere else. Twice, the Wings' medical staff had to drain fluid from his right knee, which needed major off-season surgery. To the few who questioned him for playing at the Olympics, he gave a resounding answer.

"You saw how it was," John Wharton told the Detroit News. "The first couple of games, we were all kind of holding our breath every shift he went out on the ice, just hoping he could make it back to the bench in one piece, let alone make it through the game or the series or the playoffs."

In the end, Bettman handed the Conn Smythe to the Wings' quietest superstar, Nicklas Lidstrom, who had five goals and 16 points and provided his diligent, dependable defense. Two nights after playing 34:38 in Game 2 of the finals, he played 52:03 in the Game 3 triple-overtime thriller.

"Look what Nick Lidstrom did all the way through the playoffs, the minutes he logged," Bowman said. "He's just about a perfect player on the ice. Very few mistakes. He scored some big goals for us. It's a wonderful tribute to him."

"It's about time he got some recognition," Lewis said. "What a player. He is probably, if not one of the best defensemen in hockey history, side by side with anybody."

Lidstrom was the first European to win the award.

"I think that makes it even sweeter," he said.

"WE WANT THE CUP! WE WANT THE CUP!"

The fans chanted for it, and here it came, 34 pounds of sweet silver. Bettman handed the Cup to Yzerman, and Yzerman handed it right to Bowman.

"Without him," Yzerman said, pointing to the confetti on the ice, "none of this was possible. He taught me how to win. He taught us all that the only thing that matters is getting to this point, where the only goal, the only objective that you consider acceptable, is winning the Stanley Cup."

Bowman carried the Cup triumphantly. From resting his players down the stretch, to shuffling the lineup after those first two playoff losses, to telling stories before that Game 7, he had been alert, not aloof. His last coaching performance had been one of his best.

"What a way for the greatest coach in the history of the sport to exit," Holland said. "He did an incredible job with all these egos and high-profile players. He got them all to buy into the team concept. He's the master."

Then Bowman handed the Cup to Yzerman, and Yzerman handed it to Hasek.

"You're never guaranteed another chance," Yzerman said. "So it's important that you appreciate the effort that it took to get here, as well as appreciate those who got there with you."

It was June 13—one year to the day Darcy Regier sent that fax to Holland, giving him permission to speak with Hasek's agent, making what had seemed like a pipe dream a possibility and, eventually, a reality. "It was a great honor to play with Steve," Hasek said. "I got off to a bad start in the first series, but he never lost confidence in me, and he never lost confidence that the team would be able to achieve our goal to win the Stanley Cup."

Hasek carried the Cup for the first time.

"This is my dream come true," Hasek said.

Then Hasek handed the Cup to another first-timer, Luc Robitaille, who handed it to another first-timer, Steve Duchesne, who handed it to another first-timer, Fredrik Olausson, who handed it to Chelios, who hadn't won the Cup in 16 years. Chelios handed it to another first-timer, Jiri Slegr, who handed it to another first-timer, the kid he replaced in the lineup, the suspended Jiri Fischer, who handed it to another first-timer, Boyd Devereaux.

Ilitch soaked in the scene. His gamble had paid off big-time, whether the rest of the league liked it or not. During the season, Chicago Blackhawks owner Bill Wirtz had ripped the Wings' high payroll, saying, "If the family of Mike Ilitch wants to win a Stanley Cup championship for him before he dies, that's fine. I don't expect that from my family. I don't want them to buy a Stanley Cup for Bill."

"There was so much momentum against us, of people not wanting us to win," Ilitch said. "You know that a large percentage of people just don't want you to win. It's a funny feeling. . . . I think I get a bigger thrill out of this one."

Mathieu Dandenault to Pavel Datsyuk to Manny Legace to Jason Williams the Cup went. Then it went to Lidstrom to Shanahan to Hull to the Grind Line—Kris Draper and Darren McCarty and Kirk Maltby—to Igor Larionov to Tomas Holmstrom to Fedorov to Vladimir Konstantinov, who held up the Cup in his wheelchair.

Holland had to smile. His moves had worked. The Hasek deal had created a Dominik effect, and the chemistry had clicked, the players feeding off of each other, having faith in each other, having fun with each other. After the L.A. nightmare, the Wings had a dream season.

"It's a team that I'll never forget, and I'm sure a lot of fans will never forget," Holland said.

The Wings' kids were everywhere. Little Igor Larionov. Little Manny Legace. Griffin McCarty. Steven Robitaille. Dean and Jake Chelios, who had made their dad pull his skates back on and come back onto the ice at the Joe now and then—after *games*, not practices. The team picture looked more like a family photo.

Yes, that meant the Wings were old. So what? They won.

"As you get older and you've played longer, you realize what's more fun and more important," Shanahan said. "It's a lot more fun driving home after a win than driving home after a loss in which you had a couple of goals."

"Age in today's game has zero to do with anything," Hull said. "You'd almost rather have a team with a solid mixture of veteran players, because the way teams play now, you don't have to be swift afoot or super-skilled anymore. All you have to do is be very knowledgeable. I think we proved that."

Yzerman raised the Cup, with his daughter Isabella imitating him alongside.

"What do you think would happen if I announced my retirement right now?" Yzerman joked. "What's the word I'm looking for to describe when you're really, really happy and really, really tired at the same time?"

Satisfied?

Shanahan had taken a penalty at Carolina, and while he sat in the box, a female fan put her arms up on the glass and taunted him. He retaliated by scrunching his face and motioning with his arms, saying something like, "You need to shave those pits." Now he was one of the first players to return to the dressing room. He wanted to shave off his playoff beard. Immediately.

"That was part of the incentive for ending this now," he said. "It was driving me nuts. It was just a big Brillo pad. My wife is thankful. I came in here and got it off as quickly as I could, because it's a mess."

Shanahan smiled. How great was this? He and Yzerman had won an Olympic gold medal and the Cup in the same season. Only one other man ever had done that, Ken Morrow, who played for the United States and the New York Islanders in 1980. Now Shanahan's teammates were coming in, one by one, two by two, while Slegr sat on a folding chair out on the empty ice, championship hat on his head, beer by his left foot, cell phone to his left ear, talking to his family.

Hasek turned and poured champagne on Fedorov's head.

"Hey, look!" Fedorov said, laughing. "It's raining in Detroit!"

Soon the place was packed—players and coaches, family and friends, reporters and cameramen and photographers. At 12:20 A.M., Robitaille's sons sat in his locker.

"We've gotta get the Cup!" he said. "We gotta get the Cup!"

The Cup, the thing his family had sacrificed so much time together to get, was 20 feet away, but Robitaille couldn't see it. His wife, Stacia, waded through the mob to Hull's locker and borrowed it from Chelios and Hull. Robitaille drank champagne out of it, then washed the champagne down with Miller Lite. Duchesne drank. Robitaille drank. Duchesne. Robitaille.

"Get more beer! We need more beer!"

Bowman grabbed the Cup with a big grin and took a big gulp, with Wharton and Chelios and Hull looking on. Datsyuk looked up to Hull and summoned an English word he knew: "Friend."

"That says it all," Hull said. "I feel the same way."

Hull smiled. When he signed with the Wings, he figured he would be skating with Yzerman or Fedorov or Larionov, some of the greatest centers in the game.

"And instead it ended up being one of the greatest kids on earth," he said. "I am so happy that we were a big part of this."

Maxim Kuznetsov translated for Datsyuk.

"He says it is a feeling you cannot explain, like seeing the sun coming up in the morning," Kuznetsov said. "He says it's wonderful."

At 2:00 A.M., Yzerman took the Cup up to Ilitch's suite, but he didn't stay long. The Wings had a private party at a suburban Royal Oak restaurant, Sangria. Lidstrom walked out of the Joe holding the Conn Smythe. Bowman walked out with his wife, who had been waiting for him after the game—for the final time.

"I can tell each one of these players," Bowman said, " 'Thank you very much for allowing me to ride off into the sunset in a happy manner.' "

At 2:15, Yzerman carried the Cup out into the parking lot and placed it in his Range Rover. Then, with his wife, Lisa, by his side and his buddy Darren Pang in the back, he drove off.

The season was over.

"It's been an incredible journey," Holland said.

Now that Bowman had quit, the big question was what Hasek was going to do. Asked after the final game whether he was going to retire, he said, "Give me three or four days. It was my dream to win the Cup, and now . . ."

Two days later, after the Wings took their formal team picture at Joe Louis Arena, Ilitch met with Hasek. Ilitch said he offered to go "the extra mile" for him.

"I told him a few private things I would like to do to make it as convenient as possible for him and his family to play one more year," Ilitch said. "If it was a case of money, if it was a case of anything else that is a tremendous undertaking, I'd be there. . . .

"I think it showed that I really care about him and his family. I'll respect his decision, but I just tried to show him how it would be less painful than the normal situation of a hockey player that has got a homeland overseas."

The night after that, the Wings held a rally for season-ticket holders at the Joe. As Holland headed down the hallway, he said he hadn't spoken to Hasek but was "concerned."

"Going to give him some time," Holland said. "We won the Cup Thursday night. I hate to go up Friday morning at noon and say, 'Let's have a meeting, and what are you doing next year?'

"I know his teammates want him back. I have talked to some of his teammates about him. I know a full-court press is going on."

The Wings were lobbying Hasek hard. Hasek said he talked about retirement with his wife every day, and every day there was some celebration where he was "screaming" and "having fun" and talking about coming back with his teammates.

"Drink champagne and talk about it," Hasek said. "I told them, 'Thank you, guys, but I want to make decision myself.' "

During the rally, Shanahan told Hasek the only thing better than your first Cup is your second. Hull told Hasek it was "definitely worth doing it twice." The fans chanted, "ONE MORE YEAR!" But Hasek gave no inkling of what he might do.

The parade was downtown at 11:30 A.M. the next day, a Monday. Rain fell and black clouds threatened in the morning, but about an hour before the festivities, blue skies and sunshine pushed them right down the route, across the river and out of sight. Police estimated 1.2 million people showed up, and the party was so grand that the Detroit Free Press headline the next day was: "HAPPYTOWN." After Hasek rode down Woodward and Jefferson waving from a red convertible, he said his decision had become "much harder" than he thought it would be.

"I could hear it for a half an hour," Hasek said. "They were cheering all the way: 'One more year!' I see the signs: 'One more year! One more year!' "

The parade culminated in a rally at Hart Plaza, next to the landmark Renaissance Center. In front of the throng, Legace said he wanted to back up Hasek for one more year. Hull joked that Datsyuk wanted to reiterate he wanted Hasek back for one more year.

"ONE MORE YEAR!"

The crowd chanted when Hasek came to the microphone.

"This is too much pressure," Hasek said. "Don't put too much pressure on me."

Hasek lifted the Cup and said a few words. But he didn't say he was coming back. So emcee Ken Daniels prodded him and pleaded with him.

"Just do it," Daniels said.

"ONE MORE YEAR!"

"No, no, no, no, no, no—no pressure, guys," Hasek said. "No more pressure. You're great, and I love it. I love everything. I want to enjoy the moment."

Holland said he hoped the parade and rally would be "enough to convince him to come back." Ilitch hoped they would, too, but he also worried, saying, "He's the kind of guy, you come on too strong, he doesn't like that."

"All these people, they're putting so much pressure on me," Hasek said. "It's hard, especially here with all these people cheering. I don't know. . . . I want to go home, sit with my wife and nobody else and do what is the best for me."

Hasek met with Holland the next day and hinted he was going to leave. Holland told him to take a week and think about it.

Six days later, Hasek and Holland went to dinner at Andiamo, an Italian restaurant in suburban Bloomfield Hills. Within five minutes, Holland knew there was nothing he could do: After six Vezinas, two Harts, two Pearsons, a gold medal and now a Cup, the Dominator was done—forgoing an $8-million salary. After the meal, Holland picked up the check, and they called a news conference for the next day, June 25.

Hasek stepped upon the same podium on which he had said hello to Hockeytown less than a year before—on which he refused to step during the playoffs for his own superstitious reasons—and he said good-bye.

He unfolded a piece of paper, and as the shutters clicked and cameras rolled, he said: I am here to announce my retirement from hockey. . . ."

"Winning the Cup has been everything I could ever ask for," he said. "After 12 years of playing professional hockey at the highest level, I do not feel I have enough fire in me to compete at the level I expect of myself. I achieved my final goal, and now I want to spend more time with my family and move on to new challenges."

Hasek was 37. He had a business to run, his clothing line, Dominik, which was big in the Czech Republic, which he hoped to expand to North America. His son, Michael, was six months old when he moved to the United States in 1990, and his daughter, Dominika, was born in the United States. He wanted them to at least experience what it was like to grow up as a Czech, as he had. During the season, he had tried to help Michael with his seventh-grade homework. Math was no problem, but other subjects had a language barrier for Hasek.

"I was so frustrated," Hasek said. "We explained to them that we believe they can find new friends they will like over there. We told Michael if he wants to go to college in the United States when he is 18, he can make his own decision. I hope we do the right thing. Time will show, but we believe this is right decision, and we will help them make the adjustment."

As the news conference concluded, a reporter asked Hasek whether he would play hockey ever again. Hasek said he might.

"But if I do," he said, smiling, "I'll be a forward and score goals."

Epilogue
A New Day

Ken Holland got home about 4:00 A.M. after the Red Wings won the Stanley Cup. He was back in the office about 11:00. He had much to celebrate, but he had much to do, too. As soon as the 2001-02 season ended, the '02-03 season began.

"You just work away at it," he said.

He laughed.

"Rome wasn't built in a day."

Neither was Hockeytown.

Much of the team stayed intact. Nicklas Lidstrom won his second straight Norris Trophy. The runner-up? Chris Chelios, who became a free agent for the first time in his long career, then turned down a two-year, $13-million offer from the New York Rangers and signed a new two-year contract worth about $12 million with the Wings.

"I'll be happy to keep watching Nick and finishing second as long as we keep winning," Chelios said. "There weren't many teams I wanted to go to, and I told my agent it would take a lot to leave Detroit. I love the people, my teammates, management. It's perfect. The way everything went this year, it would have been tough to leave. I did what I thought was right. I'm just glad it worked out. I can't wait to get back into it again."

Still, things were going to look a lot different when the Wings raised their 10th championship banner come opening night. The dressing room was being renovated. Steve Yzerman saw doctors all over North America about his right knee, before having the surgery he expected would keep him out into early 2003. Fredrik Olausson signed with one of his old teams, the Mighty Ducks of Anaheim. Uwe Krupp, whose arbitration case still was unresolved, got a new contract with the Atlanta Thrashers, much to the Wings' surprise. Trainer John Wharton resigned to pursue other interests, such as writing a book or a screenplay, and

Piet Van Zant was promoted to his position. Having already signed Henrik Zetterberg, the Wings signed Russian defense prospect Dmitri Bykov. As of late July, Igor Larionov was still deciding whether to re-sign with the Wings, sign somewhere else or retire. Steve Duchesne and Jiri Slegr were still free agents.

Holland promoted Dave Lewis to succeed Scotty Bowman. Holland had few options, because by the time Bowman announced his retirement, the best unemployed coaches had found jobs. Fired Dallas Stars coach Ken Hitchcock went to the Philadelphia Flyers, for example. Holland interviewed only two candidates for the job, Lewis and Barry Smith, and Lewis kept Smith as his associate. Lewis also promoted Joe Kocur from video technician to assistant coach.

"Continuity was a big factor," said Holland, who consulted with Mike Ilitch and Jimmy Devellano. "In the end, we kept coming back to the feeling that there was nobody better for the team than one of the guys that were on the team, and we made the decision that Dave was the man for the job."

After 15 years as an NHL defenseman, Lewis had spent 14 as an assistant under three Wings head coaches. Although his style was far different from Bowman's—he was a calm communicator—he wasn't afraid to follow the legend. He said his inexperience as a head coach would be balanced by the experience of his players.

"I can't think of a better opportunity," he said. "I wish it would start right away. I'm looking forward to getting on the ice and talking to the players, standing there and presenting my point of view. It's going to be fun."

As for Dominik Hasek's successor, four free agents were available: Ed Belfour, Byron Dafoe, Curtis Joseph and Mike Richter. Joseph was at the top of the list. Holland didn't think Joseph would want to leave the Maple Leafs: He was from Toronto; they were an Original Six team, too; and they were good enough to have made the Eastern Conference finals. But he called Joseph's agent, Don Meehan, as soon as he could, about 12:30 A.M. July 1—exactly one year after he had wrapped up the Hasek deal.

"When Kenny called and said, 'We'd be very interested in Curtis Joseph,' I couldn't put down the phone fast enough and then call Curtis and say, 'Kenny's called, and he's expressed a desire that the team would like to have you,' " Meehan said. "Curtis said, 'You're kidding,' and I told him Kenny is very sincere about it, and he's told me a lot of players have asked if he'd consider it. I think (Joseph) was very touched by that. Then he started to get really excited, and it started to accelerate pretty quickly."

Joseph didn't have Hasek's credentials. He had no Harts, no Pearsons and no Vezinas, and although he had an Olympic gold medal, he had earned it sitting on the bench for the most part at Salt Lake. But he was one of the top four or five goaltenders in the world, and like Hasek, he never had won a Cup and wanted one badly. He signed a three-year deal, with an option for a fourth year. Like Hasek, he accepted an $8-million salary, which was less than he could have earned elsewhere. Like Hasek, he would make $1 million more if the Wings won the Cup, although he had bonuses that started with a second-round victory, while Hasek had one all-or-nothing bonus.

The morning of July 2, Joseph teared up at a news conference in Toronto, his voice breaking as he said if the Wings didn't win the Cup, he hoped the Leafs did.

"It's not an easy decision to leave your hometown or where you played," he said. "A lot of decisions aren't easy, and this was one of the toughest I've ever had to make. But this was an offer that was tough to refuse. It's a great team. We all saw what happened not too long ago. The bottom line is: Everybody realizes Detroit has a great team. They're used to winning. The future is now, and I wanted to be a part of that. A year ago, was I going to leave Toronto? I wouldn't have thought so in my wildest dreams. But a great opportunity opened up, and here I am."

That afternoon, one year to the day after introducing the Dominator, the Wings introduced Cujo at a news conference at Joe Louis Arena. He pulled on a No. 31 sweater and smiled. A reporter reminded him of how Hasek had said: "To win the Cup, that's my goal, nothing else, nothing less."

"I think that's the only mentality in Detroit," Joseph said. "Cup or else."

Acknowledgments

I could not have written this book without the work of my Detroit Free Press colleagues, whose reporting I have used to supplement my own throughout the preceding pages. I borrowed heavily from stories by fellow Red Wings writer Helene St. James, who was at practices and games when I wasn't, who talked to people I didn't. I also borrowed a lot from columnist Mitch Albom, who unearthed anecdotes in the playoffs, whose archives were a treasure trove of background information. Others to whom I owe a thank-you include, but aren't limited to, Bill McGraw, Michael Rosenberg, George Sipple and Drew Sharp.

Information gleaned from another publication—except folklore and researchable fact—should be credited within the text. But I read several Sports Illustrated stories—most by Michael Farber—as I researched the main characters, and John Niyo's June 14, 2002, Detroit News story was particularly helpful in writing about Steve Yzerman's injured knee. Others that I should mention include, but aren't limited to, the Buffalo News, the Calgary Sun, the Dallas Morning News, ESPN.com, the Hockey News, the Los Angeles Times and the St. Louis Post-Dispatch.

I would like to thank Wings senior vice president Jimmy Devellano, general manager Ken Holland and assistant general manager Jim Nill for taking extra time to talk to me for this project, even when I asked something they didn't like or learned something they wished I hadn't. I would like to thank the coaches, players and other team officials for dealing with me day after day. Their cooperation and help are appreciated.

APPENDIX: REGULAR SEASON GAME-BY-GAME

GP	DATE	OPPONENT	SCORE	RECORD	PTS	GOALIE	GW/GT GOAL
1.	Oct. 4, 2001	at San Jose	W, 4-3 (OT)	1-0-0-0	2	Hasek	Shanahan
2.	Oct. 6, 2001	at Vancouver	W, 4-1	2-0-0-0	4	Hasek	Fischer
3.	Oct. 10, 2001	Calgary	L, 4-2	2-1-0-0	4	Hasek	Kravchuk
4.	Oct. 12, 2001	Buffalo	W, 4-2	3-1-0-0	6	Hasek	Olausson
5.	Oct. 13, 2001	at N.Y. Islanders	W, 5-4 (OT)	4-1-0-0	8	Legace	Yzerman
6.	Oct. 16, 2001	Columbus	W, 4-3	5-1-0-0	10	Hasek	Fedorov
7.	Oct. 18, 2001	Philadelphia	W, 3-2	6-1-0-0	12	Hasek	Hull
8.	Oct. 20, 2001	Los Angeles	W, 3-2	7-1-0-0	14	Hasek	Robitaille
9.	Oct. 24, 2001	Edmonton	W, 4-1	8-1-0-0	16	Hasek	Holmstrom
10.	Oct. 26, 2001	Dallas	L, 5-3	8-2-0-0	16	Hasek	Audette
11.	Oct. 27, 2001	at Nashville	W, 1-0	9-2-0-0	18	Legace	Duchesne
12.	Oct. 30, 2001	at Carolina	W, 5-2	10-2-0-0	20	Legace	Shanahan
13.	Oct. 31, 2001	at Dallas	W, 4-3 (OT)	11-2-0-0	22	Legace	Hull
14.	Nov. 2, 2001	N.Y. Islanders	W, 2-1	12-2-0-0	24	Hasek	Draper
15.	Nov. 4, 2001	at Chicago	L, 5-4	12-3-0-0	24	Hasek	Downey
16.	Nov. 7, 2001	at Phoenix	W, 3-1	13-3-0-0	26	Hasek	Fedorov
17.	Nov. 9, 2001	at Anaheim	W, 1-0	14-3-0-0	28	Hasek	Robitaille
18.	Nov. 10, 2001	at Los Angeles	L, 3-2 (OT)	14-3-0-1	29	Hasek	Palffy
19.	Nov. 13, 2001	Carolina	W, 4-3	15-3-0-1	31	Hasek	Dandenault
20.	Nov. 16, 2001	Minnesota	W, 8-3	16-3-0-1	33	Legace	Yzerman
21.	Nov. 17, 2001	Los Angeles	W, 4-2	17-3-0-1	35	Hasek	Shanahan
22.	Nov. 20, 2001	Nashville	W, 6-3	18-3-0-1	37	Hasek	Maltby
23.	Nov. 21, 2001	at Columbus	W, 1-0 (OT)	19-3-0-1	39	Legace	Robitaille
24.	Nov. 23, 2001	St. Louis	W, 3-1	20-3-0-1	41	Hasek	Yzerman
25.	Nov. 25, 2001	Chicago	T, 4-4	20-3-1-1	42	Hasek	McCarty
26.	Nov. 27, 2001	Calgary	W, 4-2	21-3-1-1	44	Hasek	Maltby
27.	Nov. 30, 2001	New Jersey	W, 4-2	22-3-1-1	46	Legace	Devereaux
28.	Dec. 1, 2001	at New Jersey	L, 4-1	22-4-1-1	46	Hasek	Salomonsson
29.	Dec. 5, 2001	Colorado	L, 4-1	22-5-1-1	46	Hasek	Vrbata
30.	Dec. 7, 2001	Phoenix	T, 1-1	22-5-2-1	47	Hasek	Langkow
31.	Dec. 10, 2001	at Calgary	L, 2-0	22-6-2-1	47	Hasek	Iginla
32.	Dec. 13, 2001	at Edmonton	W, 2-1	23-6-2-1	49	Hasek	Yzerman
33.	Dec. 15, 2001	at Vancouver	L, 3-0	23-7-2-1	49	Hasek	Bertuzzi
34.	Dec. 17, 2001	Chicago	L, 2-0	23-8-2-1	49	Legace	Zhamnov
35.	Dec. 19, 2001	Vancouver	W, 4-1	24-8-2-1	51	Hasek	Devereaux
36.	Dec. 21, 2001	San Jose	W, 3-0	25-8-2-1	53	Hasek	Draper
37.	Dec. 23, 2001	at Chicago	W, 5-0	26-8-2-1	55	Hasek	Shanahan
38.	Dec. 26, 2001	at Minnesota	T, 3-3	26-8-3-1	56	Hasek	Robitaille
39.	Dec. 27, 2001	Columbus	W, 5-1	27-8-3-1	58	Legace	Robitaille
40.	Dec. 29, 2001	at Nashville	L, 3-2 (OT)	27-8-3-2	59	Hasek	Berenzweig
41.	Dec. 31, 2001	Minnesota	W, 4-2	28-8-3-2	61	Hasek	Duchesne

207

Appendix

GP DATE	OPPONENT	SCORE	RECORD	PTS	GOALIE	GW/GT GOAL
42. Jan. 2, 2002	Anaheim	W, 5-3	29-8-3-2	63	Hasek	Fedorov
43. Jan. 5, 2002	Colorado	W, 3-1	30-8-3-2	65	Hasek	Larionov
44. Jan. 9, 2002	Vancouver	W, 5-4 (OT)	31-8-3-2	67	Hasek	Draper
45. Jan. 12, 2002	Dallas	W, 5-2	32-8-3-2	69	Hasek	Maltby
46. Jan. 15, 2002	at Phoenix	T, 2-2	32-8-4-2	70	Legace	Hull
47. Jan. 16, 2002	at Dallas	L, 3-2	32-9-4-2	70	Hasek	Nieuwendyk
48. Jan. 18, 2002	Washington	W, 3-1	33-9-4-2	72	Hasek	Hull
49. Jan. 20, 2002	Ottawa	W, 3-2 (OT)	34-9-4-2	74	Hasek	Dandenault
50. Jan. 23, 2002	San Jose	T, 2-2	34-9-5-2	75	Hasek	Hull
51. Jan. 25, 2002	Phoenix	W, 4-1	35-9-5-2	77	Legace	Yzerman
52. Jan. 26, 2002	at St Louis	W, 5-2	36-9-5-2	79	Hasek	Datsyuk
53. Jan. 28, 2002	at Edmonton	T, 1-1	36-9-6-2	80	Hasek	Holmstrom
54. Jan. 30, 2002	at Calgary	L, 4-3	36-10-6-2	80	Legace	Savard
55. Feb. 4, 2002	at Colorado	W, 3-1	37-10-6-2	82	Hasek	Maltby
56. Feb. 6, 2002	N.Y. Rangers	W, 3-1	38-10-6-2	84	Hasek	Gilchrist
57. Feb. 8, 2002	Columbus	L, 3-2	38-11-6-2	84	Legace	Vyborny
58. Feb. 9, 2002	at Ottawa	W, 3-2	39-11-6-2	86	Hasek	Fedorov
59. Feb. 11, 2002	at Montreal	W, 3-2	40-11-6-2	88	Hasek	Shanahan
60. Feb. 13, 2002	at Minnesota	W, 2-0	41-11-6-2	90	Hasek	Maltby
61. Feb. 26, 2002	at Tampa Bay	W, 4-3 (OT)	42-11-6-2	92	Hasek	Shanahan
62. Feb. 27, 2002	at Florida	W, 3-2 (OT)	43-11-6-2	94	Hasek	Hull
63. March 2, 2002	at Pittsburgh	W, 4-2	44-11-6-2	96	Hasek	Avery
64. March 6, 2002	Toronto	W, 6-2	45-11-6-2	98	Hasek	Robitaille
65. March 9, 2002	at St Louis	W, 5-2	46-11-6-2	100	Hasek	Fedorov
66. March 10, 2002	at Buffalo	L, 5-1	46-12-6-2	100	Hasek	Brown
67. March 13, 2002	Edmonton	W, 4-3 (OT)	47-12-6-2	102	Hasek	Chelios
68. March 16, 2002	at Boston	L, 2-1	48-13-6-2	104	Legace	Murray
69. March 17, 2002	at N.Y. Rangers	W, 5-3	49-13-6-2	106	Hasek	McCarty
70. March 19, 2002	Anaheim	L, 2-1	49-14-6-2	104	Hasek	Kariya
71. March 21, 2002	at Columbus	W, 3-2 (OT)	50-14-6-2	106	Hasek	Fedorov
72. March 23, 2002	at Colorado	W, 2-0	51-14-6-2	108	Hasek	Shanahan
73. March 25, 2002	at Nashville	T, 3-3	50-14-7-2	109	Legace	Shanahan
74. March 28, 2002	Nashville	T, 3-3	50-14-8-2	110	Hasek	Shanahan
75. March 30, 2002	Atlanta	W, 4-1	51-14-8-2	112	Legace	Dandenault
76. April 1, 2002	Toronto	L, 5-4 (OT)	51-14-8-3	113	Legace	Sundin
77. April 3, 2002	at Anaheim	T, 1-1	51-14-9-3	114	Hasek	Robitaille
78. April 4, 2002	at Los Angeles	L, 3-0	51-15-9-3	114	Hasek	Miller
79. April 6, 2002	at San Jose	L, 6-3	51-16-9-3	114	Legace	Marleau
80. April 10, 2002	Chicago	T, 3-3	51-16-10-3	115	Hasek	McCarty
81. April 13, 2002	at St. Louis	L, 3-2 (OT)	51-16-10-4	116	Hasek	Pronger
82. April 14, 2002	St. Louis	L, 5-3	51-17-10-4	116	Hasek	Corso

Hockey Gods

WESTERN CONFERENCE FIRST ROUND

GP	DATE	OPPONENT	SCORE	SERIES	RECORD	GOALIE	GW GOAL
1.	April 17, 2002	Vancouver	L, 4-3 (OT)	0-1	0-1	Hasek	H. Sedin
2.	April 19, 2002	Vancouver	L, 5-2	0-2	0-2	Hasek	Lachance
3.	April 21, 2002	at Vancouver	W, 3-1	1-2	1-2	Hasek	Lidstrom
4.	April 23, 2002	at Vancouver	W, 4-2	2-2	2-2	Hasek	Yzerman
5.	April 25, 2002	Vancouver	W, 4-0	3-2	3-2	Hasek	Holmstrom
6.	April 27, 2002	at Vancouver	W, 6-4	4-2	4-2	Hasek	Hull

WESTERN CONFERENCE SEMIFINALS

GP	DATE	OPPONENT	SCORE	SERIES	RECORD	GOALIE	GW GOAL
1.	May 2, 2002	St. Louis	W, 2-0	1-0	5-2	Hasek	Datsyuk
2.	May 4, 2002	St. Louis	W, 3-2	2-0	6-2	Hasek	Robitaille
3.	May 7, 2002	at St. Louis	L, 6-1	2-1	6-3	Hasek	Mellanby
4.	May 9, 2002	at St. Louis	W, 4-3	3-1	7-3	Hasek	Yzerman
5.	May 11, 2002	St. Louis	W, 4-0	4-1	8-3	Hasek	Fischer

WESTERN CONFERENCE FINALS

GP	DATE	OPPONENT	SCORE	SERIES	RECORD	GOALIE	GW GOAL
1.	May 18, 2002	Colorado	W, 5-3	1-0	9-3	Hasek	McCarty
2.	May 20, 2002	Colorado	L, 4-3 (OT)	1-1	9-4	Hasek	Drury
3.	May 22, 2002	at Colorado	W, 2-1 (OT)	2-1	10-4	Hasek	Olausson
4.	May 25, 2002	at Colorado	L, 3-2	2-2	10-5	Hasek	Drury
5.	May 27, 2002	Colorado	L, 2-1 (OT)	2-3	10-6	Hasek	Forsberg
6.	May 29, 2002	at Colorado	W, 2-0	3-3	11-6	Hasek	Shanahan
7.	May 31, 2002	Colorado	W, 7-0	4-3	12-6	Hasek	Holmstrom

STANLEY CUP FINALS

GP	DATE	OPPONENT	SCORE	SERIES	RECORD	GOALIE	GW GOAL
1.	June 4, 2002	Carolina	L, 3-2 (OT)	0-1	12-7	Hasek	Francis
2.	June 6, 2002	Carolina	W, 3-1	1-1	13-7	Hasek	Lidstrom
3.	June 8, 2002	at Carolina	W, 3-2 (3 OT)	2-1	14-7	Hasek	Larionov
4.	June 10, 2002	at Carolina	W, 3-0	3-1	15-7	Hasek	Hull
5.	June 13, 2002	Carolina	W, 3-1	4-1	16-7	Hasek	Shanahan

Appendix

2001-02 RED WINGS ROSTER

CENTERS

NO.	PLAYER	AGE	HT	WT	BIRTHPLACE	BORN
42	Sean Avery	22	5-10	185	Pickering, Ontario	April 10, 1980
22	Yuri Butsayev	23	6-1	185	Togliatti, Russia	Oct. 11, 1978
13	Pavel Datsyuk	23	5-11	180	Sverdlovsk, Russia	July 20, 1978
33	Kris Draper	31	5-11	190	Toronto	May 24, 1971
91	Sergei Fedorov	31	6-2	200	Pskov, Russia	Dec. 13, 1969
8	Igor Larionov	41	5-11	170	Voskresensk, Russia	Dec. 3, 1960
19	Steve Yzerman	37	5-11	185	Cranbrook, British Columbia	May 9, 1965

LEFT WINGS

NO.	PLAYER	AGE	HT	WT	BIRTHPLACE	BORN
21	Boyd Devereaux	24	6-2	195	Seaforth, Ontario	April 16, 1978
96	Tomas Holmstrom	29	6-0	210	Pieta, Sweden	Jan. 23, 1973
41	Brent Gilchrist	35	5-11	180	Moose Jaw, Saskatchewan	April 3, 1967
18	Kirk Maltby	29	6-0	185	Guelph, Ontario	Dec. 22, 1972
20	Luc Robitaille	36	6-1	215	Montreal	Feb. 17, 1966
14	Brendan Shanahan	33	6-3	220	Mimico, Ontario	Jan. 23, 1969

RIGHT WINGS

NO.	PLAYER	AGE	HT	WT	BIRTHPLACE	BORN
17	Brett Hull	37	5-11	205	Belleville, Ontario	Aug. 9, 1964
25	Darren McCarty	30	6-1	215	Burnaby, British Columbia	April 1, 1972
15	Ladislav Kohn	27	5-11	220	Uherske Hradiste, Czech Rep.	March 5, 1975
29	Jason Williams	21	5-11	185	London, Ontario	Aug. 11, 1980

DEFENSEMEN

NO.	PLAYER	AGE	HT	WT	BIRTHPLACE	BORN
24	Chris Chelios	40	6-1	190	Chicago	Jan. 25, 1962
11	Mathieu Dandenault	26	6-1	200	Sherbrooke, Quebec	Feb. 3, 1976
28	Steve Duchesne	36	6-0	195	Sept-Iles, Quebec	June 30, 1965
2	Jiri Fischer	21	6-5	225	Horovice, Czech Republic	July 31, 1980
71	Jiri Slegr	31	6-0	220	Jihlava, Czech Republic	May 30, 1971
4	Uwe Krupp	36	6-6	235	Cologne, Germany	June 24, 1965
32	Maxim Kuznetsov	25	6-5	235	Pavlodar, Russia	March 24, 1977
5	Nicklas Lidstrom	32	6-2	190	Vasteras, Sweden	April 28, 1970
27	Fredrik Olausson	35	6-0	195	Dadesjo, Sweden	Oct. 5, 1966
3	Jesse Wallin	24	6-2	190	Saskatoon, Saskatchewan	March 10, 1978

GOALTENDERS

NO.	PLAYER	AGE	HT	WT	BIRTHPLACE	BORN
38	Jason Elliott	26	6-2	185	Inuvik, Northwest Territories	Nov. 10, 1975
39	Dominik Hasek	37	5-11	170	Pardubice, Czech Republic	Jan. 29, 1965
34	Manny Legace	29	5-9	165	Toronto	Feb. 4, 1973

Notes: Age listed on June 13, 2002, when the Red Wings clinched the Stanley Cup. Forward Brent Gilchrist was waived before the Olympic break in February. Center Yuri Butsayev was dealt to Atlanta at the trade deadline in March. Goaltender Jason Elliott spent most of the season at Cincinnati of the AHL but periodically joined the Wings, including for the playoff run. He suited up for seven regular-season games but never played. Elliott, Jesse Wallin, Ladislav Kohn, Maxim Kuznetsov and Sean Avery did not play in the playoffs.

WINGS STATISTICS: REGULAR SEASON
(Record: 51-17-10-4)

SCORING

POS	NO.	PLAYER	GP	G	A	PTS	+/-	PM
LW	14	Brendan Shanahan	80	37	38	75	23	118
C	91	Sergei Fedorov	81	31	37	68	20	36
RW	17	Brett Hull	82	30	33	63	18	35
D	5	Nicklas Lidstrom	78	9	50	59	13	20
LW	20	Luc Robitaille	81	30	20	50	-2	38
C	19	Steve Yzerman	52	13	35	48	11	18
C	8	Igor Larionov	70	11	32	43	-5	50
D	24	Chris Chelios	79	6	33	39	40	126
C	13	Pavel Datsyuk	70	11	24	35	4	4
C	33	Kris Draper	82	15	15	30	26	56
LW	96	Tomas Holmstrom	69	8	18	26	-12	58
LW	21	Boyd Devereaux	79	9	16	25	9	24
LW	18	Kirk Maltby	82	9	15	24	15	40
D	11	Mathieu Dandenault	81	8	12	20	-5	44
D	28	Steve Duchesne	64	3	15	18	3	28
D	27	Fredrik Olausson	47	2	13	15	9	22
RW	25	Darren McCarty	62	5	7	12	2	98
RW	29	Jason Williams	25	8	2	10	2	4
D	2	Jiri Fischer	80	2	8	10	17	67
D	71	Jiri Slegr	46	3	6	9	-20	59
C	42	Sean Avery	36	2	2	4	1	68
D	32	Maxim Kuznetsov	39	1	2	3	0	40
LW	41	Brent Gilchrist	19	1	1	2	-3	8
D	4	Uwe Krupp	8	0	1	1	-1	8
D	3	Jesse Wallin	15	0	1	1	-1	13
RW	15	Ladislav Kohn	4	0	0	0	0	4
C	22	Yuri Butsayev	3	0	0	0	-1	0
TOTALS			82	251	433	684	—	1053
OPPONENTS			82	187	314	501	—	1080

GOALTENDERS

NO.	PLAYER	GP	MIN	AVG	W-L-T	SO	GA
39	Dominik Hasek	65	3872	2.17	41-15-8	5	140
34	Manny Legace	20	1117	2.42	10- 6-2	1	45
38	Jason Elliott	—	—	—	—	—	—
TOTALS		82	5008	2.24	51-21-10	7	187
OPPONENTS		82	5008	3.01	21-51-10	4	251

Appendix

WINGS STATISTICS: THE PLAYOFFS
(Record: 16-7)

SCORING

POS	NO.	PLAYER	GP	G	A	PTS	+/-	PM
C	19	Steve Yzerman	23	6	17	23	+4	10
LW	14	Brendan Shanahan	23	8	11	19	+5	20
C	91	Sergei Fedorov	23	5	14	19	+4	20
RW	17	Brett Hull	23	10	8	18	+1	4
D	5	Nicklas Lidstrom	23	5	11	16	+6	2
D	24	Chris Chelios	23	1	13	14	+15	44
LW	96	Tomas Holmstrom	23	8	3	11	+7	8
C	8	Igor Larionov	18	5	6	11	+5	4
LW	20	Luc Robitaille	23	4	5	9	+4	10
RW	25	Darren McCarty	23	4	4	8	+5	34
C	13	Pavel Datsyuk	21	3	3	6	+1	2
D	2	Jiri Fischer	22	3	3	6	+6	30
LW	18	Kirk Maltby	23	3	3	6	+7	32
LW	21	Boyd Devereaux	21	2	4	6	+5	4
D	27	Fredrik Olausson	21	2	4	6	+3	10
D	28	Steve Duchesne	23	0	6	6	+6	24
C	33	Kris Draper	23	2	3	5	+4	20
D	11	Mathieu Dandenault	23	1	2	3	+7	8
D	71	Jiri Slegr	1	0	0	0	+2	2
D	4	Uwe Krupp	2	0	0	0	-5	2
RW	29	Jason Williams	9	0	0	0	-1	2
C	42	Sean Avery	–	–	–	–	–	–
RW	15	Ladislav Kohn	–	–	–	–	–	–
D	32	Maxim Kuznetsov	–	–	–	–	–	–
D	3	Jesse Wallin	–	–	–	–	–	–
TOTALS			**23**	**72**	**121**	**193**	**—**	**308**
OPPONENTS			**23**	**47**	**75**	**122**	**—**	**284**

GOALTENDERS

NO.	PLAYER	GP	MIN	AVG	W-L	SO	GA
39	Dominik Hasek	23	1455	1.86	16-7	6	45
34	Manny Legace	1	11	5.45	0-0	0	1
38	Jason Elliott	–	–	–	–	–	–
TOTALS		**23**	**1471**	**1.92**	**16-7**	**6**	**47**
OPPONENTS		**23**	**1471**	**2.94**	**7-16**	**0**	**72**

212

Hockey Gods

2001-02 NHL CONFERENCE STANDINGS

(In the order teams qualified for the playoffs.)

WESTERN CONFERENCE

RK TEAM	W	L	T	OTL	GF	GA	HOME	AWAY	PTS
1. z-DETROIT	51	17	10	4	251	187	28-7-5-1	23-10-5-3	116
2. y-COLORADO	45	28	8	1	212	169	24-12-4-1	21-16-4-0	99
3. y-SAN JOSE	44	27	8	3	248	199	25-11-3-2	19-16-5-1	99
4. x-ST LOUIS	43	27	8	4	227	188	27-12-1-1	16-15-7-3	98
5. x-CHICAGO	41	27	13	1	216	207	28-7-5-1	13-20-8-0	96
6. x-PHOENIX	40	27	9	6	228	210	27-8-3-3	13-19-6-3	95
7. x-LOS ANGELES	40	27	11	4	214	190	22-12-6-1	18-15-5-3	95
8. x-VANCOUVER	42	30	7	3	254	211	23-11-5-2	19-19-2-1	94

Failed to make playoffs:

	W	L	T	OTL	GF	GA	HOME	AWAY	PTS
9. EDMONTON	38	28	12	4	205	182	23-14-4-0	15-14-8-4	92
10. DALLAS	36	28	13	5	215	213	18-13-6-4	18-15-7-1	90
11. CALGARY	32	35	12	3	201	220	20-14-5-2	12-21-7-1	79
12. MINNESOTA	26	35	12	9	195	238	14-14-8-5	12-21-4-4	73
13. ANAHEIM	29	42	8	3	175	198	15-19-5-2	14-23-3-1	69
14. NASHVILLE	28	41	13	0	196	230	17-16-8-0	11-25-5-0	69
15. COLUMBUS	22	47	8	5	164	255	14-18-5-4	8-29-3-1	57

EASTERN CONFERENCE

RK TEAM	W	L	T	OTL	GF	GA	HOME	AWAY	PTS
1. z-BOSTON	43	24	6	9	236	201	23-11-2-5	20-13-4-4	101
2. y-PHILADELPHIA	42	27	10	3	234	192	20-13-5-3	22-14-5-0	97
3. y-CAROLINA	35	26	16	5	217	217	15-13-11-2	20-13-5-3	91
4. x-TORONTO	43	25	10	4	249	207	24-11-6-0	19-14-4-4	100
5. x-NY ISLANDERS	42	28	8	4	239	220	21-13-5-2	21-15-3-2	96
6. x-NEW JERSEY	41	28	9	4	205	187	22-13-4-2	19-15-5-2	95
7. x-OTTAWA	39	27	9	7	243	208	21-13-3-4	18-14-6-3	94
8. x-MONTREAL	36	31	12	3	207	209	21-13-6-1	15-18-6-2	87

Failed to make playoffs:

	W	L	T	OTL	GF	GA	HOME	AWAY	PTS
9. WASHINGTON	36	33	11	2	228	240	21-12-6-2	15-21-5-0	85
10. BUFFALO	35	35	11	1	213	200	20-16-5-0	15-19-6-1	82
11. NY RANGERS	36	38	4	4	227	258	19-19-2-1	17-19-2-3	80
12. PITTSBURGH	28	41	8	5	198	249	16-20-4-1	12-21-4-4	69
13. TAMPA BAY	27	40	11	4	178	219	16-17-5-3	11-23-6-1	69
14. FLORIDA	22	44	10	6	180	250	11-23-3-4	11-21-7-2	60
15. ATLANTA	19	47	11	5	187	288	11-21-9-0	8-26-2-5	54

x - clinched playoff spot
y - clinched division
z - clinched conference

213